W9-CAZ-094

NOTRE DAME

GOLDEN MOMENTS

Twenty Memorable Events that Shaped
Notre Dame Football

John Walters

RUTLEDGE HILL PRESS®
Nashville, Tennesseee
A Division of Thomas Nelson Publishers, Inc.
www.ThomasNelson.com

Copyright © 2004 by Kestrel Communications

All rights reserved. No portion of this book may be reproduced, stored in a retrieval system, or transmitted in any form or by any means—electronic, mechanical, photocopy, recording, or any other—except for brief quotations in printed reviews, without the prior permission of the publisher.

Published by Rutledge Hill Press, a Division of Thomas Nelson, Inc., P.O. Box 141000, Nashville, Tennessee, 37214.

Library of Congress Cataloging-in-Publication Data

Walters, John (John Andrew)
   Notre Dame golden moments : 20 memorable events that shaped Notre Dame football / John Walters.
     p. cm.
   ISBN 1-59186-042-3 (hardcover)
    1. University of Notre Dame—Football—History. 2. Notre Dame Fighting Irish (Football team)—History. I. Title.
   GV958.U54W35 2004
   796.332'63'0977289--dc22

                                    2004009856

Printed in the United States of America

04 05 06 07 08—5 4 3 2 1

CONTENTS

FOREWORD

The opportunity to coach at Notre Dame was almost overwhelming. It was a huge responsibility. I was forty-one years old when I got there in December 1963 and was completely amazed at all the national attention. I got phone calls from across the country. You have to sit in that chair to appreciate it.

I had been on campus only a couple months when I was told we were having our first pep rally. Not that I was reluctant, but I wondered what we were doing showing up for an outdoor pep rally at Sorin Hall in February. At the Friday night pep rallies, I'd prepare some remarks but when I got there I realized you didn't have to have anything prepared. All you had to do was open your mouth and they'd start cheering. It was a wild scene.

When you put together a name like Knute Rockne, a tradition of winning, and a wonderful educational institution steeped in religious faith and academic and athletic excellence, you have something really special. That's why I never seriously considered taking another job, even when several NFL teams offered a lot more money midway into my Notre Dame years. And that's why my wife Katie and I have a home five miles from Notre Dame Stadium and live there six months of the year.

I was an emotional guy. I'd like to think some of that rubbed off on my teams. We won more than our share of games. We prepared our players to anticipate anything that might happen over sixty minutes. They were taught to win with dignity, respect their opponent, don't make excuses, play by the rules, work like hell to prevent penalties and set standards for honesty and integrity.

There were many great moments, but two that stand out are the 1966 Michigan State game, the 10-10 tie, and the 24-23 victory over Alabama in the 1973 Sugar Bowl. I remember both for their tremendous pre-game attention involving undefeated teams. Those two games are among the twenty memorable events depicted in this book, a work that covers eighty years and has something for every Notre Dame fan.

Fortunately, it all worked out for me in my eleven years there, and at eighty-one years old, I'm absolutely honored that I became the head football coach at Notre Dame.

—Ara Parseghian, June 2004

PREFACE

AFTER MY FIRST TWO AUTUMNS AS A NOTRE DAME STUDENT, I was resigned to the fact that I'd never witness a truly memorable football moment. Then Lou Holtz arrived. Even then it was not until the final contest of that 1986 season, when the Irish recovered from a 37-20 fourth-quarter deficit at USC to win, 38-37, that my classmates and I felt as if we'd truly been initiated into the Fighting Irish family.

That game did not make the *Golden Moments* Top Twenty list (it tops mine), but it is emblematic of nearly all that did. For, if there is a pervasive theme coursing through the decades of Notre Dame football, it is this: the paradox of the most successful college football program in history repeatedly playing the role of the underdog. Time and time again, old Notre Dame does win over all.

From their helmets to their heroes; from Rockne to the Rocket; from a dossier that includes the most national championships, most Heisman Trophy winners, and one of the highest winning percentages in college football history, Notre Dame has a tradition that is unmatched in college football. That is not news.

What you will learn as you read this book is that the Notre Dame mystique has less to do with what the Fighting Irish have accomplished on the gridiron as it does with how they have done it: by consistently performing, within the context of a football game, heroically. And that is why millions of people, for more than a century, have invested so much emotion into them.

This book could not have been completed without: Jerry Klein, whose many years of covering both college football and the NFL made him the perfect prototype quarterback for this project; Charles Lamb, assistant director of the University of Notre Dame Archives and archivist Erik Dix, who both understand what it means to be on deadline; John Heisler, associate athletic director for media relations, and assistant Carol Copley, cooperation at its best; Michael Bennett of Lighthouse Imaging, a wizard in all areas of photography; photographer Joe Raymond of the *South Bend Tribune*, thirty-two years of documenting Irish football; Mike "Monte" Towle, a fellow alum and sportswriter who served as project editor; Linda Wachtel and the friendly staff at the *Sports Illustrated* Library.

—*John Walters*

JOHN LATTNER
1953 – HEISMAN TROPHY WINNER

NOTRE DAME 31, MIAMI 30

OCTOBER 15, 1988

THERE APPEARED TO BE SO MUCH MORE AT STAKE THAN A WIN or a loss. Or even a national championship.

Good vs. Evil? Hyperbole.

Catholics vs. Convicts, as the popular campus T-shirt espoused? Not exactly, as many a wag noted that Miami's quarterback, Steve Walsh, as well as its entire starting offensive line, was Catholic, while Fighting Irish signal-caller Tony Rice was Baptist.

Icon vs. Iconoclast? Definitely. Notre Dame represented the bedrock of college football lore, from "Win One for the Gipper" to the Victory March to the gold helmets to the unadorned natural-grass field. The Hurricanes, in hindsight, were the harbinger of the modern sports team: brash, in-your-face trash talkers who had no interest in humbly going about their business. The Canes added insult to your injury, and with glee. But they won. Oh, how the Hurricanes won.

The banners and special T-shirts were out in full force to welcome the Hurricanes, but not all of the messages were G-rated.

Miami, which had played for the national championship in four of the previous five seasons, entered the game with a thirty-six-game, regular-season win streak, a sixteen-game overall win streak, and, most daunting of all, a twenty-game road winning streak.

> "I felt like crawling under a rock and dying," said senior Irish defensive end Frank Stams, who had been a freshman starting at fullback that day. "I STILL HAVE NIGHTMARES ABOUT THAT."

Along the way the Hurricanes had taken much of the shine off Notre Dame's gold helmets and mystique. The Irish had lost four straight to the Hurricanes, including their only two shutouts of the 1980s. The nadir came in former Notre Dame coach Gerry Faust's final game, a 58-7 rout at the Orange Bowl. The fifty-one-point defeat represented the worst Irish loss since a 59-0 drubbing by Army in 1944. At least the loss to the Cadets had not been nationally televised.

"I felt like crawling under a rock and dying," said senior Irish defensive end Frank Stams, who had been a freshman starting at fullback that day. "I still have nightmares about that."

The Hurricanes, under coach Jimmy Johnson, delighted in debunking the myth of Notre Dame. Defensive back Donald Ellis said that playing Notre Dame wasn't special but rather "like playing Wisconsin or Central Florida." When the Hurricanes hosted the Irish in 1987 for a rematch, they shut out the Irish, 24-0, and shut down Heisman Trophy winner Tim Brown, taunting him with terms like "punk."

Little wonder, then, that Notre Dame players, students, and fans penciled in October 15, 1988, as their day of redemption. Six months before the Hurricanes even visited Notre Dame Stadium on the most sun-splashed October afternoon you'll ever see, the Notre Dame student magazine *Scholastic* ran a full-page ad that read, "Avoid the Rush. Hate Miami Early. Only 198 Days Left!" When the two schools' baseball teams played a two-game series in early October, a Notre Dame pitcher hit the first three Hurricane batters he faced and beaned the leadoff Miami hitter in the second inning.

The animus reached absurd extremes. Notre Dame fans and students sent piles of hate mail to Johnson ("As avid college football fans," wrote five Dillon Hall residents,

> Miami was street tough and cocky. THE CANES RELISHED THEIR PUBLIC ENEMY NUMBER ONE REPUTATION, but no school had a better record over the previous five seasons than Miami's 56-9 mark.

"we hate to see our sport ruled by your team of hooligans."), while a Miami student columnist printed the private office phone number of Notre Dame coach Lou Holtz. The third-year Irish coach wrote a letter to the Notre Dame student body encouraging them to impress the Hurricanes with "the classiness of our program and fans." Holtz penned the letter almost two weeks prior to the game, before the Irish even ventured east to play Pittsburgh.

In the national media and to those legions with a passion for sport, the game was not only a clash of cultures, but of eras. Could Notre Dame, the most storied program in college football, return to prominence, or were the Fighting Irish a quaint relic? The school had recently spent three hundred thousand dollars regilding its signature edifice, the golden dome atop the Administration Building, but was that the only type of luster that Notre Dame could still summon?

Then there were the Hurricanes, who had caused a furor before their 1987 Fiesta Bowl showdown with Penn State by arriving at a dinner wearing fatigues. Miami was street tough and cocky. The Canes relished their Public Enemy Number One reputation, but no school had a better record over the previous five seasons than Miami's 56-9 mark. Moreover, they had not lost a network-televised regular-season game in nine years, that being a 30-0 loss in 1979 to top-ranked Alabama in Tuscaloosa.

Holtz knew that top-ranked Miami (4-0) had more talent and more battle-tested players than his number-four Irish (5-0). A brilliant motivator, Holtz hoped to publicly plant a seed of doubt in the Hurricanes while bolstering the confidence of his own troops.

"Without a doubt, Miami is better than Notre Dame," he said a few days before the game. "But what we don't know and what Miami doesn't know is whether they'll be better on Saturday."

At the Friday night pep rally, held outdoors to accommodate the huge throng of students, who had just finished a week of midterms, as well as thousands of others, Holtz went even further: "We're going to beat the living dog out of Miami," he said.

Lou Holtz told his players to leave Miami coach Jimmy Johnson to him.

Twenty-four hours later, Holtz would recall his uncharacteristically brazen oath. "I woke up at 4:45 A.M. this morning," he confided, "and I couldn't believe what I had said."

Everyone was itching for this fight. A pregame melee erupted outside the tunnel leading to both teams' locker rooms. Apparently, a Miami player bumped a Notre Dame player as he was making his way toward the tunnel. Both squads were in close quarters in the north end zone. Words were exchanged and soon a brawl, lasting nearly a minute, was in high gear.

"This is our house and we don't take any of that [taunting]," said Notre Dame offensive tackle Andy Heck, "so we just shoved them into the tunnel."

"There was pushing and shoving, punching, poking eyes, everything," said Notre Dame's six-foot-seven freshman tight end Derek Brown.

"I don't know what precipitated it," said police sergeant James Campbell, one of three officers assigned to protect Johnson, "but I'll tell you there was a helluva fight going on there."

Inside the Notre Dame locker room, Holtz gathered his players together, instilling them with confidence and a laugh. "Men, you're gonna take care of the Canes today," freshman speedster Raghib "Rocket" Ismail recalls the wispy coach saying. "But do me one favor: *Leave Jimmy Johnson's ass for me!*"

Outside, the atmosphere on this sublime day (temperatures in the midseventies) was, as the *Washington Post*'s Sally Jenkins termed it, "unmitigated bedlam." The students, now enjoying their first day of fall break, provided the impetus for the loudest crowd in Notre Dame history (the 110 decibels registered on the sideline was the equivalent of standing fifty yards away from a 747 during takeoff). The din was repeatedly stoked by a game replete with thrills and turnabouts: five lost fumbles, four interceptions (one returned for a touchdown), a snuffed-out fake punt, a blocked punt, and a failed last-minute two-point conversion. Over the course of three hours, the frenzy never did wane.

"This," said Stams, who played all afternoon like a man possessed, "is what college football is all about."

On Miami's first series the Hurricanes quickly advanced from their own 16 to their 42 in four plays. Then Stams jarred the ball loose from Walsh. Irish nose tackle Chris Zorich recovered at the Miami 41. After the teams exchanged punts, the Irish began from their own 25, and churned out a six-minute touchdown drive. The final play saw Irish option quarterback Tony Rice fake a belly dive to fullback Braxston Banks and then scoot around right end untouched for seven yards. The score, coming with 3:36 left in the opening period, represented the first rushing touchdown the Hurricanes had surrendered all season.

The teams then exchanged turnovers—Walsh tossed an interception to Irish defensive back D'Juan Francisco, but Rice lost the ball on a fumbled exchange from center on the very next play at the Miami 32. Walsh, a junior who entered the game 16-0 as a collegian, led the Hurricanes on a 68-yard scoring drive that featured a pair of 20-yard pass completions. Wideout Andre Brown scored on an eight-yard pass, stretching his body out for the final yard to tie the score at 7.

Walsh would complete passes seemingly at will all afternoon. His stat line would read 31-of-50 for 424 yards, four touchdowns, and three interceptions. The 424 yards represented the most yards the Irish had surrendered, while the thirty-one completions, a

Miami record, were all the more impressive considering who Walsh's immediate Hurricane predecessors had been: Jim Kelly, Bernie Kosar, and Heisman Trophy winner Vinny Testaverde. Cleveland Gary caught a school-record (for a running back) eleven passes for 130 yards, but Miami's air assault neither surprised nor scared Holtz.

"We went into the game knowing Walsh would complete a lot of passes," Holtz said, "but we had to stop their running game. And we did." The Hurricanes gained just 57 net yards on twenty-eight carries.

> "We went into the game knowing Walsh would complete a lot of passes," Holtz said, "BUT WE HAD TO STOP THEIR RUNNING GAME. AND WE DID." The Hurricanes gained just 57 net yards on twenty-eight carries.

In the second quarter Rice, whose passing ability was constantly questioned, faded back to pass near his five-yard line. The junior from Woodruff, South Carolina, took a step or two up in the pocket and launched a rainmaker that traveled at least 60 yards in the air. "I had no idea he has that strong of an arm," said Hurricane linebacker Bernard Clark.

The pass fell into the arms of Ismail, the speedy freshman, who stumbled and fell at the Hurricane 25. Seven plays later Rice tossed a nine-yard touchdown pass to Banks and the Irish were again ahead, 14-7. Less than two minutes later Stams, rushing from the right end, deflected a Walsh pass into the arms of safety Pat Terrell. The junior, who had made his first defensive start only a week earlier at Pitt, raced 60 yards untouched to put the Irish ahead, 21-7, with less than six minutes remaining in the first half. Walsh, diving in vain after Terrell near the goal line, opened a gash on his chin that would require five stitches.

Miami, at last truly aroused, responded quickly. Walsh led the Hurricanes on a 61-yard drive culminating with a 23-yard touchdown pass to running back Leonard Conley with 2:16 left until halftime. The Irish quickly punted, and again the Hurricanes traveled downfield with impunity. This drive of 54 yards took seven plays, the last a Walsh-to-Gary 15-yarder that tied the score at 21 with 0:21 showing on the clock.

Inside the Notre Dame locker room at halftime, feelings were mixed. The Irish knew that they could play with the Hurricanes, and yet Miami had recovered from the

Notre Dame safety Pat Terrell sets sail for the end zone on a 60-yard interception return that put the Irish up, 21-7

fourteen-point deficit with ease. It would be hard to imagine the Irish, whose entire offensive line was comprised of first-year starters, doing the same.

"If we got the lead," Johnson said later, "I thought we could control the game."

The Hurricanes never did. After a Notre Dame defensive assistant put his fist through a blackboard at halftime, the Irish returned to the field full of fight in the third quarter. With Miami facing fourth and three from their 47 midway through the period, Johnson decided to gamble. Holtz's punt-return team was prepared.

"Jimmy Johnson," Holtz said, "always tries a special-teams trick on national TV."

Indeed, the ball was snapped to upback Matt Britton, who ran right. Notre Dame backup quarterback Steve Belles dropped Britton for a one-yard loss on what Holtz would later call "the most important play of the game."

"It was supposed to run to the right," Johnson said, "but it was run to the left."

On the next play Rice hit sophomore flanker Ricky Watters for a 44-yard gain down to the Miami two. Then Pat Eilers, a transfer from Yale, cut back on a sweep right and stumbled in for a 28-21 lead with 8:09 left in the third quarter to the thunderous roar of the crowd.

Again Miami came right back, as Walsh led them down to the Irish 23. Then Walsh threw his third interception of the afternoon as defensive tackle Jeff Alm used all of his six-foot-seven frame to snare a lob pass out of the sky. Rice then led the Irish on a drive of their own, with freshman tight end Brown, a south Florida native who had nearly signed with Miami, making one big catch for 26 yards. The drive stalled at the Hurricane 11, but kicker Reggie Ho converted a 27-yarder with 0:37 left in the third to make the score 31-21.

> "The official said, 'Son, the ball is dead,'" Gary recalled. "Then all of a sudden, they're calling it a fumble. IF IT'S DEAD, HOW COULD IT BE A FUMBLE?"

Anyone who had watched Miami under Johnson knew that the game was far from over. The Hurricanes of recent vintage may have been the most dangerous fourth-quarter road team anyone had ever seen. A year earlier in Tallahassee the Canes had trailed number-four Florida State, 19-3, at the start of the final stanza and won, 26-25. Four Saturdays earlier Miami had trailed number-fifteen Michigan, 30-14, with 5:37 remaining, but came back to win, 31-30. As one unidentified Miami lineman told his Notre Dame counterpart, "This one's going down to the wire."

Four times in the fourth quarter the Hurricanes would advance beyond the Irish 25-yard line. First, Walsh completed three straight passes for 47 yards for a first and goal at the Irish nine. The Notre Dame defense, led by linebackers Ned Bolcar, Wes Pritchett, and Michael Stonebreaker, held, though. Miami settled for a 23-yard Carlos Huerta field goal that cut the deficit to 31-24.

Minutes later Miami was right back near the south end zone, facing fourth and seven from the Irish 11. With just more than seven minutes left, Walsh completed a pass to Gary, who dove for the end zone as Tracy Graham put a lick on him. The ball came loose and Stonebreaker recovered, but had Gary's knee already touched the ground? Had the ball already broken the plane of the goal line?

"The official said, 'Son, the ball is dead,'" Gary recalled. "Then all of a sudden, they're calling it a fumble. If it's dead, how could it be a fumble?"

Johnson vehemently protested the call. "It wasn't a fumble," he snapped afterward,

Miami quarterback Steve Walsh threw for 424 yards, but he also turned the ball over a number of times, including this fumble. Frank Stams forced the fumble and Chris Zorich would recover at the Notre Dame 28.

though he refused to blame the outcome of the contest on one call, "and if someone comes back now and says it was a fumble, they're full of bull."

The Irish escaped that parry, but minutes later Walsh had the Hurricanes back at the Notre Dame 24 following a 12-yard completion to tight end Rob Chudzinski and a late-hit penalty. Again, Stams rescued the Irish, blindsiding Walsh and forcing a fumble. As happened when Stams forced Walsh's first fumble, Zorich was there to pounce on it, this time at the Notre Dame 28.

The miracle seemed almost complete. All Notre Dame had to do was kill the final three-plus minutes and this victory would go down with all of the classic streak-busters in Fighting Irish lore: the 0-0 tie with Army in 1946 that ended the Cadets' twenty-five-game win streak; the 27-14 defeat of Georgia Tech in 1953 that ended the Yellow Jackets' thirty-one-game unbeaten streak; Oklahoma, 1957, the forty-seven-game win streak, college football's longest; Texas's thirty-game win streak, ended at the Cotton Bowl on New Year's Day 1971; and USC's twenty-three-game unbeaten string, nullified in 1973. All that, plus the fact that Notre Dame had not upended the nation's No. 1 team in South Bend since Northwestern in 1936.

On third and 17 from the Irish 21, Rice fumbled. The crowd hushed. Miami had the ball on the Irish 14 with 2:10 remaining. Four plays later the Hurricanes faced fourth and seven from the 11 with 0:51 left. Walsh, tossing his fiftieth pass of the day, hit Brown in the right corner of the end zone to bring the Hurricanes within one. The score was 31-30.

Five years earlier Miami had won its first national championship by a 31-30 score over Nebraska. Tom Osborne, the Cornhusker coach, had gone for two in the game's dying moments when a tie likely would have assured him a national championship. Johnson had not been the Hurricanes coach then, but he too disdained the prospect of a tie. "We always play to win," he said.

In the Notre Dame huddle, safety George Streeter, a cocaptain, reminded his teammates, "Don't flinch!" The Hurricanes expected a zone pass defense, but Irish defensive coordinator Barry Alvarez called for a mix of man and blitz. The defensive backs would jam the wideouts on the line. Miami lined up trips right with Brown, Conley, and Dale Dawkins. Across from Conley stood Terrell. The two players had both grown up in Tampa and played against one another in high school. Terrell caught Conley's eye. They grinned at one another.

"Back to throw," said Westwood One radio play-by-play man Tony Roberts. "Walsh looks . . . looks . . . looks . . . has the time . . . lobs the ball!"

Walsh, who had been briefly confused by Notre Dame's alignment, tossed the ball in the same area that he had thrown his touchdown pass the previous play. Conley was the intended receiver, but Terrell was in front of him. He leaped up and batted the ball harmlessly toward the ground before being buried under a crush of friendly, dark blue jerseys.

Pat Terrell's day would have been almost complete with his interception return for a touchdown, but it was his game-saving breakup of a two-point conversion toss with under a minute left that truly made his, and the Irish's, day.

"I felt like a magnet," Terrell said, "around a bunch of paper clips."

Anthony Johnson recovered the Miami onside kick on the next play. Notre Dame ran out the clock and, in avenging perhaps its most humiliating loss, had scored its greatest victory.

"Notre Dame has a tradition of rising to the occasion," Holtz said. "A lot of people lose games because they don't really believe deep down inside that they can win. We told the players all last week to forget who they were playing, that the important thing was to believe from the bottom of their hearts that if we all worked together, we had a chance to beat Miami."

Where there had been vitriol before, the postmortem on the game saw two teams with mutual respect for one another. "I must give Notre Dame credit," said Walsh. "They caused some of the turnovers and played a great game. It was a great game between two great teams."

It was a game that nobody will ever forget.

"It's strange," said Zorich, "but before, during, and after the game, it was like we could feel all of the Irish legends out there. I kept hearing those lines from our fight song about shaking down the thunder and waking up the echoes."

And if Notre Dame's incredible 31-30 win was not Good triumphing over Evil, it was something equally important. As the cover of *Sports Illustrated*, featuring a determined-looking Tony Rice, declared the following week, "NOTRE DAME IS BACK."

Notre Dame 31, Miami 30
Notre Dame Stadium, South Bend, Indiana
October 15, 1988

SCORING SUMMARY

	1	2	3	4	
Miami	0	21	0	9	30
Notre Dame	7	14	10	0	31

Team	Qtr.	Time Left	Play	Score
ND	1	3:36	Tony Rice 7 run (Reggie Ho kick)	ND 7-0
UM	2	12:40	Andre Brown 8 pass from Steve Walsh (Carlos Huerta kick)	7-7
ND	2	7:34	Braxston Banks 9 pass from Rice (Ho kick)	ND 14-7
ND	2	5:42	Pat Terrell 60 interception return (Ho kick)	ND 21-7
UM	2	2:16	Leonard Conley 23 pass from Walsh (Huerta kick)	ND 21-14
UM	2	0:21	Cleveland Gary 15 pass from Walsh (Huerta kick)	21-21
ND	3	8:09	Pat Eilers 2 run (Ho kick)	ND 28-21
ND	3	0:37	Ho 27 FG	ND 31-21
UM	4	13:07	Huerta 23 FG	ND 31-24
UM	4	0:45	Brown 11 pass from Walsh (Walsh pass failed)	ND 31-30

Attendance: 59,075

TEAM STATISTICS

	UM	ND
First Downs	26	16
Total Net Yards	481	331
Rushes-Yards	28-57	49-113
Passing	424	218
Punt Returns	2-21	0-0
Kickoff Returns	6-74	2-41
Interceptions-Returns	1-0	3-72
Comp-Att-Int	31-50-3	10-18-1
Sacked By-Yards Lost	0-0	0-0
Punts	1-25.0	4-37.7
Fumbles-Lost	4-4	3-2
Penalties-Yards	6-34	5-39
Time of Possession	28:59	31:01

INDIVIDUAL STATISTICS

Rushing: ND: Brooks, 13-56, Banks 7-21, Rice 21-20, Green 4-6, Watters 1-5, Johnson 2-3, Eilers 1-2. UM: Gary 12-28, Conley 10-27, Crowell 3-7, Walsh 2-(-4), Britton 1-(-1).

Passing: ND: Rice, 8-16-1-195, K. Graham 2-2-0-23. UM: Walsh, 31-50-3-424.

Receiving: ND: Ismail 4-96, Brown 2-46, Watters 1-44, Green 1-21, Banks 1-9, K. Graham 1-2. UM: Gary 11-130, Brown 8-125, Chudzinski 6-85, Conley 3-41, Dawkins 2-35, Hill 1-8.

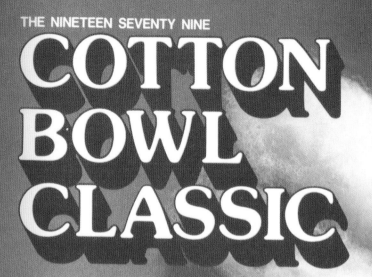

THE NINETEEN SEVENTY NINE

COTTON
BOWL
CLASSIC

Houston vs
Notre Dame

Official Souvenir Program

January 1 / Dallas, Texas $2.50

2

NOTRE DAME 35, HOUSTON 34 1979 COTTON BOWL

JANUARY 1, 1979

JOE MONTANA'S GRIDIRON PERFORMANCES WERE LESS EVOCATIVE of a gifted athlete than of a Saturday matinee idol. In fact, he was both. The Monongahela, Pennsylvania, native was the Notre Dame quarterback, but he was also the Lone Ranger, Mighty Mouse, and every other cartoon or celluloid hero who never saved the day until the day absolutely, positively needed saving.

Joe Montana! Even the name evokes images of a new sheriff riding into town. But every hero needs an alias, and so his was The Comeback Kid. By the beginning of his fifth autumn in South Bend, Montana had already earned that moniker. On New Year's Day 1979, in the Forty-third Cotton Bowl Classic against the University of Houston, he would take that nickname to its climactic apogee. In his final college game, on the final play, with 0:00 showing on the clock, Montana would consummate what was statistically, and dramatically, the greatest comeback in Notre Dame history.

As a Notre Dame freshman four years earlier, Montana had found himself listed seventh on the quarterback depth chart. Although popular with his teammates, who called him "Montanalow" due to his resemblance to pop singer Barry Manilow (whose fame was never greater than at this time), Montana was reputedly a poor practice player. That may have been what kept Coach Dan Devine from allowing him to start a game, although Devine never shied away from allowing Montana to finish one. The Comeback Kid had already bailed the Irish out of numerous fourth-quarter perils. Trailing unranked North Carolina, 14-6, at Chapel Hill in 1975, Montana, then a sophomore, entered the game and tossed a pair of touchdowns in the final 5:11 for a 21-14 win.

> "What he would do," remembers center Dave Huffman, "was kneel down in the middle of the huddle, lick his fingers, and say, 'OKAY, LET'S WIN THIS GAME.' And that's what would happen."

The very next Saturday in Colorado Springs, Notre Dame trailed unranked Air Force, 30-10, with 13:00 left. Again Montana got the call. He led the Irish to three touchdowns, running for one and tossing seven yards to tight end Ken MacAfee for another, as the Irish edged the Falcons, 31-30. There would be other such heroics.

"What he would do," remembers center Dave Huffman, "was kneel down in the middle of the huddle, lick his fingers, and say, 'Okay, let's win this game.' And that's what would happen."

Fast forward to the 1979 Cotton Bowl. The defending national champion Irish were headed to Dallas for the second straight year, albeit this time with an 8-3 record. Southwest Conference champ Houston, which had won the Cotton Bowl two years earlier, would be the foe.

The weather reflected the contrast in Notre Dame's two visits to Dallas in as many years. The Irish had awakened on January 2, 1978, to a morning as shiny as their prospects. Notre Dame defeated Texas, 38-10, to win the national title. On January 1, 1979, the Irish woke up to a city besieged by the worst ice storm it had suffered in thirty years. The sky was barren and gray. Meteorological data do no justice to the bone-numbing chill. They provide merely a starting point. The temperature ranged between sixteen and twenty-two degrees. Coupled with a wind of between eighteen and thirty miles per hour, the wind chill was somewhere around minus-six to minus-ten degrees.

Most of the 72,000 thousand Cotton Bowl seats were encrusted in ice. As was Dallas. Power lines and trees fell, leaving 10,000 residents without power. There were 39,500 no-shows and only 32,500 inside the stadium.

"I got a hundred tickets here, and I'm selling them from twenty-five cents to a hundred dollars," complained one ticket broker. "I've lost two to three thousand dollars in a day of work. It's a gamble, and it's part of the business. Sometimes you just have to eat them. I like 'em sautéed; I like 'em barbecued. Doesn't matter."

The game began as bizarrely as it would end. It was delayed ten minutes after both the Notre Dame and Houston kicking units lined up across from one another for the opening kickoff. "We told [tri-captain Bob] Golic if we won the toss to defend the north goal, because that put the wind at our backs," Devine explained later. "We told him five times not to say 'and kick.' But he's excitable, and he added 'and kick.'"

MOST OF THE 72,000 THOUSAND COTTON BOWL SEATS WERE ENCRUSTED IN ICE. As was Dallas. Power lines and trees fell, leaving 10,000 residents without power.

When that confusion was sorted out—and nothing was less welcome on this frostbitten afternoon than an unnecessary delay—the Cougars kicked off. Randy Harrison returned the kick 56 yards on the ice-slicked artificial turf, but the Irish drive stalled. On its second series, Notre Dame took over on its own 34. Aided by a 27-yard completion to fullback Jerome Heavens and a 28-yard completion to tight end Dean Masztak, the Irish went 66 yards in nine plays. Montana

A wicked ice storm the night before the game resulted in more empty seats than spectators, and many, if not most, were gone by halftime.

skated in for a touchdown around right end from three yards out for the touchdown. Kicker Joe Unis, a Dallas native, missed the extra point and Notre Dame led, 6-0.

On the ensuing kickoff Terry Elsten of the Cougars fumbled. Notre Dame freshman Bob Crable recovered at the Houston 25. Six plays later fullback Pete Buchanan rumbled in from the one for another Notre Dame score. The two-point conversion

Joe Montana, handing off to Vagas Ferguson (No. 32) following the block of Pete Pallas (No. 45), turned the ball over three times in the second quarter. As we discovered, he was feeling as bad as he played. A bowl of hot chicken soup came to his rescue.

attempt failed, but the Irish led, 12-0, with barely ten minutes elapsed.

Then it was the Irish who played as if their fingers were frozen. First, an official ruled that a Houston punt had touched Notre Dame's Dave Waymer. Chuck Brown of the Cougars recovered on the Irish 12-yard line. Three plays later quarterback Danny Davis threw a 15-yard touchdown pass to Willie Adams. At the end of the first quarter, Notre Dame led, 12-7.

In the second quarter Montana, whose own body temperature was beginning to drop, committed three turnovers. Houston scored off each one. First, Montana lost a fumble at his own 21. Six plays later Houston's Randy Love scored from one yard out to make it 14-12. Then Montana tossed two interceptions late in the quarter, leading to Kenny Hatfield of the Cougars kicking field goals of 21 and 34 yards. The latter came with 0:03 left in the half and gave Houston a 20-12 lead.

Houston's four first-half scores all were the direct results of Notre Dame turnovers. The Cougars' longest scoring march, its last one, was only 39 yards. Meanwhile, the Cougars' ground attack, led by 1,000-yard rusher Emmitt King, had already gained 155 yards.

Inside the Notre Dame locker room, Montana was a worrisome sight. Wrapped in blankets, Montana was suffering from hypothermia as his body temperature had dropped nearly three degrees, to ninety-six. Earlier in the week it had been reported that Montana was fighting the flu. "I wasn't sick," he would say later. "I was just cold. I was chilled."

When the Irish ventured back outside to the Cotton Bowl tundra for the second half, Montana did not join them. Would The Comeback Kid be coming back? "We were told that Joe wasn't coming back in the second half," Huffman said, "and we thought it was over."

Houston scored a touchdown midway through the third quarter to take a 27-12 lead. Inside the Notre Dame locker room, team doctor Les Bodnar was heating up a packet of chicken broth powder mix for Montana. That Bodnar even had such a remedy was fortuitous and, appropriately for this day, bizarre. Notre Dame had arrived in Dallas two days before Christmas. In the Bodnar family's hotel suite, the doctor's youngest daughter had placed a packet of Mrs. Grass's soup in her father's Christmas stocking. Bodnar brought the packet with him to the game. After adding its contents to boiling water, Bodnar gave the instant soup to Montana.

Inside the Notre Dame locker room, team doctor Les Bodnar was heating up a packet of chicken broth powder mix for Montana. THAT BODNAR EVEN HAD SUCH A REMEDY WAS FORTUITOUS AND, APPROPRIATELY FOR THIS DAY, BIZARRE.

Bodnar's broth might as well have been spinach and Montana might as well have been Popeye. "I was coming back no matter what," Montana later said. "The doctors might have tried to hold me back, but I don't think they could have. This was my last game."

With 6:11 remaining in the third quarter, Montana reappeared on the Notre Dame sideline. His backup, Tim Koegel, had failed to move the Irish past their own 21-yard line and was 0-3 passing in the admittedly miserable conditions.

"When Joe came back to the field," said split end Kris Haines, "I started thinking this was a fairy tale."

Or was it? Moments after Montana got to the sideline, Houston's Bobby Harrison blocked Dick Boushka's punt. (Boushka was a backup; regular punter Joe Restic had been knocked out of the game earlier.) The Cougars recovered on the Irish 19 and quarterback Davis scored three plays later on a five-yard run. Now the score was 34-12 with 4:40 to play in the third quarter. Houston had scored thirty-four unanswered points. If the score was not enough motivation for the Cotton Bowl fans to exit the stadium, Montana threw an interception on his sixth play back in the game. Early in the fourth quarter, he threw another one.

Notre Dame's Jim Browner didn't let the sub-zero wind chill slow him down going after the Cougars.

After nearly three and a half quarters on this day, Montana's passing stats read like this: 7-for-26 passing, four interceptions, no touchdowns. The nadir came early in the fourth quarter when Haines, who was supposed to run a post pattern, changed his route. Montana took a sack on the play and Haines was flagged for shoving a Cougar defensive back, resulting in a loss of 15 more yards.

On the sideline Haines and Montana, who had stayed in South Bend the previous summer and been roommates, got into it. "Why don't you run the patterns?" a frustrated Montana asked.

Haines barked back. "Then we looked at each other," Haines would later say, "and said, 'Why are we arguing?'"

The comeback began with 7:37 remaining. Six-foot-three Notre Dame freshman Tony Belden blocked a Houston punt and yet another freshman special teams player, Steve Cichy, returned it 33 yards for a touchdown. Montana then found Vagas Ferguson on a pass for the two-point conversion. The score was 34-20.

The Notre Dame defense held and the Irish got the ball back on their own 39 with 5:40 left. This time Montana was masterful, completing passes of 17 and 30 yards. After a pass-interference call added on another 11 yards, Montana took it in himself around left end from two yards out. Again he converted the two-point try, this time finding Haines on a busted route. There was plenty of time and the Irish only trailed by six, 34-28.

In fact, The Comeback Kid may have had too much time. After the Irish defense, now playing without Restic (the punter was also a safety) and All-American middle linebacker Bob Golic, who had twisted his knee earlier in the game, held yet again, Notre Dame had the ball on the Cougar 36 with more than two minutes left. Montana, flushed from the pocket, scrambled 16 yards but had the ball jarred loose by Houston linebacker David Hodge.

Cougar Tommy Ebner recovered at the Houston 20 with 1:50 left. Getting up,

Montana pressed both hands against the side of his gold helmet in frustration. "You couldn't print what I was saying," he said. "I called myself a few names."

Montana trudged to the sideline. His knees and elbows were bloodied from the frozen turf that had been sprinkled with salt to melt the ice [trainers would cut his pants off after the game]. He looked beaten. The Southern Cal loss had been excruciating. Now this. He looked at Haines.

"It's all over," said The Comeback Kid.

"No, it's not," Haines replied.

Again, the Irish defense held. Houston, faced with a fourth and six at its 24 with less than a minute left, punted. Jay Wyatt, who already had two punts blocked in this game, sent a 21-yard kick into the gusty wing. Then someone noticed the yellow flag. The Irish had jumped offside.

Would Houston decline the penalty, giving Notre Dame first down at the Cougar 45 with 0:35 left? Or would they take the five yards and go for it on fourth and one? Houston coach Bill Yeoman chose to go for the first down and, in effect, the win. "We rushed for 260 yards this afternoon," Yeoman would later say. "I figured we should try for one more."

Yeoman called for a run off left-tackle. Davis handed the ball to King, but the exchange was clumsy. Irish linemen Joe Gramke and Mike Calhoun stopped King inches short of the first down.

Said Gramke, "They'd been running that play on short yardage. I wasn't crashing, but I crashed anyway. They didn't pick me up, and I had a clear shot at him. I wrapped him up high and somebody cut his legs out low."

The Comeback Kid, with the ball on the 29, 0:28 on the clock, and no time-outs left, had one last chance. He gained 11 yards on a keeper, then tossed to Haines for 10. Now the Irish were on the Cougar eight with six seconds left. No more than ten thousand fans were still inside the Cotton Bowl.

The two had worked on this out pattern countless times the previous summer. Haines's feet were barely inbounds, and his hands were low and reaching out of bounds. THE CLOCK READ 0:00.

The Cougars called time-out. Devine and Montana huddled and decided to call 91, a quick out by both wide receivers. This might afford the Irish a second play if it failed.

Montana took the snap and tossed to Haines in the right corner, but the ball whizzed by him as he was turning. Two seconds remained. Back in the huddle, Montana looked at his friend. "Can you beat your man again?" he asked. Haines said yes. Montana called the same play.

Haines, lined up wide right, ran into the end zone, then sharply to the outside. Montana's pass, low and to the outside to avoid any defender, was already in the air. The two had worked on this out pattern countless times the previous summer. Haines's feet were barely inbounds, and his hands were low and reaching out of bounds. The clock read 0:00.

"It might have looked like a bad pass," Haines would later say, "but it wasn't."

"He knew what I wanted him to call," Devine said. "He looked over to the sideline, and I just waved him back. That may be the first time all year we didn't send the play in from the bench."

Touchdown. The Comeback Kid had done it again. Still, the drama was not over. Unis kicked the extra point (his first of the game), but the Irish were called for illegal

Split end Kris Haines gets a celebratory hug from Dave Huffman after making a diving catch of a Montana pass for the touchdown that tied the game with no time on the clock.

motion. Again, both sides lined up with no time remaining. Unis, now attempting the game-winning point from 25 yards away, kicked the ball straight and true. It sailed through the uprights, putting the finishing touch on a remarkable twenty-three-point comeback in the Cotton Bowl's final 7:37.

Earlier in the week, Yeoman had dispelled the concept of the Notre Dame mystique. He told his Cougars that such talk was "garbage." Huffman, the Irish's All-American center, had respectfully disagreed.

"It's there even when you don't want to believe it," Huffman said. "There comes a time when skeptics turn around and, bang, there it is. Right in front of them. And they know it."

Notre Dame 35, Houston 34
Cotton Bowl, Dallas, Texas
January 1, 1979

SCORING SUMMARY

	1	2	3	4	
Notre Dame	12	0	0	23	35
Houston	7	13	14	0	34

Team	Qtr.	Time Left	Play	Score
ND	1	6:55	Joe Montana 3 run (Joe Unis kick failed)	ND 6-0
ND	1	4:40	Pete Buchanan 1 run (Montana pass failed)	ND 12-0
UH	1	0:17	Willis Adams 15 pass from Danny Davis (Kenny Hatfield kick)	ND 12-7
UH	2	6:27	Randy Love 1 run (Hatfield kick)	UH 14-12
UH	2	3:00	Hatfield 21 FG	UH 17-12
UH	2	0:03	Hatfield 34 FG	UH 20-12
UH	3	6:29	Davis 2 run (Hatfield kick)	UH 27-12
UH	3	4:40	Davis 5 run (Hatfield kick)	UH 34-12
ND	4	7:25	Steve Cichy 33 blocked punt return (Vagas Ferguson pass from Montana)	UH 34-20
ND	4	4:15	Montana 2 run (Kris Haines pass from Montana)	UH 34-28
ND	4	0:00	Haines 8 pass from Montana (Unis kick)	ND 35-34

Attendance: 32,500

TEAM STATISTICS

	ND	UH
First Downs	13	16
Total Net Yards	294	289
Rushes-Yards	40-131	63-229
Passing	163	60
Punt Returns	5-48	2 (-2)
Kickoff Returns	6-136	2-33
Interceptions-Returns	0-0	4-43
Comp-Att-Int	13-37-4	4-13-0
Punts	7-26.3	10-25.5
Fumbles-Lost	3-3	6-3
Penalties-Yards	8-74	6-39
Time of Possession	26:12	33:48

INDIVIDUAL STATISTICS

Rushing: ND: Heavens 16-71, Montana 7-26, Ferguson 10-19, Pallas 4-11, Mitchell 1-3, Buchanan 2-I.
UH: Davis 19-76, King 21-74, Love 22-73, Brown 1-6.

Passing: ND: Montana 13-34-4-163, Koegel 0-3-0-0.
UH: Davis 4-12-0-60, Brown 0-1-0-0.

Receiving: ND: Heavens 4-60, Haines 4-31, Masztak 3-49, Holohan 1-14, Ferguson 1-9.
UH: Adams 2-35, Herring 2-25.

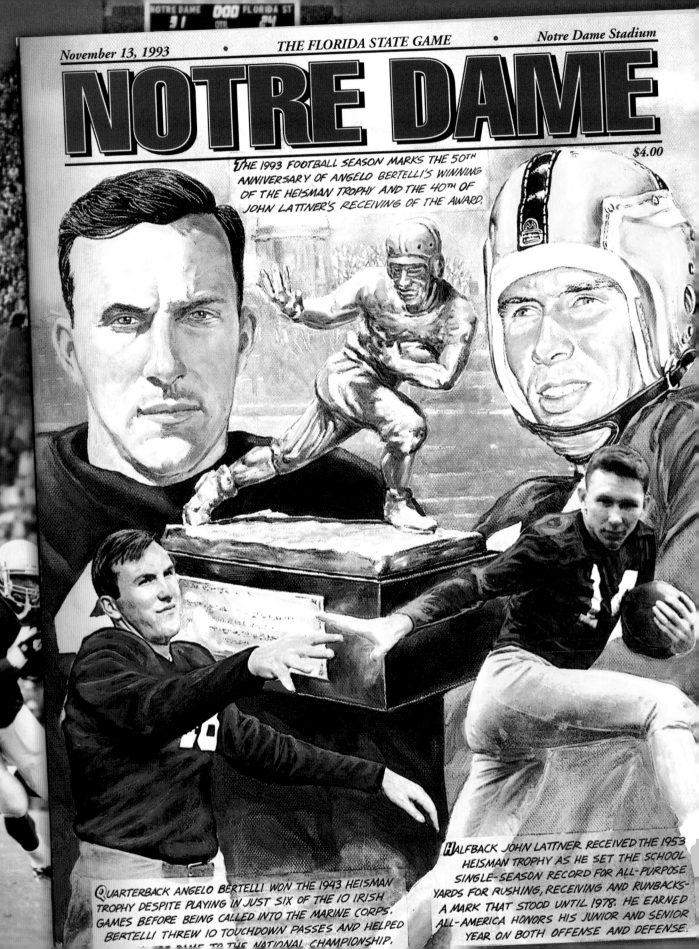

NOTRE DAME

November 13, 1993 • THE FLORIDA STATE GAME • *Notre Dame Stadium*

$4.00

THE 1993 FOOTBALL SEASON MARKS THE 50TH ANNIVERSARY OF ANGELO BERTELLI'S WINNING OF THE HEISMAN TROPHY AND THE 40TH OF JOHN LATTNER'S RECEIVING OF THE AWARD.

QUARTERBACK ANGELO BERTELLI WON THE 1943 HEISMAN TROPHY DESPITE PLAYING IN JUST SIX OF THE 10 IRISH GAMES BEFORE BEING CALLED INTO THE MARINE CORPS. BERTELLI THREW 10 TOUCHDOWN PASSES AND HELPED NOTRE DAME TO THE NATIONAL CHAMPIONSHIP.

HALFBACK JOHN LATTNER RECEIVED THE 1953 HEISMAN TROPHY AS HE SET THE SCHOOL SINGLE-SEASON RECORD FOR ALL-PURPOSE YARDS FOR RUSHING, RECEIVING AND RUNBACKS- A MARK THAT STOOD UNTIL 1978. HE EARNED ALL-AMERICA HONORS HIS JUNIOR AND SENIOR YEAR ON BOTH OFFENSE AND DEFENSE.

3

NOTRE DAME 31, FLORIDA STATE 24

NOVEMBER 13, 1993

"This might be the biggest game ever in college football."
—Florida State defensive end Derrick Alexander

FIVE YEARS AFTER THE UNIVERSITY OF MIAMI SWAGGERED INTO South Bend with a No. 1 ranking and the nation's longest win streak, their in-state neighbors arrived at Notre Dame with similarly impressive bona fides. The Seminoles of Florida State University strutted onto campus a day before their November 13 showdown versus the Irish with a No. 1 ranking, a sixteen-game win streak (tied with Notre Dame at the time for longest in the nation), and an arrogant-bordering-on-comical disdain for their host's historic imprints on the sport.

"Mystique?" asked Seminole wide receiver Kevin Knox. "There is no mystique. They should be scared of our mystique. We're a dominating team. We could be the best college team ever."

"Rock Knutne?" quipped linebacker Chris Cowart, when asked to name Notre Dame's greatest coaching legend. "Right? Rock Knutne?"

One could forgive these Seminoles their vainglory. Coached by the undeniably like-able Bobby Bowden, sixty-four, Florida State had endured an arduous climb to the summit. FSU was in the midst of its seventh consecutive ten-win season under Bowden, but because in-state rival Miami had won six of the two schools' past seven meetings prior to 1993, the Seminoles had yet to sniff a national championship. This year, though, FSU had clobbered the Hurricanes, 28-10, in Tallahassee.

"**MYSTIQUE?**" said Seminole wide receiver Kevin Knox. "There is no mystique. They should be scared of our mystique."

"Write this down," said cornerback Clifton Abraham, the most garrulous of the Seminoles. "Miami was the final obstacle. We're not going to beat Miami and lose to someone else."

Besides, who expected Lou Holtz's Irish to be here, ranked No. 2 and, like the Seminoles, 9-0 and with a sixteen-game win streak? Notre Dame had lost nine players to the NFL from its 1992 squad that had finished 10-1-1. Moreover, the season had begun turbulently. Before the final preseason scrimmage, Holtz had informed senior quarter-back Kevin McDougal, who had waited patiently behind Rick Mirer three years for his opportunity to start, that he was naming true freshman Ron Powlus as the starter. Then, during that very scrimmage, Powlus broke his collarbone.

Unphased, McDougal told Holtz, "I think I can lead this team to a national championship."

"Goodness gracious," Holtz said, "you can't even get us a first down."

Besides the loss of those nine players to the NFL, a brief stay in the hospital due to chest pains, and the release of a book *Under the Tarnished Dome* that alleged

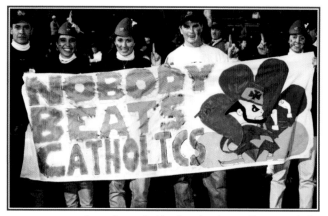

For another week at least, such a sign would prove prophetic.

he did everything from turning a blind eye to improprieties in his program to spitting on a player, Holtz had never been happier. "I could walk away from this game now," he said, "and I'd be at peace."

Then, in the season's second week, the No. 11 Irish rumbled into Ann Arbor a seven-point underdog to No. 3 Michigan. The Irish won, 27-23, and carried their embattled coach off the field. Holtz, brittle from having undergone so much scrutiny in the past few months, approached the FSU game with an uncharacteristic bravado and candor.

"We didn't get to be 9-0 and get to play in this game because we won the lottery," Holtz said. "We're here because we belong here. We've earned it and tomorrow we're going to prove it."

The Seminoles, meanwhile, betrayed a bemused annoyance with their opponent's legacy. The media, intrigued with what ESPN *College Gameday* host Chris Fowler called a "history mismatch," clearly enjoyed quizzing the Seminoles on Fighting Irish Football 101.

"I've heard of the Four Horsemen," said Seminole center Clay Shiver, "but we haven't watched any film of them."

> Unphased, McDougal told Holtz, "I think I can lead this team to a national championship." "Goodness gracious," Holtz said, "YOU CAN'T EVEN GET US A FIRST DOWN."

"We're playing this game in the present, aren't we?" wide receiver Kez McCorvey asked.

On Friday afternoon the Seminoles toured Notre Dame Stadium. Many of them mockingly donned green baseball caps with a gold interlocking *FSU* on the front. On the side of the caps were shamrocks. That evening some thirteen thousand Fighting Irish faithful crammed into the Joyce Athletic Center for a boisterous pep rally during which Holtz addressed them. "I've heard Florida State say they don't know anything about mystique," Holtz said. "They've never been around mystique. How would they recognize it?"

The audience roared its approval. Later, Holtz would say that he took his cue from a television documentary he had recently watched featuring former U.S. Army general and president Dwight D. Eisenhower. "The one thing Dwight Eisenhower said was, 'If you don't have a positive attitude with the commander, victory is impossible,'" Holtz said.

It was difficult for anyone facing the Seminoles, even Holtz, to maintain a positive attitude. Florida State was averaging 44.3 points per game, and their average margin of victory was thirty-eight points. The Seminoles had the nation's No. 1 defense, anchored by aggressive outside linebacker Derrick Brooks.

FSU quarterback Charlie Ward showed why he was worthy of the Heisman Trophy. The best the Irish defense could do was contain him, which they did well. Even then, Ward nearly pulled it out in the end and may have just run out of time.

Their No. 2-ranked offense was led by senior quarterback Charlie Ward, a shoo-in for the Heisman Trophy. He entered the game with a 69 percent completion rate and sixteen touchdown passes against only one interception. "They need to play the most perfect game Notre Dame has ever played," the Seminoles' Abraham said, "if they plan on beating us."

Holtz agreed. He believed that the 1993 Seminoles were the best team he had seen in twenty-four years of coaching, which is exactly why he puffed out his chest so brazenly in the days before the contest. "I really thought for us to have a chance to win," Holtz said, "our team had to believe it had a chance."

Holtz did believe it. So did Bowden, an old friend eight years Holtz's senior who, as an FSU assistant in 1961, had hosted Holtz and his new bride, Beth, for a night or two as they passed through Tallahassee on their low-budget honeymoon. "Number one, [Lou] will be the underdog," Bowden said. "Oh Lord, he eats that up. Number two, he's got an extra week of practice. He's playing in his own backyard. He ought to be feeling pretty good."

He was. In reviewing film Holtz had discovered his advantage. His talented offensive line outweighed FSU's defensive line by an average of thirty-nine pounds per man. "He really felt that they were small," McDougal said. "They were really fast, but he thought we just had to pound them."

Or, as *Washington Post* columnist Michael Wilbon wrote in his game preview, "Can you spell *smashmouth*?"

The hype for this No. 1-vs.-No. 2 matchup, the first in Notre Dame Stadium in twenty-five years (No. 1 Purdue had beaten the second-ranked Irish, 37-22, in 1968), set new precedents. Notre Dame issued a record 810 media credentials; *College Gameday* set up shop in the Joyce Center, the first of many times Fowler et al would do so for a regular-season game. NBC added the ace of its staff, Bob Costas, to the production as well as a second sideline reporter: O. J. Simpson. More than fifty million viewers would tune in at some point to see the most-watched regular season college football game since Alabama–Auburn in 1981.

Cash flowed. Imprudent ticket seekers were bilked out of an estimated fifty thousand dollars by scalpers hawking counterfeit tickets. Authentic tickets were going at anywhere from four hundred to a thousand dollars per. One desperate fan traded his 1991 Honda for a pair of tickets at midfield. At least eight thousand fans would watch the game on closed-circuit TV across the street from Notre Dame Stadium inside the Joyce Center. In Las Vegas oddsmakers were projecting more than ten million dollars in bets. "I anticipate this to be the largest college football game ever bet on in the state of Nevada," said the sports director at Bally's casino.

The atmosphere, if not the overcast skies, was reminiscent of the 1988 Miami contest: a No. 1, unbeaten, smack-talking squad from the Sunshine State that happened to have the nation's longest win streak; a Notre Dame quarterback in whose arm Holtz professed to have little faith; and an underground T-shirt that was selling briskly (this one read: CATHOLICS *vs.* CREMINOLES). Would the outcome be the same? Only time—to be precise, a commercial-laden-telecast three hours, forty-six minutes—would tell.

Florida State struck first. After the Irish took the opening kickoff and ran off six plays before punting, the Seminoles took over on their own 11. Ward, who was also the starting point guard for the Seminole basketball team, calmly directed his offense 89 yards in ten plays for a touchdown. He rushed twice for 34 yards and completed five passes for 43 yards, the last a 12-yard touchdown to Knox. The visitors led, 7-0.

The Irish responded right away on this unseasonably warm (fifty-nine degrees) and blustery afternoon, marching 80 yards in seven plays to tie the score, 7-7. On the first

play of the drive, fullback Ray Zellars burst straight up the middle for an 18-yard gain. On the seventh play senior punter/flanker Adrian Jarrell, running left to right, took the ball on a reverse and galloped 32 yards up the right sideline for the touchdown. The carry was only the third of Jarrell's career.

Jarrell's jaunt was accompanied by a crushing downfield block from six-foot-four, 299-pound left tackle Aaron Taylor, who crossed the field to do so. Taylor and center Tim Ruddy were in the midst of All-American seasons. Along with left guard Mark Zataveski, right guard Ryan Leahy (a grandson of former Irish coach Frank Leahy), and right tackle Todd Norman, they were responsible for the Irish gaining 99 first-quarter rushing yards. The Seminole defense began the day having yielded only 97 rushing yards per game.

Flanker Adrian Jarrell finishes off his 32-yard scoring run, coming on only his third career carry.

"That's really the core of the team, right there," Zataveski said, alluding to his linemates.

The entire first half was a humbling experience for the Seminoles, who trailed at intermission, 21-7. Florida State entered the contest having allowed two rushing touchdowns all season. The Irish ran for three touchdowns in the first half, the latter two on a 26-yard sprint by tailback Lee Becton and a six-yard burst by Jeff Burris. An All-American free safety, Burris lined up as a halfback in short-yardage T-formations this afternoon.

Notre Dame's offensive supremacy was only half the tale. Defensive tackle Bryant Young twice sacked Ward, equaling the number of times the

Tailback Lee Becton ran 26 yards for one of three rushing touchdowns the Irish would put on the board in the first half.

elusive signal-caller had been sacked all season. Before the game Holtz had made sport of his defense's lack of speed. "Play-action passes won't work against us," he said. "Our line-backers are too slow to get out of position." But the Irish did pressure Ward into tossing his first inter-ception (picked off by strong safety John Covington) in 159 attempts, and Burris dropped at least three more in the first half.

> "Play-action passes won't work against us," Holtz said. "OUR LINEBACKERS ARE TOO SLOW TO GET OUT OF POSITION."

Florida State did itself no favors. With a rush-ing offense that averaged 8.2 yards per carry, the 'Noles went to the air twenty times in their twenty-five first-half plays following their initial score. "I didn't think we ran enough," said McCorvey—and this from the Seminoles' leading receiver (eleven catches) on this day.

The lowest point for Florida State came with 10:42 left in the second quarter. From their own 20 the 'Noles attempted a cross-field, double-lateral pass. Ward lateraled to tailback Sean Jackson (6.8 yards per carry on the season), who then threw backward to Ward, who slipped to the turf at his own six yard-line. A 14-yard loss. On the next play Ward threw a rainbow into the twenty-mile-per-hour southerly wind that was intercepted by Covington. The Irish had the ball at the FSU 23, and four plays later they scored on Burris's six-yard run. As had Jarrell and Becton before him, Burris crossed the goal line standing up.

For the first time in twenty-three games, the Seminoles were losing at halftime.

"We waited 'til halftime before we even started to play," linebacker Ken Alexander angrily spat afterward. "Notre Dame shouldn't have scored a point on us. Not one point."

Inside the FSU locker room, Bowden found himself in the unusual role of having to rally his team. Asked later what he said, Bowden replied, "Told 'em the same thing Knute would've."

In the third quarter the Irish, moving with the wind, extended their lead to 24-7. Kicker Kevin Pendergast split the uprights with a career-long 47-yard field goal. FSU trimmed the lead back to seven points thanks to a pair of freshmen. With 4:45 to play, Ward tossed a six-yard pass to tailback Warrick Dunn. Then, with 10:40 remaining in the contest, Dunn's classmate Scott Bentley, who had missed a first-quarter field-goal attempt, converted a 24-yarder with the wind at his back to close the gap to 24-17.

The Irish then put together their most impressive scoring drive of the day. With McDougal, who would finish 9-of-18 passing for 108 yards, showing poise in the pocket, Notre Dame marched 80 yards for a touchdown. The key play was a third-down completion of 14 yards to wideout Lake Dawson in which McDougal, whom Holtz had briefly kicked out of practice that Tuesday for making a bad read on a pass, stepped under a Seminole blitz and calmly double-pumped before making his toss. A few plays later Burris scampered into the end zone from 11 yards out. The Irish led, 31-17, with 6:53 left.

Ward, finally displaying his Heisman pedigree, rallied the Seminoles yet again. As the Florida State and Notre Dame fans waged a literal extended-arms battle with one another—FSU's "tomahawk chop" mimicking Notre Dame's "LOU!" cheer—Ward brought the Seminoles to a first and goal at the Irish five. Alas for FSU, a 15-yard dead-ball foul was called on offensive lineman Jesus Hernandez. Three plays later the Seminoles faced fourth and goal from the Irish 20, the game and more hanging in the balance.

Irish defensive coordinator **RICK MINTER INSERTED WOODEN,** whose good hands had cradled FSU's onside kick two minutes earlier, as a sixth defensive back.

"The perfect season for the Seminoles, coming down to this play," said NBC play-by-play announcer Charlie Jones. Ward dropped back and fired a missile into the middle of the end zone. The ball landed in Notre Dame cornerback Brian Magee's hands, then miraculously ricocheted out and into the fortunate arms of McCorvey. The 20-yard touchdown completion was Ward's longest of the day, but more importantly, with 2:26 left, it made the score 31-24.

Notre Dame defensive back Shawn Wooden recovered Bentley's onside kick at the Florida State 47, but the Irish were unable to run out the clock. After three rushing plays gained five yards, Notre Dame was forced to punt. Jarrell shanked his partially blocked kick against the wind, and the ball traveled only five yards. As darkness enshrouded the stadium, the Seminoles had the ball at their own 37 with 0:51 showing on the clock. Plenty of time.

Ward, operating with no time-outs, wasted none of it. He completed four straight passes, one to Dunn and three to McCorvey, totaling 49 yards. Ten seconds remained. The Seminoles had the ball on the Irish 14. Time for two more plays.

Ward's first pass was batted up in the air by defensive end Thomas Knight. Three seconds remained. Irish defensive coordinator Rick Minter inserted Wooden, whose good hands had cradled FSU's onside kick two minutes earlier, as a sixth defensive back. The game would come down to this play.

It was déjà vu for long-time Notre Dame fans. Five years earlier Miami had trailed by the same score, 31-24, when quarterback Steve Walsh threw an 11-yard touchdown pass to Andre Brown with 0:45 seconds left. Miami lost, 31-30, though, and Walsh ended the day with 31-for-50 passing. Now Ward, who had already completed thirty-one passes, was about to attempt his fiftieth with the Seminoles trailing, 31-24.

On the Notre Dame sideline, McDougal and Becton held hands and looked away. "I had watched the drive where they got the touchdown before," McDougal said, "so I said I'll switch up and not watch it. On the last play I just waited for the crowd reaction."

Ward dropped back in the pocket, scanning the end zone for either Knox or McCorvey. Neither were open. Ward rolled left. Wooden, in the end zone, drifted in the same direction.

Jubilant Notre Dame fans celebrated their team's huge victory, although the sentiment would turn to heartbreak a week later.

"My job was to read Charlie," Wooden said. "Coach Holtz just told us to stay fundamentally sound, read your keys. When he scrambled to my side, I said over and over, 'Just stay home.'"

Ward, nearing the sideline, was running out of room. The clock already read 0:00. FSU flanker Matt Frier, mirroring Ward, was open at the five-yard line but the Heisman Trophy candidate threw the ball toward Dunn in the back of the end zone.

Wooden, positioned perfectly, batted the ball down harmlessly to the turf in the northwest corner of the end zone, right in front of the student section. "The pass was right to me," he said. "I was surprised. I just wanted to knock it down and make sure."

A moment later Wooden and the rest of the Irish disappeared in the wave of humanity as the student section celebrated the 31-24 victory. Wooden injured his knee in the pandemonium and was forced to miss the following week's Boston College game.

Notre Dame had not played a perfect game, but they had come pretty darn close. The Irish did not commit a turnover (for a fourth straight game) and were penalized only four times for 38 yards. Becton alone outrushed Florida State, gaining 122 yards to their 96. The Seminoles, who despite playing erratically had made a valiant comeback and nearly won, were in disbelief.

"For every one person they have," said Abraham, as if it might alter the outcome, "we have three people better."

That might have been true. "I think FSU is the best football team we have beaten since I've been coaching," Holtz said.

Ward would win the Heisman Trophy. The Seminoles, beneficiaries of Notre Dame's stunning 41-39 loss to Boston College the following Saturday, would win Bowden his well-deserved first national title. Still, as Bowden freely admitted as dusk faded to darkness, "The better team won today."

It was a thrilling game, if not quite the Game of the Century. It was, however, the comeuppance of the century.

Notre Dame 31, Florida State 24
Notre Dame Stadium, South Bend, Indiana
November 13, 1993

SCORING SUMMARY

	1	2	3	4	
Florida State	7	0	7	10	24
Notre Dame	7	14	3	7	31

Team	Qtr.	Time Left	Play	Score
FS	1	7:09	Kevin Knox 12 pass from Charlie Ward (Scott Bentley kick)	FS 7-0
ND	1	4:30	Adrian Jarrell 32 run (Kevin Pendergast kick)	7-7
ND	2	10:42	Lee Becton 26 run (Pendergast kick)	ND 14-7
ND	2	7:48	Jeff Burris 6 run (Pendergast kick)	ND 21-7
ND	3	9:41	Pendergast 47 FG	ND 24-7
FS	3	4:45	Warrick Dunn 6 pass from Ward (Bentley kick)	ND 24-14
FS	4	10:40	Bentley 24 FG	ND 24-17
ND	4	6:53	Burris 11 run (Pendergast kick)	ND 31-17
FS	4	2:26	Kez McCorvey 20 pass from Ward (Bentley kick)	ND 31-24

Attendance: 59,075

TEAM STATISTICS

	FS	ND
First Downs	26	20
Total Net Yards	403	347
Rushes-Yards	27-96	49-239
Passing	307	108
Punt Returns	2-19	1-1
Kickoff Returns	3-64	1-33
Interceptions-Returns	0-0	1-7
Comp-Att-Int	32-53-1	9-18-0
Sacked By-Yards Lost	1-9	2-22
Punts	6-36.8	7-34.0
Fumbles-Lost	1-1	0-0
Penalties-Yards	7-70	4-38
Time of Possession	29:40	30:20

INDIVIDUAL STATISTICS

Rushing: ND: Becton 26-122, Zellars 11-44, Jarrell 1-32, Burris 3-19, McDougal 6-12, Failla 1-10, Kinder 1-0.
FS: Ward 11-38, Floyd 5-31, Jackson 7-18, McCorvey 1-9, Dunn 3-0.

Passing: ND: McDougal 9-18-0-108.
FS: Ward 31-50-1-297, Jackson 1-2-0-10, McCorvey 0-1-0-0.

Receiving: ND: Becton 2-39, Miller 2-30, Johnson 2-22, Dawson 2-20, Zellars 1-(-3).
FS: McCorvey 11-138, Jackson 5-26, Frier 4-46, Vanover 4-30, Dunn 3-18, Knox 2-30, Floyd 2-9, Ward 1-10.

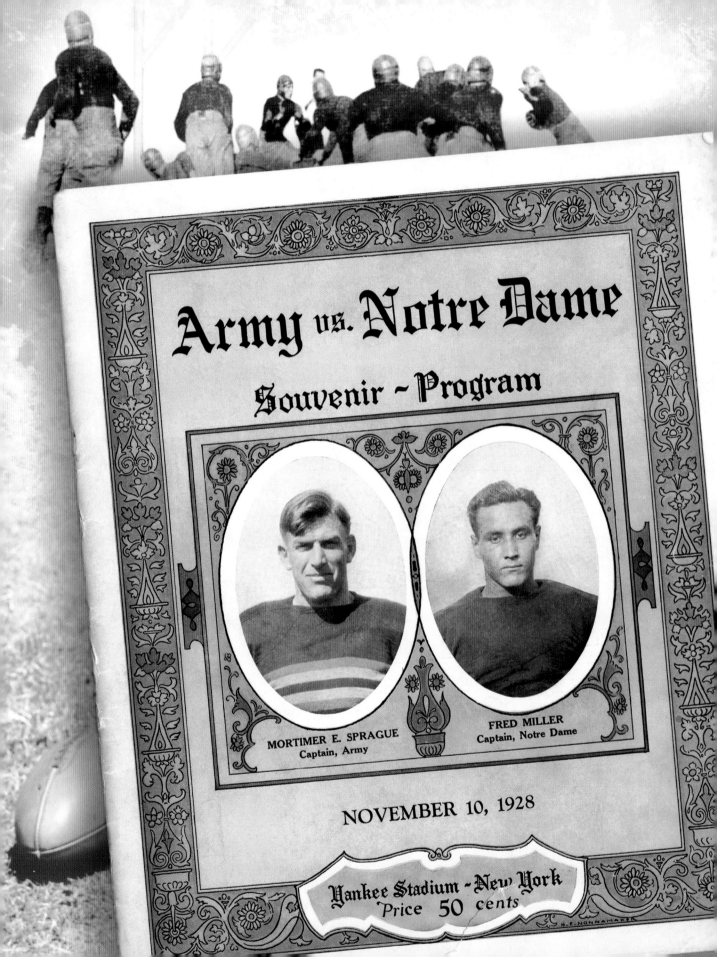

4

NOTRE DAME 12, ARMY 6

NOVEMBER 10, 1928

IN DECEMBER 1924 A PSYCHOLOGY PROFESSOR BY THE NAME of Coleman Griffith wrote a letter to Notre Dame football coach Knute Rockne. The letter, in part, read:

> Dear Coach Rockne:
>
> I have been interested for some years in many of the problems of psychology and athletics.
> I have heard it said that you do not key your men up to their games.

Four days later Rockne penned the following response:

> Dear Mr. Griffith:
>
> I do not make any effort to key them (my players) up, except on rare, exceptional occasions.

Four years later, in a cold, dank locker room in Yankee Stadium, Rockne alighted upon that rare, exceptional occasion. Either during pregame or halftime (there is dispute as to when it occurred) of Notre Dame's November 10, 1928, game against Army, Rockne delivered the immortal "Win One for the Gipper" speech. It remains to this day not only the defining pep talk in American sports but also certainly one of the most recognizable moments in American rhetoric. Rockne's dramatic appeal to his team ranks right up there with Abraham Lincoln's Gettysburg Address ("Four score and seven years ago . . . ") and Martin Luther King Jr.'s speech in front of the Lincoln Memorial ("I have a dream . . . ").

How did a locker room speech delivered to a squad that would finish the 1928 season with a 5-4 record ever gain such renown in American culture? This is a testament to many things: to Rockne and Notre Dame, certainly; to the era, to the dying moments of the Roaring Twenties and the Golden Age of Sports (the stock market crash of 1929 would occur less than a year later); and to the universal sentiment that Rockne invoked in his monologue, the idea that some battles matter more than others and, in those moments, there exists a reserve of strength and resolve that one can—and must—draw upon in order to win.

Even the most casual sports fan, as well as many folks who are completely apathetic about sports, recognize the phrase "Win One for the Gipper." How many people know, however, that this was Rockne's worst team, that the 1928 Fighting Irish would lose four games, representing one-third of Rockne's losses in his unparalleled thirteen-year career? Rockne had not lost his magic. His talent pipeline was just experiencing a one-year hiccup. The 1927 squad had finished 7-1-1, its only loss coming to the Cadets, 18-0. The 1929 and 1930 teams (the latter being Rockne's last) would not lose or even tie a game.

With trusted friends, Rockne, forty years old, was more candid. In a letter to his former student press assistant, George Strickler, Rockne wrote, "OUR TEAM LOOKS TERRIBLE. WHETHER WE GO ANYWHERE OR NOT IS DOUBTFUL."

The 1928 team, then, was a year away in either direction. Nine of the previous season's eleven starters had graduated. Only seven seniors remained. Future greats and All-Americans, such as quarterback Frank Carideo and fullback Joe Savoldi—the cornerstones of the 1929 and 1930 national championship teams—were inexperienced sophomores.

Rockne had no misconceptions about the luster of his '28 squad. In fact, he was in a sardonic humor when assessing Notre Dame's chances, referring to his lads as "the Minutemen" in a preseason interview. "They'll be right in the game one minute," he told Paul Gallico of the *New York Daily News*, "and then the other team will score."

With trusted friends, Rockne, forty years old, was more candid. In a letter to his former student press assistant, George Strickler, Rockne wrote, "Our team looks terrible. Whether we go anywhere or not is doubtful."

The Irish, alas, wasted little time in proving their coach correct. After eking out a 12-6 victory against unheralded Loyola of New Orleans in the home opener at Cartier Field, Notre Dame traveled to Madison, Wisconsin, and lost, 22-6, to the University of Wisconsin. Three fumbles did the Irish in against the Badgers. An unimpressive 7-0 win against Navy was followed by a 13-0 shutout loss at Georgia Tech. After four games the Irish were 2-2. One more loss and they'd have their most losses in a season since 1905.

Victories against Drake (32-6) and Penn State (9-0) put Notre Dame at 4-2 heading into the Army game. The Cadets were 6-0 and marching toward a national championship. Halfback Chris Cagle was the nation's most impressive all-around back and would be the best rusher ever to wear a Cadet uniform until the Blanchard and Davis era of the 1940s. Tackle Mortimer "Bud" Sprague was not only the team captain; a few days before the game he would be promoted to cadet lieutenant and commander of the First Battalion's A Company.

The men from West Point were, if not *prohibitive* favorites, certainly *heavy* favorites. And yet Rockne appeared more self-assured before the Army game than he had all autumn. On Wednesday night, the eve of the team's departure from South Bend, Rockne's friend and next-door neighbor on Saint Vincent's Street, Tom Hickey, stopped by to wish him good luck. Rockne, cigar in hand, told him, "We'll whip Army on Saturday, Tom."

Despite, or perhaps because of, Notre Dame's underdog status, the game was a nexus of ballyhoo. Senators and celebrities alike planned on attending. Notre Dame ticket manager Arthur Haley reported that his office was "returning over a thousand dollars a day for Army tickets." More than seventy-eight thousand fans jammed themselves into Yankee Stadium. This despite the fact, or again, perhaps due to the fact, that in 1928 Notre Dame allowed the fledgling radio networks of CBS and NBC to broadcast its games for free.

The Cadets, sent off with a rousing pep rally from West Point, arrived in New York City on Friday. After practicing at Travers Island, the team sequestered itself at the Astor

Hotel in Times Square. The Irish stayed outside the city at the Westchester–Biltmore Country Club. Earlier in the week the presidential election had been held, with Republican Herbert Hoover defeating Democratic candidate Al Smith, a Catholic. The election had been a catalyst for demonstrative anti-Catholic fervor across the country. In a story headlined "AFTER ELECTION . . . ROCKNE'S REVENGE," the preeminent sportswriter of the era, Grantland Rice, penned the following words:

"If there is any such thing as firing all your barrels in one game this will be the Notre Dame idea on Saturday. Both Rockne and Notre Dame understand that here is one game that can wipe out every adverse mark made (against N.D. and against Catholics) this year."

Rice's piece was probably not the only sports story that caught Rockne's eye that week. On Thursday, Francis Wallace, Rockne's original student press assistant and now a reporter at the *New York Daily News*, wrote a story about the 1919 and 1920 Notre Dame–Army contests. Wallace emphasized the role that halfback George Gipp had played in those Irish victories. Indeed, Gipp had accounted for 332 all-purpose yards against the Cadets in 1920, the year in which he became Notre Dame's first consensus All-American—and the year in which he died.

> Earlier in the week the presidential election had been held, with Republican Herbert Hoover defeating Democratic candidate Al Smith, a Catholic. THE ELECTION HAD BEEN A CATALYST FOR DEMONSTRATIVE ANTI-CATHOLIC FERVOR ACROSS THE COUNTRY.

George Gipp. If the Heisman Trophy had existed before 1935, surely he would have won it. At least Gipp *was* named by Walter Camp as the outstanding college player in America for 1920. Rockne once wrote of the six-foot, 180-pound specimen, "George Gipp was the greatest football player Notre Dame ever produced. He was unequaled in the game by anybody save, perhaps, Jim Thorpe. Gipp was Nature's pet, and, as with many of her pets, Nature also punished him."

Like Rockne, Gipp never graduated high school. Like Rockne, Gipp worked a few years before enrolling at Notre Dame in his twenties (Rockne was twenty-two; Gipp, twenty-one). Like Rockne, Gipp's first football experience at Notre Dame was as a member of an interhall team. Finally, like Rockne, he had entered Notre Dame a non-Catholic but would later convert. Unlike Rockne, Gipp was a sublimely gifted athlete. In a freshman football game in 1916, Gipp dropkicked a 62-yard field goal against Western State Normal of Michigan. It is said that as a defensive back he never allowed a pass to be completed in his zone during his entire career. Gipp was an outstanding runner and passer, as well, simply a legend in all phases of the sport. His school career rushing record of 2,341 yards lasted nearly sixty years.

But, as Rockne wrote, Nature punished Gipp. Highly undisciplined as a student and an athlete, Gipp actually was expelled from Notre Dame for six weeks in the spring of 1920. A teammate called Gipp, a pool hustler and card shark, "the greatest free-lance gambler in Notre Dame history." Gipp came down with strep throat or pneumonia in late November of his senior year, supposedly after a night or two of carousing in Chicago. He died on December 14, 1920, at the age of twenty-five, just two weeks after being named All-American.

It didn't take a Knute Rockne locker room pep talk to make George Gipp famous. His exploits and clippings preceded Rockne's memorable speech by about seven years.

Wallace's piece on Gipp was the first of two about the tragic hero written in the days immediately preceding the Army contest. The New York *Herald Tribune* columnist W. O. McGeehan had a story on Friday morning in which he called Gipp "the greatest individual football player I ever saw."

Perhaps Rockne already knew what he was going to say to his troops at the next day's game with Army. Perhaps he read Wallace's and McGeehan's stories and found inspiration. Nobody knows. What is not in dispute, though, is that at some point during the Army game (some say it was a pregame speech; others claim, as did the film *Knute Rockne: All-American*, that it was delivered at halftime) Rockne delivered the greatest address in sports history and made the late, great Gipp its centerpiece.

Rockne ordered the locker room doors closed. All visitors, with the exception of New York City mayor Jimmy Walker and two Irish New York City policemen, were ordered out. Rockne had blankets (Army blankets from World War I, curiously enough) placed atop the cold cement floor and had his players lie on them. Then, speaking slowly and softly at first, Rockne told them the tale of Gipp. He told them that Gipp was the greatest player to ever suit up for the Irish and that they should always remember his name. He told them that he had been at Gipp's bedside when he died. And now, Rockne's voice rising, his cadence quickening, he shared with them Gipp's last request:

"'I've got to go, Rock,' he said. 'It's all right, I'm not afraid. Some time, Rock, when the team is up against it and the breaks are beating the boys, tell them to go out and win just one for the Gipper. I don't know where I'll be then, Rock, but I'll know about it and I'll be happy.'"

As tears streamed down his players' faces, Rockne paused. "This is the day," he told them, "and you are the team."

"There wasn't a dry eye in the room," line coach Ed Healey would later recall. "I don't give a damn who it was. And they almost tore the door off the hinges when they raced toward the field. They were all ready to kill someone."

The game was equal to the hype that surrounds it to this day. Notre Dame dropped Army's Cagle for a 15-yard loss on the Cadets' first play from scrimmage, setting a tone. The West Pointers failed to cross midfield in the first half. The Irish mounted one serious offensive drive in the first half, that in the second quarter. Behind the blocking of team captain Fred Miller, a tackle and heir to the Miller Brewing Company fortune (he would later become the company president), Notre Dame halfbacks Jack Chevigny and Fred Collins ripped up chunks of yardage. On second and goal from the Army two-yard line, Collins, who

> If, as many believe, Rockne delivered his **"WIN ONE FOR THE GIPPER"** address at halftime, the impassioned speech failed to produce immediate results. Army, in its black jerseys, marched down the field in the third quarter and scored first.

had broken his right wrist in the season opener and was playing this game with arm in cast, ripped into the right side of the line. A pair of Army tacklers converged upon Collins, stopping him cold. The ball, however, squirted out of Collins's grasp and into the end zone. Cadet back Johnny Murrell fell on the pigskin for a touchback. The half ended, 0-0.

If, as many believe, Rockne delivered his "Win One for the Gipper" address at halftime, the impassioned speech failed to produce immediate results. Army, in its black jerseys, marched down the field in the third quarter and scored first. After Cagle completed a 40-yard pass to right end Ed Messenger to the Notre Dame 14, Murrell bulled in from a yard out. Bud Sprague missed the extra point and Army led, 6-0.

Notre Dame replied swiftly. Chevigny got the call on fourth and one inside Army's three-yard line and made it by inches. Two plays later Chevigny plunged in for the tying score and is reputed to have said, "That's one for the Gipper!"

Did Chevigny really say that? Probably. He was someone who played with emotion and was probably

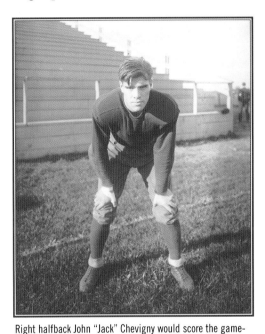

Right halfback John "Jack" Chevigny would score the game-tying touchdown, immediately after which he was reported to have said, "That's one for the Gipper."

as touched as anyone in the gold satin pants by Rockne's locker-room histrionics that day. Chevigny would go on to be the head coach at Texas (his Longhorns beat the Irish, 7-6, in 1934) and then enlist with the marines in World War II. A member of the Twenty-seventh Regiment, he was killed on the first day of the battle of Iwo Jima, February 19, 1945.

Chevigny would figure prominently in the game-winning touchdown, though he was not in on the play. Because Notre Dame had had its point-after blocked, the teams were deadlocked, 6-6, in the fourth quarter. After Chevigny missed a 50-yard field-goal attempt, Army couldn't move and once again punted to the Irish.

Notre Dame picked up three first downs. The ball was on the Army 16-yard line when an errant snap sailed 16 yards back to the 32. Chevigny fell on the ball and then, it seemed, twenty-one players fell on top of him. He emerged from the pileup woozy, and Rockne had to replace him. Rockne also took the opportunity to replace left end Johnny

Colrick with sophomore Johnny O'Brien, a lanky six-foot-two sophomore who was also a hurdler on the track team.

This was in the era before teams huddled between plays. One of the rules of this time was that a replacement was prohibited from talking with his teammates until one play had been run. Instead, as Carideo, the Notre Dame quarterback at this point in the game (Jimmy Brady had started), later explained, "We signaled outright by numbers. Each man had a play that he was outstanding in, and that particular week, we (had) worked on a pattern with O'Brien."

It was third and 26 from the Army 32. Less than two minutes remained. Carideo called signals and the ball was snapped to halfback Butch Niemiec. O'Brien faked a cut, losing Cagle in the process, then sprinted across the field to the right. Niemiec faded back to the 43-yard line, then launched a high, hovering spiral. O'Brien outdueled Murrell, Army's five-foot-nine defensive back, for the ball near the 10-yard line, bobbled it momentarily, then fluttered into the end zone.

The Yankee Stadium stands erupted. Notre Dame led, 12-6. Rockne shook the hand of O'Brien, who reacted as if he'd just caught a pass in practice and nothing more, and the coach helped drape a blanket over him. Forever after he would be known as "One

One of these two similarly posed figures would become the inspiration for a Knute Rockne speech and one would become president of the United States. Ronald Reagan was a relatively obscure actor when he took on the role of George Gipp in *Knute Rockne: All-American,* although in his later years Reagan would be affectionately known as "The Gipper."

Actor Pat O'Brien did well to capture much of Rockne's nuanced motivational style playing the lead role in *Knute Rockne: All-American.*

Play" O'Brien, as that was his lone play of the game. A few years later O'Brien would be killed in a car crash in Chicago.

Army, a most worthy nemesis, did not quit. Cagle fielded the kickoff at his own 10 and returned it 55 yards to the Notre Dame 35. After an incomplete pass, Cagle ran around end to the Notre Dame 10-yard line. It was a valiant effort, but it was Cagle's last of the day. Visibly exhausted, he was taken out of the game to a rousing ovation.

Cagle's replacement, Dick Hutchinson, completed a pass to Charlie Allan to the Notre Dame four. How much time was left? Army lined up quickly and Hutchinson called his own number and picked up three yards. The ball was spotted inside the one-yard line. Again, the Cadets lined up quickly, but referee Walter Eckersall called the game over.

There was some controversy, as Eckersall only moonlighted as a referee. As was the custom at the time, many refs were sportswriters who were hired by coaches to officiate their games. Eckersall had refereed many Notre Dame contests in the 1920s (bringing him ancillary income), and certainly anyone could see that this arrangement presented the potential for a conflict of interest.

PERHAPS THE ENTIRE TALE WAS A MOTIVATIONAL PLOY by Rockne, who like Gipp, would die tragically and prematurely.

What was done was done, however. Two days later Wallace broke the story of the Gipper speech. Joe Byrne Jr., an eyewitness, had shared the tale with Wallace, whose piece ran under the headline "GIPP'S GHOST BEAT ARMY." A legend, perhaps the most storied in all of college football, was born.

What if Hutchinson had scored on his final run? What if Eckersall had allowed one more play to be run? Would Rockne's famous speech ever have made news? Would the phrase "Win One for the Gipper" have entered the American lexicon? Would the film *Knute Rockne: All-American* have cast the spell that it did, and would Notre Dame have ever assumed the stature in college football that it has?

Maybe not. And, perhaps, as some people who have researched this event claim, Gipp never uttered his deathbed request. Perhaps the entire tale was a motivational ploy by Rockne, who, like Gipp, would die tragically and prematurely. Former Notre Dame president John W. Cavanaugh, C.S.C., said, "There never was a greater showman than Knute Rockne. All his long life he was a play actor." Even Rockne himself, the former thespian, once confided to an old buddy that "there is an awful lot of ham in the old Swede."

Then again, Rockne, despite still possessing the highest career winning percentage (105-12-5, .881) in college or professional football history, is best known for this game. And for this team, which was the worst of the Rockne era. Or, as Rockne called them, "the greatest—for that afternoon."

Notre Dame 12, Army 6
Yankee Stadium, Bronx, New York
November 10, 1928

SCORING SUMMARY

	1	2	3	4	
Notre Dame	0	0	6	6	12
Army	0	0	6	0	6

Attendance: 78,188

Team	Qtr.	Play	Score
A	3	Johnny Murrell 1 run (Bud Sprague kick failed)	A 6-0
ND	3	Jack Chevigny 1 run (John Niemiec kick failed)	6-6
ND	4	Johnny O'Brien 38 pass from Niemiec (Niemiec kick failed)	ND 12-6

SPECIAL COLLECTORS ISSUE

J.R.Wainwright

SOUTHERN CAL • NOTRE DAME

October 22, 1977 • Notre Dame Stadium • $2.00

NOTRE DAME 49, SOUTHERN CAL 19

OCTOBER 22, 1977

"Look at the jerseys!" roared ABC's Keith Jackson over the din at Notre Dame
Stadium. "That's the Notre Dame football team for the first time wearing green.
You talk about stretching emotions. Looking for an asset. Finding any
advantage. Whatever it takes. . . . Listen to this crowd!"

IN 1925 TWO OFFICIALS FROM THE UNIVERSITY OF SOUTHERN
California made a pilgrimage to South Bend to hire Notre Dame coach Knute Rockne.
The Irish had just capped their first national championship season with their first trip to
California, where Rockne's Ramblers (a popular nickname then) beat Stanford, 27-10, in
the Rose Bowl. USC, duly impressed, told Rockne to name his own terms.

Rockne declined their offer, but the two schools did agree to play each other in 1926. And
they have every year since, except for three years during World War II. USC's loss was college
football's gain. Besides, the Trojans didn't really lose: USC hired Duke's Howard Jones on
Rockne's recommendation. Jones would lead the Trojans to four national championships.

Beginning on December 4, 1926, with a 13-12 Notre Dame victory at the Los Angeles Coliseum, a tilt Rockne called "the greatest game I ever saw," the Fighting Irish and the Trojans have met seventy-five times. As of 2004, Notre Dame leads the series, 42-28-5.

Any USC fan will tell you that the most memorable game in the series' long history occurred in 1974. The sixth-ranked Trojans trailed the fifth-ranked Irish, 24-0, late in the first half at the Los Angeles Coliseum. Then, in one of the all-time great turnabouts in sports, the Trojans scored fifty-five unanswered points to win, 55-24. In little more than one half, USC surfed a wave of emotion the likes of which had rarely been seen in a sporting event and would not be seen again . . . for three years.

Dan Devine was in his third season at Notre Dame in 1977. The fifty-three-year-old head coach was of Irish ancestry, but he still seemed like an outsider at Notre Dame. Devine was invariably described as taciturn or moody, whereas his predecessor, Ara Parseghian, had been charismatic and intense. Consecutive 8-3 and 9-3 seasons did little to warm the cool relationship Devine had with fans, media, and even some of his players.

Then, on the season's second Saturday, Notre Dame, a preseason No. 1 squad with four returning All-Americans (defensive ends Ross Browner and Willie Fry, cornerback Luther Bradley, and tight end Ken MacAfee), lost to unranked Mississippi, 20-13. Patience was running thin. Outside Devine's office at the Athletic and Convocation Center, someone had painted over his name in his parking space and replaced it with the words "5 minute parking." Bumper stickers that read "Dump Devine" became a popular item.

The heat was on as the 4-1 Irish prepared for the 5-1 University of Southern California Trojans in October. The men of Troy had lost only once to their intersectional rival since 1966. A one-point loss at home to Alabama earlier in the season was all that separated USC from being the nation's No. 1 team. Devine should have been concerned. He wasn't. He had a secret weapon.

"We thought something might be up," quarterback Joe Montana later said, "when they gave us socks with two green stripes around the top."

Notre Dame wore its standard dark blue home jerseys for warmups against Southern Cal on October 22, 1977. The Irish then retreated to their locker room and discovered two of their co-captains, Terry Eurick and Fry, clad in emerald green jerseys with gold numerals. A similar green jersey rested at each player's locker. Bedlam followed.

"We went absolutely wild when we saw those jerseys," said cornerback Ted Burgmeier, whose play this day would be as much a welcome surprise as the sartorial switch. "We were so anxious to put them on that the scene in the locker room was wild."

Devine's inspiration had been months in the planning. That summer he had ordered the green jerseys, sharing his secret with no one except Notre Dame basketball coach Digger Phelps (who had suggested the ploy two years earlier), his four team captains, and equipment manager Eugene O'Neill.

Devine's message was clear: Anyone who had battled adversity or prejudice was "Irish." And, while the school colors may be gold and blue (in honor of the Virgin Mary), green is the color of the Irish. No matter what your background.

> The Irish then retreated to their locker room and discovered two of their co-captains, Terry Eurick and Willie Fry, clad in emerald green jerseys with gold numerals. A SIMILAR GREEN JERSEY RESTED AT EACH PLAYER'S LOCKER. Bedlam followed.

"Green," Devine would tell them, "is a sacred color."

On campus, pep rallies were staged on both Thursday and Friday nights, the latter drawing ten thousand people at a school with sixty-six hundred undergraduates. There Phelps urged the student body to wear green the next day, to become, in his words, "A green machine."

After warmups on Saturday, a buzz began to circulate among the 59,075 fans filling Notre Dame Stadium. At the north end zone tunnel, a wooden Trojan horse was wheeled out. Then a trapdoor opened and Notre Dame's four captains—Eurick, Fry, Browner, and Steve Orsini—emerged in their green jerseys. Their teammates, who had stood behind the horse, raced behind them.

"The reaction was unbelievable," defensive back Nick DeCicco said. "It was better than any pep talk any coach ever gave in the history of the game."

Southern Cal took the opening kickoff and, despite the hysteria surrounding them and second-year coach John Robinson, advanced the ball steadily. The Trojans featured sophomore tailback Charles White, the latest dazzling runner to carry the pigskin on USC's famed Student Body Right and Left sweeps.

Notre Dame countered with a defense that had yet to allow a rushing touchdown this season. Browner and Fry, both two-time All-Americans, anchored a line that also featured middle guard Bob Golic. Southern Cal would gain 42 yards on its opening drive, but a 52-yard field goal attempt by Frank Jordan fell short.

The Irish took over on their 20 behind junior quarterback Joe Montana, who had opened the season third on the depth chart. Notre Dame had not scored a first-quarter TD all season; USC had not allowed a first-half point all season. Methodically, though, Montana marched the green shirts 80 yards in eleven plays, with fullback Dave Mitchell blasting in for the score from four yards out. Notre Dame led, 7-0.

Southern Cal was no stranger to big games, though. With 10:44 remaining in the first half, Notre Dame had the ball in the shadow of its own goal line. Eurick took the handoff from Montana, but was popped by Trojan noseguard Tyrone Sperling at the five-yard

Students swarmed around the Trojan Horse that was pulled onto the field before the game. The roar of the crowd would get near-deafening when they saw the green-clad players come out of hiding and onto the field.

line. The ball squirted loose and was plucked from midair by linebacker Mario Celotto. Three Celotto steps later, the game was tied at seven.

The first half was played at a fever pitch, and less than flawlessly. USC had advanced to the Notre Dame nine in the first quarter. The drive stalled, and Jordan missed his second field-goal attempt, from 26 yards. Fumbles abounded. Midway through the second quarter the Irish drove 79 yards to the Southern Cal five. Mitchell lost the ball and USC linebacker Ed Gutierrez recovered.

But White fumbled it back to Notre Dame's Bobby Leopold on the USC 14. Six plays later Montana scored from one yard out on a quarterback sneak with 2:37 remaining. The snap on the extra point was poor. Holder Burgmeier, a starting cornerback who was only holding because the regular holder, Joe Restic, was injured, grabbed the ball and yelled, "Fire!"

"We practice the bad snap every day," said Burgmeier, a former high school southpaw quarterback in Iowa. "When that happens, I yell 'Fire' and two men on each side release with the tight ends going short and the halfbacks long."

Burgmeier scurried right. Then left. He sprinted toward the pylon, but a USC defender was waiting. He shot-putted the ball over the defender's helmet and into the arms of halfback Tom Domin, who caught it barely inbounds. Notre Dame led, 15-7.

"It was a terrible pass," Burgmeier said, "but it got there."

A few plays after Bradley intercepted USC quarterback Rob Hertel's pass, tying the school record for career interceptions with fifteen, Notre Dame faced fourth and six from the Trojan 33. The field goal unit trotted onto the field, but again there was no kick. The snap was perfect and kicker Dave Reeve swung his leg, but Burgmeier had already scooped up the ball and was racing around the right flank.

Joe Montana threw for 167 yards and two touchdowns, and no fourth-quarter heroics were necessary.

"That play was called from the bench," Burgmeier said. "We gambled they would rush from our left. They did. So I had open field to the right."

Burgmeier picked up 21 yards and a first down. On the next play Montana connected with MacAfee, who had Trojan safety Dennis Thurman draped all over him, for a 13-yard touchdown pass with only twenty seconds remaining in the half. This time, as the kicking unit made its way onto the field, press-box announcer Jack Lloyd proclaimed, "Burgmeier will hold—we think."

He did and the Irish clattered into the north end zone tunnel leading, 22-7. Inside the Notre Dame locker room someone had posted the December 9, 1974, cover of *Sports Illustrated.* Former USC tailback Anthony Davis was featured running through the Irish defense. The cover billing read, "WHAT A COMEBACK!" and underneath, "USC and Anthony Davis shatter Notre Dame." Not that anyone in a green jersey needed reminding.

"Well," Burgmeier would later say, "they have humiliated us the last three years."

BURGMEIER SCURRIED RIGHT.

Then left. He sprinted toward the pylon, but a USC defender was waiting. He shot-putted the ball over the defender's helmet and into the arms of halfback Tom Domin, who caught it barely inbounds.

The second half, though it featured more scoring, played out like an epilogue. Golic blocked USC's Marty King's punt early in the third quarter. Backup defensive tackle Jay Case scooped it up at the Trojan 30 and ran it in for a touchdown. Notre Dame 29, USC 7. There were still more than twenty-five minutes remaining, but this particular Trojan war was, in effect, over. Montana would throw another touchdown pass to MacAfee and score on another sneak. For the afternoon Montana would go 13-of-24 for 167 yards and two touchdown passes, both to MacAfee. The senior tight end would catch eight passes.

The green-clad defenders were the real stars, though. Notre Dame's defense set up or scored three of the team's first four touchdowns, while USC's lone score was scored when the Irish offense was on the field. White, USC's outstanding tailback, would gain 135 yards on twenty-five carries, but he never did score.

On the first play of the fourth quarter Southern Cal fullback Lynn Cain scored on a four-yard run. It was the first touchdown anyone had scored against the Notre Dame defense in thirteen quarters.

Burgmeier, the day's unlikely hero, had one more memorable play. On a long pass intended for Trojan All-American wideout Randy Simmrin, Burgmeier, who at the time held the Iowa high school pole-vault record, leaped high in the air and snatched it away at the Irish 13-yard line. As if straight out of a Marx Brothers film, Burgmeier zigzagged three times across the field while returning the ball 38 yards.

"I'm not usually the one in the sun," said the five-foot-eleven, 186-pound senior. "I'm kind of tickled."

Everyone was giddy following the 49-19 upset. The students stormed the field and tore down the north goal post. Inside the Notre Dame locker room, shouts of "Green Machine! Green Machine!"—a play on the team name Mean Machine from the popular Burt Reynolds prison football film *The Longest Yard*—sounded like a battle cry. Devine, who had been showered with Coca-Cola by his players, had experienced something of a transformation.

> This time, as the kicking unit made its way onto the field, press-box announcer Jack Lloyd proclaimed, "Burgmeier will hold WE THINK."

Tight end Ken MacAfee (No. 81), who caught two touchdown passes, leads one of many celebratory charges on the field.

The final score left no doubt as to what had transpired. The thirty-point loss was the Trojans' worst in eleven seasons (a 51-0 loss to the Irish in '66), while the forty-nine points were the most that the Irish had scored in Devine's twenty-nine games there.

Even on the sideline, Montana and Dan Devine kept a little bit of distance between them. This would be one of several times during the 1977 season that they were on the same page during Notre Dame's national-title run.

Robinson was characteristically gracious in defeat. "We just got the hell beat out of us," he said. "We lost to an inspired opponent. They outplayed us and outcoached us. We have no excuses."

Notre Dame had worn green jerseys before this day, contrary to what Jackson told the national television audience. The earliest known appearance was November 3, 1928, back when teams did not use home and away jerseys. Penn State was the opponent and, like the Irish, wore blue jerseys. To avoid confusion Rockne, then the Notre Dame coach, outfitted his squad in the green practice jerseys used by his freshman team. Notre Dame won, 9-0.

The green jersey reappeared over the years. During the Frank Leahy era (1941–43, 1946–53) the Irish made green the preferred home jersey color. The last time Notre Dame had donned green was on Thanksgiving Day 1963 at Yankee Stadium. There in New York the Irish lost to Syracuse, 14-7, in Hugh Devore's final game as the Fighting Irish coach.

It was Devine who resurrected the green jersey and, in so doing, restored the spirit to a program that had been moribund since Parseghian's departure after the 1974 season. Devine would hear none of it. "Let's get underneath them," he said of the jerseys. "There's an awful lot of heart under those jerseys."

That was true, but Devine was not foolish. The Irish would wear green at home for the rest of his six-year tenure as the Notre Dame coach. But they would not beat Southern Cal again.

Notre Dame 49, Southern Cal 19
Notre Dame Stadium, South Bend, Indiana
October 22, 1977

SCORING SUMMARY

	1	2	3	4	
Southern Cal	0	7	0	12	19
Notre Dame	7	15	13	14	49

Team	Qtr.	Time Left	Play	Score
ND	1	8:22	Dave Mitchell 4 run (Dave Reeve kick)	ND 7-0
USC	2	10:44	Mario Celotto 5 fumble return (Pat Jordan kick)	7-7
ND	2	2:37	Joe Montana 1 run (Tom Domin pass from Ted Burgmeier)	ND 15-7
ND	2	0:20	Ken MacAfee 13 pass from Montana (Reeve kick)	ND 22-7
ND	3	10:45	Jay Case 30 run with blocked punt (Reeve kick)	ND 29-7
ND	3	6:02	MacAfee 1 pass from Montana (Reeve kick failed)	ND 35-7
USC	4	14:57	Lynn Cain 4 run (Rob Hertel pass failed)	ND 35-13
ND	4	7:39	Montana 1 run (Reeve kick)	ND 42-13
USC	4	4:21	Calvin Sweeney 14 pass from Hertel (White run failed)	ND 42-19
ND	4	0:12	Kevin Hart 4 pass from Rusty Lisch (Reeve kick)	ND 49-19

Attendance: 59,075

TEAM STATISTICS

	USC	ND
First Downs	19	24
Total Net Yards	347	386
Rushes-Yards	41-167	62-192
Passing	180	194
Punt Returns	1-9	2-43
Kickoff Returns	8-150	3-24
Interceptions-Returns	1-8	2-42
Comp-Att-Int	12-29-2	16-27-1
Punts	5-30.2	4-41.7
Fumbles-Lost	4-3	4-4
Penalties-Yards	5-50	3-36

INDIVIDUAL STATISTICS

Rushing: ND: Heavens 32-83, Mitchell 8-30, Eurick 10-22, Burgmeier 1-21, Montana 3-14, Ferguson 2-7, Knott 1-5, Waymer 1-4, Stone 1-3, Pallas 1-3, Orsini 2-0.
USC: White 25-135, Tatupu 6-20, Cain 5-19, Ford 3-10, Hertel 2-(-17).

Passing: ND: Montana 13-24-1-167, Lisch 3-3-0-27.
USC: Hertel 12-29-2-180.

Receiving: ND: MacAfee 8-97, Mitchell 2-29, Orsini 2-23, Haines 1-27, Eurick 1-8, Heavens 1-6, K. Hart 1-4.
USC: Sweeney 5-114, Simmrin 1-18, White 1-17, Studdard 1-14, Ford 1-8, Tatupu 1-7, Shipp 1-2, Gay 1-0.

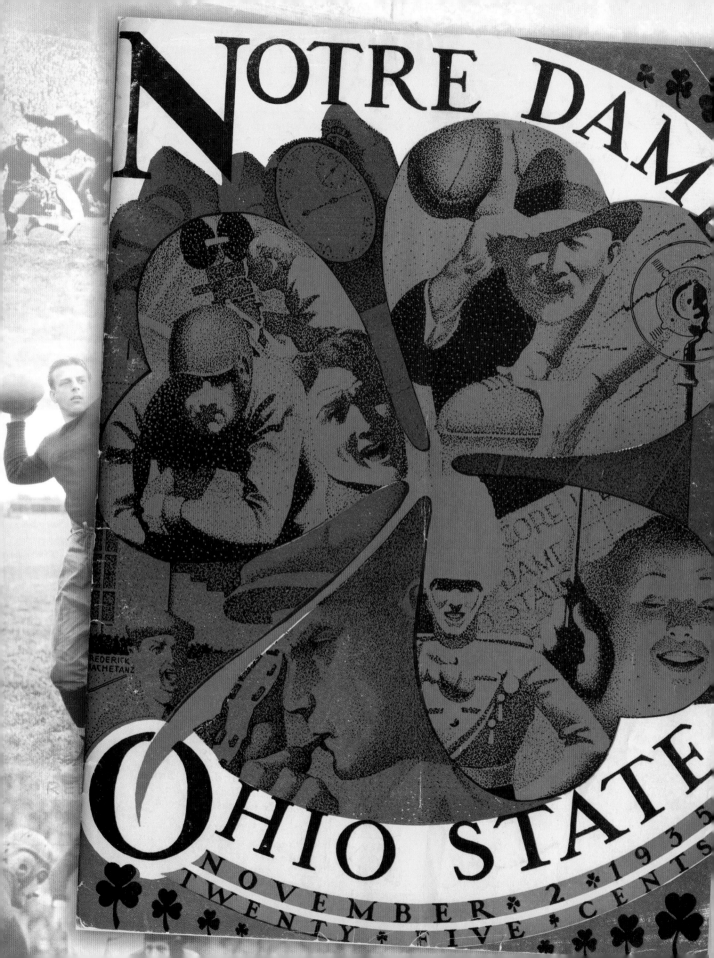

NOTRE DAME 18, OHIO STATE 13

NOVEMBER 2, 1935

THEY WOULD LATER CALL THIS "THE GAME OF THE CENTURY." None of the 81,018 fans who witnessed it in person at Ohio Stadium, none of the estimated eight million radio listeners—most of them tuned to Ted Husing of CBS—who sat close by their radios on the afternoon of November 2, 1935, would argue with that appellation. The first meeting between Ohio State and Notre Dame had it all: heartbreak and ecstasy; heroes and goats; razzle-dazzle and blood-and-guts; high comedy, and, in the context of the event, tragedy.

This one game is reminiscent of every memorable sports film that has been made in its wake. It out-Rudy's *Rudy* in terms of a player getting one play of glory, and it out-Rockne's Rockne (i.e., *Knute Rockne: All-American*) in that the Fighting Irish were actually trailing at halftime. It was a contest drunk with drama and unforgettable characters, and if it just so happened that the person who tossed the game-winning touchdown pass was named Bill Shakespeare, well, it only proves that God is in the details. Folks in Columbus, Ohio, and South Bend, Indiana, had been scrambling for tickets to this match-up for three years, since the game had first been announced. In the depth of the Great Depression, five-dollar tickets were being scalped for ten times that price.

COUNTERFEIT TICKETS, THOUSANDS OF THEM, were found as far away as Pittsburgh. Officials at both schools went into hiding in the weeks before the contest to escape the constant badgering for tickets.

Counterfeit tickets, thousands of them, were found as far away as Pittsburgh. Officials at both schools went into hiding in the weeks before the contest to escape the constant badgering for tickets. A sports editor in Columbus went so far as to have his phone disconnected.

Why? Notre Dame, five seasons after Rockne's death, was still a magnet of attention. The Irish, under head coach Elmer Layden, one of the Four Horsemen, were also 5-0. Ohio State had been a titan in the Big Ten for years, and the 1935 edition, under second-year coach Francis Schmidt, was 4-0 and averaging fifty points per contest. Schmidt's offense had as many as eleven offensive formations and one hundred plays. Laterals were as intrinsic to his offense as downfield blocking, and just as spontaneous. After an 85-7 drubbing of Drake, the Buckeyes were being hailed as "point-a-minute monsters" and "the Scarlet Scourge." Schmidt, who made few friends in the coaching ranks with his blowout victories and could not have cared less, was known as "Close-the-Gates-of-Mercy."

"Schmitty was an offensive genius," said Nick Wasylik, a sophomore quarterback on that Buckeye squad. "He was way ahead of his time. It was wonderful to come to practice. You never knew what he was going to try next."

Coach Layden told reporters that his Irish would have difficulty holding the Scarlet Scourge to fewer than forty points. The sports editor of the *Columbus Evening Dispatch* agreed with him, forecasting a 36-0 Ohio State victory. A minor earthquake rocked Columbus and parts of the northeastern United States on Friday, November 1, but who cared? "CITY GOES FOOTBALL CRAZY" screamed one headline, as parades and rallies broke out throughout Columbus that day. The town's two plushest hotels, Neal House and the

Deshler, had removed all breakable furniture and valuable portraits from their lobbies. Layden, wary of the hysteria, opted to have his squad work out miles away from the Ohio State campus at the Seminary of Saint Charles Borromeo. Even then, according to backup halfback Andy Pilney, "there must have been fifteen thousand people there. That's how big a secret we had. And of course they were yelling, 'Catholics, go home!'"

The game was less than ten plays old when Ohio State incited the first great rumble since the previous day's temblor. After both teams exchanged punts, Notre Dame had possession in Buckeye territory. Halfback Mike Layden, the coach's younger brother, hurried a pass that was intercepted by Buckeye fullback Frank Antenucci, who ran a few yards before lateraling the ball to teammate Frank Boucher, who sped the rest of the way for a 68-yard touchdown return. Halfback Dick Beltz kicked the extra point for a 7-0 Ohio State lead. Pandemonium erupted inside Ohio Stadium, as all but 500 or so of the 81,018 fans were in support of the home team.

Reserve halfback Andy Pilney had a career game in the fourth quarter alone, engineering the Irish to three touchdowns in the final minutes.

Late in the first quarter Stan Pincura of Ohio State intercepted a second Irish pass. The Buckeyes then commenced a 50-yard scoring drive that again dazzled their faithful. One play included two downfield laterals. When sophomore sensation "Jumpin" Joe Williams ran the ball in from three yards out, Ohio State led 13-0. The point-after was missed. There the score remained until the fourth quarter. Observers, including a press box filled with all the heavyweight bylines of the era, writers such as Grantland Rice, Paul Gallico, and Damon Runyon, were stunned. "This Ohio State team has shown me the greatest display of football I have ever witnessed," said Rice, the man who launched the Four Horsemen.

Others concurred. "I had never seen a Notre Dame offense so completely stopped," said *New York Daily News* writer Francis Wallace. Inside the locker rooms, one could be forgiven for thinking, if he observed each coach's demeanor, that it was the Buckeyes who were in trouble. Schmidt, whose Scarlet Scourge had gained nearly 200 yards and had nine first downs to Notre Dame's two, was apoplectic at only being ahead by two touchdowns. "You should be ahead by thirty-five points!" he screamed.

On the other hand, Layden, a Rockne disciple, made no attempt to mimic the old master. He was even-tempered and analytical. "We didn't need to be roused up," said the younger Layden, whose pass had been intercepted in the game's early minutes. "That had been our trouble. He calmed us down."

If these Irish had been a little overwhelmed both by the passion of the Buckeye fans and the talent of their foes, they were not unfamiliar with adversity. The previous March the team captain, tackle Joe Sullivan, had died of pneumonia. The squad chose not to elect a new captain but to dedicate each game to their deceased leader. "The '35 Irish team was one that believed in itself to an extraordinary extent," Coach Layden would recall years later. "It was fired [up] emotionally because death walked with it in every game."

Tackle Joe Sullivan should have been playing in the Ohio State game, but tragically he had passed away the previous March from pneumonia.

Layden spared the rah-rah speech, but he did make solid adjustments. First, to counteract Buckeye All-American linebacker Gomer Jones, a 220-pound behemoth whose stunts and blitzes had paralyzed the Irish, he ordered his quarterbacks and halfbacks to periodically check off to a different play at the line of scrimmage. "Looking back," Pilney recalled, "it was really the first check-off system I ever heard of."

Just before the end of the half, with no fanfare, Layden told his club, "Gaul's team will start." Gaul was Frank Gaul, the quarterback of the second unit. In other words, Layden was substituting out his entire first string. In truth, the two units were fairly even, but in an era when a player could not re-enter a game after being taken out until the next quarter, it was a bold risk.

"My first-team players . . . looked as if they were going to go for my throat," Layden recalled. "They were white with anger."

Just before the Irish left the locker room, Layden told his players, "They won the first half. Now it's your turn. Go out and win this half for yourselves."

Layden's lads did not overwhelm the Buckeyes in the third quarter, but they did stop them. The third quarter was primarily a punting duel, but here the Irish had the edge. Punter Bill Shakespeare, who would be named an All-American at the end of the season and finish third in voting for the first Heisman Trophy, had gotten off a 90-yard punt against Pittsburgh two weeks earlier that had proved the difference in Notre Dame's 9-6 victory. Shakespeare, known, yes, as "the Bard," continually pinned Ohio State near its goal line. Schmidt later would call his punting the difference in the game.

On the final play of the third quarter Notre Dame's Pilney, a five-foot-eleven, 175-pound senior from Dillonvale, Ohio, fielded a punt over his shoulder while near midfield. "It was a bad mistake," he would remember. "The ball was going over my head. I should have let it go, but I was so gung-ho I said, 'I'm going to take this thing.'"

Pilney, a tremendous broken-field runner, was also prone to fumbling. For that reason, and because he played the same position, left halfback, as Shakespeare, he never cracked the starting lineup. Cooling his heels on the bench only minutes earlier, Pilney had said, "If they'll put me in there now, I'll win this game for them."

"Knowing Andy," Layden would later say, "I knew that meant something."

So Pilney fielded the punt . . . and returned it 28 yards to the Buckeye twelve. "It lit the Irish fire," Pilney recalled. "They came into the huddle eyes blazing."

Thus began the fourth quarter. And, in some ways, when people would reconsider every wild thing that transpired in the final fifteen minutes, thus began the game. A Pilney pass to Gaul got the Irish to the two-yard line. Then fullback Steve Miller plunged

It was called The Game of The Century. Even in the midst of the depression, tickets were being scalped at ten times their face value.

forward to put the Irish on the board. Ken Stilley's extra point hit the crossbar, however, and wobbled back. Ohio State 13, Notre Dame 6.

The Irish second-unit line had solved the Buckeyes' offense. In fact, Ohio State, after its near-200-yard first half, would net only two yards (an all-time low for them) in the second half. The Notre Dame offense, alas, stymied itself just as much. Twice in the second half, Irish fumbles ended drives agonizingly close to the end zone. First, on fourth and one from the Buckeye fourteen, halfback Vic Wojcihovski fumbled. He recovered, but for no gain. Then, in the series after Miller's touchdown, Pilney ran and passed the Irish down to the Buckeye one-yard line. Again, Miller's name was called. He plunged into the line, but during the pileup Ohio State's Jim Karcher wrestled the ball away from Miller (which was perfectly legal), and the Buckeyes recovered in the end zone for a touchback.

On the next play Ohio State's Williams ran around end for a 24-yard gain. Only Pilney's tackle saved a touchdown and probably defeat. The Irish defense stiffened, and, with a little more than three minutes remaining, Ohio State punted. Beginning at their own 20, the Irish mounted a drive. Fullback Wally Fromhart, whom the Buckeyes only thought of as a blocking back, was open for easy dump passes over the middle. One of them went for a 39-yard gain. Then Pilney tossed a 15-yard touchdown pass to Mike Layden and suddenly it was 13-12 with only ninety seconds remaining.

Notre Dame lined up for the tying extra point. Schmidt sent in six-foot-four Fred Crow Jr., calling him by his nickname. "Goon," said Schmidt, "get in there and block that kick."

The ball glanced off Crow's left arm and sailed wide. The Buckeye faithful were ecstatic. Up in the stands Notre Dame vice president Fr. John O'Hara, C.S.C., tried to console Coach Layden's wife. "Don't worry, Edythe," he said. "Elmer and the boys have done a marvelous job."

> "That's easy for you to say," Mrs. Layden replied. "YOUR JOB DOESN'T DEPEND ON IT."

"That's easy for you to say," Mrs. Layden replied. "Your job doesn't depend on it."

Notre Dame's onside kick failed. All Ohio State needed to do was run out the clock. On the first play, however, Beltz, who had not fumbled all season, took a direct snap and raced off tackle. He crashed through the line but then was pummeled by Larry Danbom and—that name again—Pilney, who had come up from the secondary like a tornado. The ball squirted loose and bounced ominously toward the sideline.

In those days, possession on a fumble that went out of bounds was given not to the last team that possessed the football, but rather to the last one that touched it. Notre Dame center Henry Pojman managed to get a paw on the ball before it rolled out of bounds. Notre Dame had the ball on the Ohio State 49, with a minute left.

Chaos reigned. Layden crouched on the sideline, chain-smoking cigarettes. His coach in the press box, Joe Boland, called plays in to the sideline to another assistant coach (and former Irish quarterback), Chet Grant, who would relay them to Layden. Boland pleaded "Fifty-seven! Fifty-seven!" but the throng of fans who had dripped onto the sidelines made it impossible for Grant to relay the call to Layden. Telekinetically, though, Layden and Boland were on the same wavelength. Layden sent in Fifty-seven.

Pilney dropped back to pass. No one was open, or it was a quarterback draw. Regardless, Pilney took off. He scampered 32 yards, squirming free of scarlet-clad tacklers at least four times before being driven out of bounds at the 19. It was one of the epic open-field runs of the pre-television age, but it was also the last football play of Pilney's career. He tore ligaments in his left knee on the play. In came Shakespeare for Pilney. Layden sent in a quarterback (at that time, quarterbacks were the ones who called the signals, but halfbacks threw just as many passes) with the play. It was a pass. Shakespeare's throw found a man all alone and wide open: Ohio State's Beltz. The pigskin landed right in Beltz's arms, but he dropped it. The Irish had a reprieve, but Layden had a problem. Who was left to run in a play to Shakespeare? Layden spotted Jim McKenna, a fifth-string quarterback who had twice been cut from the team and not been placed on the traveling squad for this game. McKenna sneaked aboard the team train to Columbus, and with his teammates' help, hid in a berth. When he was unable to scrounge a ticket for the game, he talked his way into the Notre Dame locker room.

So there was McKenna with half a minute remaining in the game of the century, reporting in for the only play of his Notre Dame career. The trainer had forgotten to pack his pads, but this did not deter him. "Thirty-seven!" he told Shakespeare.

> Boland pleaded "FIFTY-SEVEN! FIFTY-SEVEN!" but the throng of fans who had dripped onto the sidelines made it impossible for Grant to relay the call to Layden.

Pojman snapped the ball to right halfback Tony Mazziotti, who turned and lateraled to Shakespeare. Ends Marty Peters and Wayne Millner ran a crisscross pattern, and Shakespeare's pass found Millner in the corner of the end zone with thirty-two seconds remaining.

The scene was pure Hollywood. Pilney was being carried off the field on a stretcher just beyond the end zone where the touchdown occurred. He never saw the play, only heard the reaction of the crowd and then a trainer telling him, "Andy, it's over. We won." Then he passed out.

End Wayne Millner caught the winning touchdown pass from Bill Shakespeare with less than a minute to go.

Pilney, in the fourth quarter alone, had carried five times for 45 yards, and was five of six for 121 passing. Though he missed the game's climactic score, he engineered Notre Dame's three touchdowns in the fourth quarter, two in the final three minutes.

In the press box broadcaster Red Barber, calling the game for Cincinnati station WLW, was unable to identify the name of the Irish end who had made the game-winning catch. His student spotter from Notre Dame had raced out to celebrate as soon as Millner cradled the pigskin. Meanwhile the *Columbus Dispatch*, which had gone to press with an "OHIO STATE WINS" headline as soon as the Buckeyes' tackle Chuck Gales had recovered the onside kick, now had stopped the presses.

When Pilney came to in the Notre Dame locker room, Layden, wiping tears of joy from his eyes, introduced him to a stranger. "Andy, I'm Grantland Rice," the man said. "I just want you to know that I've been writing and watching football for over forty years, and that was the greatest single performance that I've ever seen."

> Red Barber, calling the game for Cincinnati station WLW, was unable to identify the name of the Irish end who had made the game-winning catch. His student spotter from Notre Dame had RACED OUT TO CELEBRATE.

Rice was referring to Pilney, but he might as well have been talking about the game itself. No one who was there ever forgot it.

Epilogue: Notre Dame suffered a huge letdown, a foreshadowing of what would transpire fifty-eight years later (Chapter 3) and lost the following weekend at home to Northwestern, 14-7. The Irish would finish 7-1-1 . . . Andy Pilney never played football again, but he was an outstanding baseball player. In 1936 Pilney was called up for a brief stint in the big leagues with the Boston Braves (known as the Bees at the time). . . . Fred Crow, Ohio State's kick-blocking "Goon," had it in his will that when he died his left arm (the kick-deflecting limb) would be severed, cremated, and deposited in the end zone in Ohio Stadium. . . . Nine years later Notre Dame fullback Fred Carideo would take part in the Normandy invasion as a naval captain and live to tell about it. . . . Twenty-three years later Irish end Chuck Sweeney would officiate in the 1958 NFL Championship game, which is widely regarded as the greatest NFL game ever played. . . . In 1969 a panel of Associated Press voters, on the centennial of college football, would vote the 1935 Notre Dame-Ohio State game "the Game of the Century."

Notre Dame 18, Ohio State 13
Ohio Stadium, Columbus, Ohio
November 2, 1935

SCORING SUMMARY

	1	2	3	4	
Notre Dame	0	0	0	18	18
Ohio State	7	6	0	0	13

Attendance: 81,018

Team	Qtr.	Play	Score
OS	1	Frank Boucher 68 run with lateral after interception (Dick Beltz kick)	OS 7-0
OS	2	Joe Williams 3 run (Sam Busich kick failed)	OS 13-0
ND	4	Steve Miller 2 run (Ken Stilley kick failed)	OS 13-6
ND	4	Mike Layden 15 pass from Andy Pilney (Wally Fromhart kick failed)	OS 13-12
ND	4	Wayne Millner 19 pass from Bill Shakespeare (Marty Peters kick failed)	ND 18-13

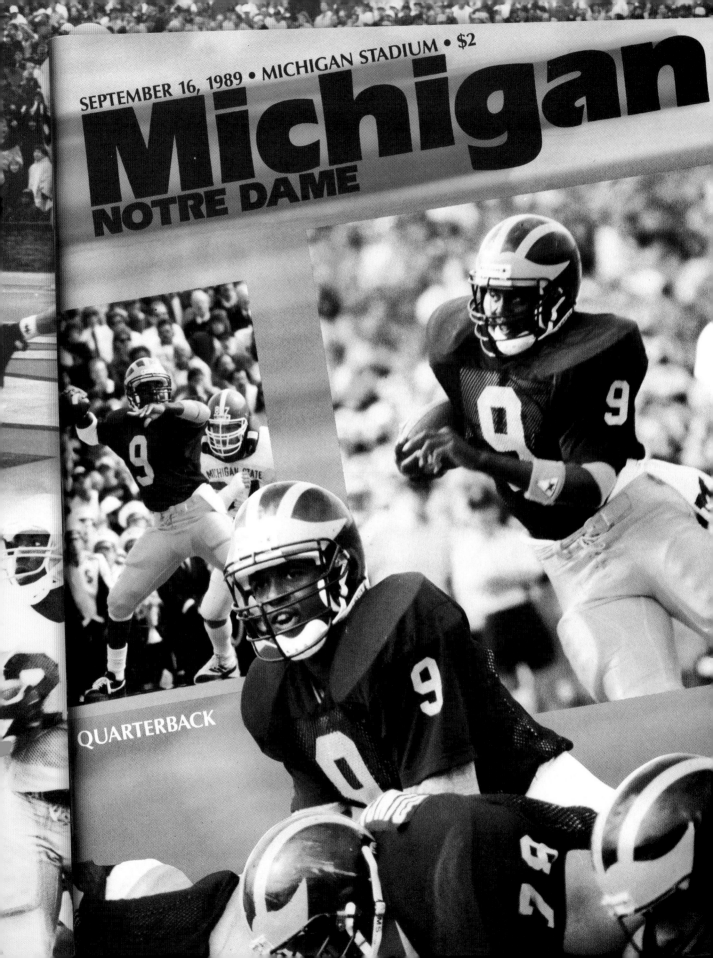

SEPTEMBER 16, 1989 • MICHIGAN STADIUM • $2

Michigan
NOTRE DAME

QUARTERBACK

NOTRE DAME 24, MICHIGAN 19

SEPTEMBER 16, 1989

AT THE DAWN OF THE 1989 SEASON, MICHIGAN HEAD COACH Bo Schembechler had much about which to be pleased. Schembechler, sixty, had guided the Wolverines to a Big Ten championship and a Rose Bowl win the previous New Year's Day. His team entered the season with a ten-game win streak and was ranked No. 1 in the Associated Press preseason poll. He was the winningest active coach in college football. His autobiography, *Bo* ($17.95, 281 pages), was eleventh on the *New York Times* best-seller list. And, as the athletic director at Michigan, Schembechler could be proud of the Wolverine men's basketball team, which had made an unlikely run with a late-season replacement coach, Steve Fisher, to the NCAA championship.

Schembechler did not sound happy.

"People say, 'You won the [Big Ten] championship,'" Schembechler told *Sport Detroit Magazine* that summer. "'You went to the Rose Bowl. You won the Rose Bowl. Hot damn, the national championship in basketball!' So everyone thinks we're going to sit around on our asses here and pat ourselves on the back—like they're doing at Notre Dame. And the answer is, No! We're not going to do that."

Schembechler's ire for the Irish was understandable. The Wolverines had lost two games the previous season by a total of three points to Notre Dame and Miami, who finished first and second, respectively, in the AP poll. The 19-17 loss to Notre Dame in South Bend was particularly agonizing, as senior Mike Gillette barely missed a game-winning 48-yard field goal on the final play. Earlier in the game Gillette had made a 49-yarder.

Michigan had gone on to win the Big Ten. Notre Dame had gone on to win the national championship—a prize that had eluded Schembechler during his illustrious twenty-one-year tenure at Michigan.

Michigan had a ten-game win streak. Notre Dame had a thirteen-game win streak, the nation's longest.

Michigan had "Hail to the Victors." The Irish had the "Notre Dame Victory March."

Michigan, without even playing a game, had dropped to No. 2 in the AP poll by mid-September. Notre Dame, which had beaten Virginia, 36-13, in its season opener, was No. 1.

At least Schembechler was still Lou Holtz's literary superior. The Notre Dame head coach also had a new book out, coauthored by sports information director John Heisler and entitled *The Fighting Spirit: A Championship Season at Notre Dame* ($18.95, 380 pages). Holtz's tome had yet to crack the *New York Times*'s top twenty.

Their September 16 meeting in Ann Arbor was a circle-the-date moment for college football fans. The twenty-fifth regular-season, No. 1-versus-No. 2 game since the introduction of the AP poll in 1936, this edition would be the earliest in a season. In Ann Arbor, you could almost feel the Wolverines chomping at the bit.

"All we have heard is Notre Dame, Notre Dame," Michigan linebacker J. J. Grant said. "I'm getting sick of it. This is a big game for us and we want to win it badly."

When Lou Holtz and Michigan coach Bo Schembechler met at midfield before the game, they had plenty to talk about, perhaps starting with their respective new books.

The Wolverines' massive offensive tackle, six-foot-eight, 330-pound Greg Skrepenak, was even more blunt. Referring to the two consecutive losses Michigan had suffered to the

Irish, and knowing that Michigan had never lost three games in a row to the same foe during Schembechler's tenure, Skrepenak promised, "Notre Dame's not going to beat us again!"

Michigan was hot. A few hours to the southwest in South Bend, the Irish sounded cool. "We're preparing hard, but we've played in big games before," said cornerback Todd Lyght, mindful that Michigan represented Notre Dame's fourth No. 3-or-above opponent in its last nine games. "To us it's another game."

"Oh, I don't know," said linebacker and tri-captain Ned Bolcar when asked if the hype was getting to him. "Is the hype getting to you? Go down to the Grotto. Say a prayer."

More maddening for Schembechler, Michigan, and their fans, Holtz was at it again. The coach of the top-ranked, defending national champion, longest-win-streak-in-the-nation Irish, was reprising his

> "WE'RE PREPARING HARD, but we've played in big games before," said cornerback Todd Lyght, mindful that Michigan represented Notre Dame's fourth No. 3-or-above opponent in its last nine games. "To us it's another game."

Chicken Little routine. Holtz likened his squad, which was returning two-thirds of its starters, to a "fragile embryo, a young colt." He mentioned that Michigan's offensive line, the largest in school history at an average of 293 pounds per man (give or take a meal), outweighed his by forty pounds per man. He noted that if backup 220-pound defensive tackle Eric Jones played, he'd be lined up against the behemoth Skrepenak. "I've never had a player give up a hundred pounds before," Holtz wailed. "And Jones missed breakfast this morning. Can you believe that? He should have eaten breakfast three times, under assumed names."

At a Thursday practice, Raghib Ismail offered, "There's really nothing different about the Michigan game. Coach Holtz preaches that all the games are the same. You want to be mentally and physically prepared. And after those two-a-day summer workouts, man, are we prepared."

In his book Schembechler offered a stunning revelation. "Now it hurts me to say this," Schembechler, along with coauthor Mitch Albom, wrote, "but my dream back [in high school] was to play college football for Notre Dame. Fortunately, for both of us,

Notre Dame wasn't interested in me. I wasn't very big [five-foot-ten, 193 pounds], and I wasn't very good."

Schembechler's words, framed against a dreary September afternoon in Michigan Stadium, would prove ironic. On this afternoon Notre Dame would frustrate Schembechler yet again, primarily due to the fleet steps of a not-very-big (five-foot-ten, 175-pound) sophomore whom Holtz had been skeptical about in the initial stages of recruiting.

"I'd never heard of a good football player named Raghib," Holtz said, referring to Raghib "Rocket" Ismail. "At his size, how good could he be? I wasn't high on him."

Ismail, from Wilkes-Barre, Pennsylvania, was a unique performer. His 4.28 speed in the 40 made Rocket perhaps the fastest college student in shoulder pads. But there was more to Ismail than that, Holtz came to realize. "I could sense this was someone people genuinely loved," said Holtz, who moved Rocket from his high school position of tailback to wide receiver and kick returner. "There was some-thing special about him. Intensity. Awareness. Unselfishness."

And speed. "At the beginning of last season," Holtz said, referring to Ismail's fresh-man year, "we put him in only on long passes. That changed when the defensive backs started pedaling the moment we broke the huddle. Rocket is beyond quick."

Notre Dame's turbo-powered weapon was by no means a secret weapon. As a freshman in 1988, Ismail had led the NCAA in kickoff return average at 36.1 yards per return. By comparison Tim Brown, who had won the Heisman Trophy a year earlier, averaged 19.8 yards per kickoff return. Ismail had even returned two kickoffs for touchdowns in one game, on dashes of 87 and 89 yards. That feat, though, had been performed against Rice, which had the longest losing streak in the nation. And that game had not been nationally televised.

September 16 began cold and wet. Morning and afternoon rains preceded the 3:30 P.M. kickoff. By then the showers would subside, but the 105,912 fans who stuffed themselves

> "I could sense this was someone people genuinely loved," said Holtz, who moved Rocket from his high school position of tailback to wide receiver and kick returner. "There was something special about him. **INTENSITY. AWARENESS. UNSELFISHNESS."**

"The Three Blocks of Granite"? Jeff Alm (No. 90), Chris Zorich (No. 50), and Bob Dahl (No. 93) were part of a Notre Dame defense that managed to keep the Wolverines off the scoreboard until late in the first half.

into Michigan Stadium, as well as the national television audience watching and listening to Keith Jackson on ABC, would bear witness to a dark and gloomy day. After a breakfast of spaghetti and sliced ham, the Irish departed from the Holiday Inn at 1:25 P.M. for the half-hour bus ride to Michigan Stadium.

At 3:30 P.M. the Fighting Irish clambered out of the midfield tunnel at Michigan Stadium full of fists and fury, ready to play. The Wolverines were scheduled to appear one minute later. They did not. Two minutes passed. Three. Still no maize-and-blue football team emerged. The Irish, standing around in the cold and rain, began to lose some of their steam. Two years earlier on this field Michigan had pulled this same ploy, and Holtz had vowed not to allow it to happen again. It had, however, and Holtz was still giving an earful to the referees when Michigan sprinted out of the tunnel at 3:35 P.M.

What followed was a fairly dull first half. On its opening series the Irish marched to the Michigan three-yard line using nothing but running plays. The drive stalled there. Freshman Craig Hentrich then shanked a 20-yard field-goal try, and the Irish had squandered their chance to take an early lead.

Nearly midway through the second quarter, Michigan quarterback Michael Taylor fumbled the ball on his own 24-yard line. Notre Dame defensive end Scott Kowalkowski, who had grown up just thirty minutes from Ann Arbor, pounced on the ball. Eight plays and nearly four minutes later, the Irish faced a third and goal from the Michigan six.

Quarterback Tony Rice, who had yet to attempt a pass, finally tossed one underneath Michigan's linebacker coverage to fellow tri-captain Anthony Johnson. The senior fullback caught it at the four, then rumbled into the end zone. Hentrich converted the point-after and the Irish led, 7-0, with 5:05 remaining in the first half.

Inside the Notre Dame locker room, Holtz was determined not to be the first coach out of the tunnel for the second half. "I told them WE WEREN'T COMING OUT UNTIL MICHIGAN GOES OUT," Holtz said.

Michigan's Desmond Howard, who two seasons later would win the Heisman Trophy, returned the ensuing kickoff 38 yards to the Michigan 41. A 14-yard completion on third and four to Chris Calloway moved the ball to the Irish 39. Taylor sought out Calloway again, this time in the end zone. Though the pass fell incomplete, Notre Dame safety Pat Terrell was flagged for pass interference. Five plays later, on third and goal from the nine, Taylor lofted a wobbly but perfectly placed pass to Calloway, who had beaten cornerback Stan Smagala, in the corner of the end zone. Touchdown, Michigan, with 0:25 remaining.

A wet field and a Michigan pursuit somewhere behind him couldn't keep Notre Dame's Rocket Ismail from another of his appointed rounds with the Wolverines' end zone.

Kicker J. D. Carlson's extra-point try hit the right upright dead-on and ricocheted back into the end zone. At halftime the score stood Notre Dame 7, Michigan 6.

After four years of Gillette handling both the kicking and punting duties for Michigan, Schembechler was ill at ease with how his special teams unit would perform. "If we have some problems with our kicking game," he had said in August, "then that could cost us the season."

Carlson's errant extra point had only further rattled the combustible coach.

Inside the Notre Dame locker room, Holtz was determined not to be the first coach out of the tunnel for the second half. "I told them we weren't coming out until Michigan goes out," Holtz said.

The staring contest would delay the second-half kickoff—Michigan came out first—and leave the players less time to

Rodney Culver often excelled running the ball for the Irish, but his biggest play in this game was contributing a block that allowed Ismail to break free on one of his kickoff returns.

loosen up once they stepped onto the soggy artificial turf. As Ismail waited inside the cramped locker room, he began to stretch his legs. "I knew I wouldn't have much time once we got out there," he said.

Ismail fielded Carlson's second-half kickoff at the 12-yard line. Eleven seconds later, number twenty-five was standing in the opposite end zone, having raced 88 yards virtually untouched. Ismail sprinted straight upfield, then, abetted by a Ryan Mihalko block, sprinted toward the right sideline. Michigan's swift freshman defensive back Corwin Brown appeared to have an angle on Ismail for a moment, but then the Rocket put on the afterburners and . . .

"Ismail up the middle. He . . . is . . . gone!" said Keith Jackson of ABC. "They call him 'Rocket' . . . and you just saw why."

No one had ever run back a kickoff against Michigan in Schembechler's previous twenty seasons in Ann Arbor. In fact, the last time the Wolverines had surrendered a touchdown on a kickoff return had been October 26, 1957—a span of thirty-two years. Ron Engel of Minnesota had returned one 95 yards for a score in a 24-7 Wolverine victory.

"Our front line made the initial contact and created a decent-sized crease," said Ismail, "and then the back wall in front of me surged through and picked up the guys who were left. It was nice."

Nice and easy.

Later in the third quarter, Hentrich's 30-yard field goal extended the Irish lead to 17-6. That was the score at the start of the fourth quarter, as the Irish were frustrating the Wolverines on both sides of the line of scrimmage. Offensively, Notre Dame's Rice had attempted only two passes and would attempt no more. Rice would rush for 79 yards and fullback Johnson for 80. More importantly, the conservative Notre Dame attack would not commit a turnover. Just as Holtz had planned.

Back on Planet Earth, Ismail enjoys a sideline celebration with teammates after one of his two kickoff-return touchdowns.

"We didn't throw the ball," Holtz said, "because we didn't want to open things up and give Michigan anything they didn't earn." And because the Irish were never trailing, Holtz added, "We were never forced to open things up."

Defensively, the Wolverines were unable to exploit their forty-pounds-per-man advantage up front. Despite a trio of talented backs, including Tony Boles, who had finished fourth in the nation in rushing in 1988 with 1,408 yards, the Wolverines would gain only 94 yards rushing on the afternoon. That would be their lowest output on the ground in more than two seasons.

"Size," said Notre Dame's Kowalkowski, who lined up at defensive end despite weighing just 226 pounds, "isn't everything."

The Wolverines were learning that, much to their chagrin. After backup quarterback Elvis Grbac threw a five-yard touchdown pass to wide receiver Derrick Walker to close the gap to 17-12 (Grbac's two-point conversion attempt pass to Howard fell incomplete) with 12:58 remaining, Michigan lined up for another kickoff. Displeased with Carlson,

Schembechler inserted backup kicker Gulam Khan, a premed student who had never appeared in a game, to kick off.

"They're going to squib it," Holtz told his kickoff return team. "They're not going to kick it to Rocket again. Move up a little bit."

"But," Schembechler would later lament, "we kicked it right to him."

Holtz watched the ball sail toward Rocket. From behind him he heard one of his players remark, "Oh, here we go."

Ismail fielded the ball at his eight. Twelve seconds later he crossed the goal line. Again, he headed straight upfield. Just past the 25-yard line, Michigan linebacker Brian Townsend got both arms around Rocket's legs for an instant. "I felt someone brush by my legs," said Rocket, who had been dubbed that by his eighth-grade track coach, "and then I felt myself breaking free."

Again Rocket veered toward the Notre Dame sideline, which, because it was a different quarter, was now to his left. Near midfield Notre Dame fullback Rodney Culver laid out Khan with a block, breaking his arm in the process. Rocket raced the last 50 yards with the wind and the forlorn Wolverines at his back.

> ## "NINETY-TWO YARDS!"
> Jackson bellowed to the television audience. "Eighty-nine yards! Give him the rest of the day off, Lou."

"Ninety-two yards!" Jackson bellowed to the television audience. "Eighty-nine yards! Give him the rest of the day off, Lou."

"They should never score twice like that," Skrepenak said. "After it happens once, you figure they're going to buckle down and make sure it doesn't happen again. It's so frustrating, standing there on the sidelines watching that and knowing you can't do anything about it."

Michigan, behind the brilliant passing of Grbac, would score again. With 4:08 remaining in the game Grbac, who would finish 17-of-21 for 134 yards after relieving Taylor, found tight end Greg McMurtry on a four-yard touchdown pass to make the score 24-19. Taylor had left the game in the third quarter after Bolcar hit him in the back while he was scrambling on a third-and-eight play.

"I probably should have started Elvis Grbac," Schembechler said, "and let the chips fall where they may."

The final mishap for the Michigan kickoff team came next. Carlson attempted an onside kick but the ball feebly rolled just three yards. Possession, Irish. After Johnson picked up one yard on a gritty fourth-and-one play at the Wolverine 29, the Irish ran out the clock for their fourteenth straight victory. Schembechler, for the first time since arriving in Ann Arbor in 1969, had lost to the same school three straight times (adding insult to injury, Holtz's book would catapult to number six on the *New York Times* list the following week, while *Bo* would drop to number fourteen). In defeat Schembechler was gracious and, like the rest of the nation, awed by the performance of one of the smallest players who had suited up.

"That may be the fastest guy I've ever seen," said Schembechler, who had coached three-time All-American wide receiver Anthony Carter a decade earlier. "He's faster than the speed of sound."

Asked what the Irish called the kickoff return play that had yielded two touchdowns, Holtz replied, "Middle. We're not really clever on kickoffs."

Afterward, Ismail attempted to deflect praise. "I have the easiest job on the unit," he said. "I just catch the football and run with it. The other ten guys have the hard part because they have to open the holes for me while getting banged around from all sides."

Holtz, who had considered Rocket special from the very first day he'd seen him in practice, noted, "He's so unselfish. We gave Rocket a game ball and he wanted to give everyone else one, too. We told him that it wasn't in our budget."

Almost two years earlier Notre Dame senior Tim Brown had galvanized football fans, as well as Heisman voters, by returning two punts for touchdowns at home on national television against Michigan State. Now Rocket, only a sophomore, had returned two kickoffs for touchdowns (the third and fourth of his Notre Dame career, breaking Brown's school record) on the road against a better Michigan team. Charismatic and mature beyond his years, Ismail understood that it was unlikely Heisman voters would reward such a performance, by someone from the same school, again so soon.

"Not this year," said Rocket, when asked about his Heisman chances.

Time would prove Ismail correct, even though he did appear dashing across the cover of *Sports Illustrated* that week under the heading, "ROCKET MAN." He failed, however, to appreciate the imprint his feat had made on the legacy of Notre Dame greats. "It was nice," he said, "but people probably won't even remember this when the season is over."

Notre Dame 24, Michigan 19
Michigan Stadium, Ann Arbor, Michigan
September 16, 1989

SCORING SUMMARY

	1	2	3	4	
Notre Dame	0	7	10	7	24
Michigan	0	6	0	13	19

Team	Qtr.	Time Left	Play	Score
ND	2	5:05	Anthony Johnson 6 pass from Tony Rice (Craig Hentrich kick)	ND 7-0
UM	2	0:25	Chris Calloway 9 pass from Michael Taylor (J. D. Carlson kick failed)	ND 7-6
ND	3	14:49	Raghib Ismail 88 kickoff return (Hentrich kick)	ND 14-6
ND	3	4:28	Hentrich 30 FG	ND 17-6
UM	4	12:58	Derrick Walker 5 pass from Elvis Grbac (Grbac pass failed)	ND 17-12
ND	4	12:46	Ismail 92 kickoff return (Hentrich kick)	ND 24-12
UM	4	4:08	Greg McMurtry 4 pass from Grbac (Carlson kick)	ND 24-19

Attendance: 105,912

TEAM STATISTICS

	ND	UM
First Downs	13	15
Total Net Yards	219	272
Rushes-Yards	54-213	34-94
Passing	6	178
Punt Returns	1-2	2-14
Kickoff Returns	3-192	3-86
Interceptions-Returns	0-0	0-0
Comp-Att-Int	1-2-0	22-28-0
Sacked By-Yards Lost	0-0	3-20
Punts	3-37.3	6-33.8
Fumbles-Lost	1-0	1-1
Penalties-Yards	5-45	8-70
Time of Possession	30:23	29:37

INDIVIDUAL STATISTICS

Rushing: ND: A. Johnson 20-80, Rice 18-79, Culver 7-35, Ismail 4-14, Watters 5-5. UM: Hoard 15-56, Boles 5-17, Bunch 5-12, Taylor 6-11, Howard 1-6, Grbac 2-(-8).

Passing: ND: Rice 1-2-0-6. UM: Grbac 17-21-0-134, Taylor 5-6-0-44, Hoard 0-1-0-0.

Receiving: ND: A. Johnson 1-6. UM: Calloway 7-72, McMurtry 4-51, Bunch 4-8, Hoard 3-12, D. Walker 2-12, Howard 1-17, Boles 1-6.

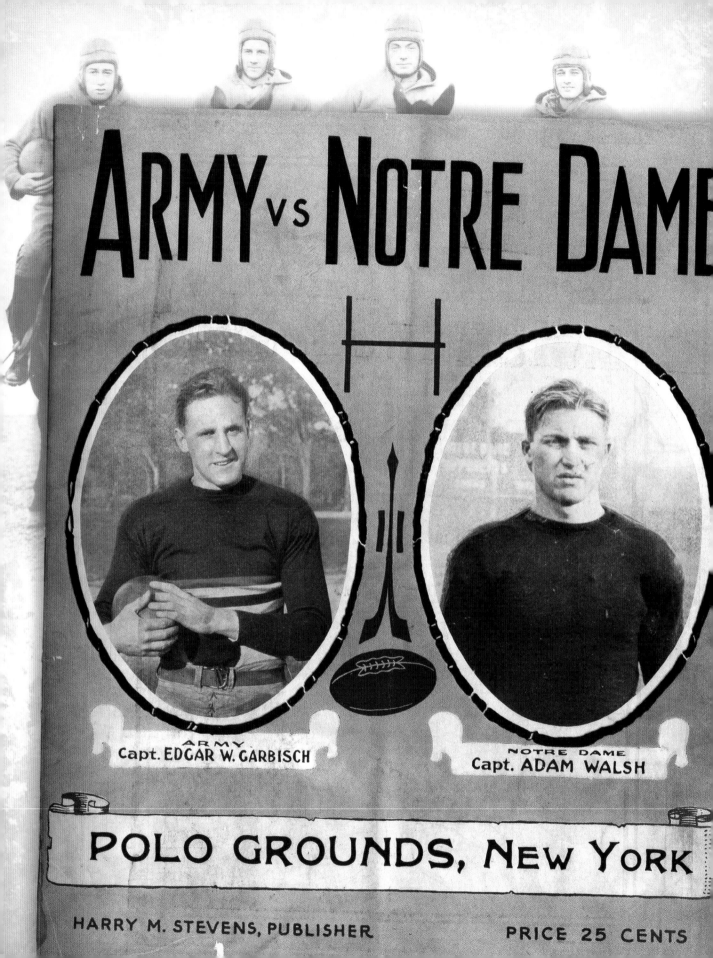

#8

NOTRE DAME 13, ARMY 7

OCTOBER 18, 1924

NONE OF THE FOUR HORSEMEN KNEW HOW TO RIDE A HORSE. That irony, in the context of the mystique that has enveloped the 1924 Notre Dame backfield, and indeed the school itself, ever since Grantland Rice typed the words "Outlined against a blue, gray October sky . . . ," is only fitting.

For, if ever there were an example of not letting the truth get in the way of a good story, Notre Dame's 13-7 victory against Army is it. Or, more accurately, Rice's now legendary account of that game, featuring the most famous lead in sports-writing history, is it.

Rice's story ran on the front page of the October 19, 1924, edition of the *New York Herald Tribune*, under the headline "NOTRE DAME BEATS ARMY'S CYCLONE." The first paragraph is the best-known lead in the annals of sports writing:

> *Outlined against a blue, gray October sky the Four Horsemen rode again. In dramatic lore they*
> *are known as famine, pestilence, destruction, and death. These are only aliases. Their real*

names are: Stuhldreher, Miller, Crowley, and Layden. They formed the crest of the South Bend cyclone before which another fighting Army team was swept over the precipice at the Polo Grounds this afternoon as 55,000 spectators peered down upon the bewildering panorama spread out upon the green plain below.

That paragraph changed Notre Dame football forever. Coupled with a photograph of the four backfield stars atop horses that appeared later that week in newspapers from coast to coast, it lent, in that era before television, a sense of grandeur, if not immortality, to what was simply a quartet of talented yet undersized gridders. This was the first of many episodes in which the marriage of myth and magnificence, as managed—some might say manipulated—through the media, would accrue to the Fighting Irish.

"Like many romantics," writes Murray Sperber in his myth-shattering book *Shake Down the Thunder*, "Rice's infatuation with his words led him far from reality."

Consider, for example, that after the 1922 Army–Notre Dame contest, Rice had written, "Notre Dame's attack is more like a modern war offensive than anything we have seen." This in the aftermath of a 0-0 tie.

The 1924 game's combatants were nearly worthy of Rice's prose. The Fighting Irish squad that took the field at the Polo Grounds in New York on October 18, 1924, had won forty-seven of its past fifty-one games (including one tie) over the previous five-plus seasons. Notre Dame, playing mostly substitutes, had won its first two contests of the 1924 season, against Lombard and Wabash, by a combined score of 74-0. Army,

Outlined against a blue-gray October sky, the Four Horsemen rode again. In dramatic lore they are known as Famine, Pestilence, Destruction and Death. These are only aliases. Their real names are Stuhldreher, Miller, Crowley and Layden. They formed the crest of the South Bend cyclone before which another fighting Army football team was swept over the precipice at the Polo Grounds yesterday afternoon as 55,000 spectators peered down on the bewildering panorama spread on the green plain below.

A cyclone can't be snared. It may be surrounded, but somewhere it breaks through to keep on going. When the cyclone starts from South Bend, where the candle lights still gleam through the Indiana sycamores, those in the way must take to storm cellars at top speed.

Yesterday the cyclone struck again as Notre Dame beat the Army, 13 to 7, with a set of backfield stars that ripped and crashed through a strong Army defense with more speed and power than the warring cadets could meet.

Notre Dame won its ninth game in twelve Army starts through the driving power of one of the greatest backfields that ever churned up the turf of any gridiron in any football age. Brilliant backfields may come and go, but in Stuhldreher, Miller, Crowley and Layden, covered by a fast and charging line, Notre Dame can take its place in front of the field.

Coach McEwan sent one of his finest teams into action, an aggressive organization that fought to the last play around the first rim of darkness, but when Rockne rushed his Four Horsemen to the track they rode down everything in sight. It was in vain that 1,400 gray-clad cadets pleaded for the Army line to hold. The Army line was giving all it had, but when a tank tears in with the speed of a motorcycle, what chance had flesh and blood to hold? The Army had its share of stars in action, such stars as Garbisch, Farwick, Wilson, Wood, Ellinger and many others, but they were up against four whirlwind backs who picked up at top speed from the first step as they swept through scant openings to slip on by the secondary defense. The Army had great backs in Wilson and Wood, but the Army had no such quartet, who seemed to carry the mixed blood of the tiger and the antelope.

Compared to the no-stone-left-unturned reporting of today's newspaper reporters, the ink-stained scribes of the Grantland Rice era rarely would let the facts get in the way of crafting a good story. Rice was no exception, and he had no peers in his day when it came to hyperbole, even if he did have a little help along the way in picking up on the Four Horsemen reference.

The shot of the Four Horsemen—left to right, Don Miller, Elmer Layden, Jim Crowley, and Harry Stuhldreher—saddled atop ol' plow horses is intimately familiar to Notre Dame fans. Less recognizable are the same four back on terra firma and without their leather helmets.

meanwhile, had lost just two games (to Yale and Notre Dame, both in 1923) in the past two seasons.

That afternoon some fifty-five thousand fans (the most Notre Dame had ever drawn until then) assembled at the stadium that normally housed the New York Giants baseball team. Not one but two different New York radio stations—WJZ and WEAF—broadcast the game live, a first for an Army–Notre Dame matchup.

Famine, pestilence, destruction, and death, a.k.a. quarterback Harry Stuhldreher, halfbacks Don Miller and Jim Crowley, and fullback Elmer Layden, all arrived on campus as callow freshman in the autumn of 1921. "The football epic of the Four Horsemen is the story of an accident," their coach, Knute Rockne, would write in 1931. "The four did not play as a backfield in their freshman year—remember, I had seen them in practice and survived the experience."

Stuhldreher, a five-foot-seven, 151-pound quarterback from Massillon, Ohio, had strongly considered attending Princeton. However, Stuhldreher had an older brother at Notre Dame. Also, as a lad he had toted the football headgear of a member of the semipro

Massillon Tigers as a means of entrance into their games. The Tiger for whom Stuhldreher had acted as valet was Rockne. Halfback Crowley, five-foot-eleven, 162 pounds, had been a high school star in Green Bay, Wisconsin. There a new pro football team named the Packers was starting up, under the guidance of Earl "Curly" Lambeau, who had played one season for Rockne in 1918. Lambeau steered the languid-looking Crowley, who would distinguish himself as a punishing blocker and a caustic wit, to South Bend.

The other halfback was Miller, five-foot-eleven, 169 pounds, from Defiance, Ohio. Don was the fourth Miller brother, behind Red, Ray, and Walter, to play for the Irish. A fifth brother, Gerry, was a classmate and teammate of Don's. When Don first got to the equipment counter as a freshman, all the uniforms had already been distributed. He was given a hand-me-down jersey, though there is evidence that Rockne was using it as a psychological ploy. He would later call Miller "the greatest open-field runner I've ever seen," and Miller's 6.8 yards per carry would be the school standard for the next seventy years.

> Layden wrote, "By today's standards, WE WERE ALMOST MIDGETS. We'd probably have trouble getting on most of today's college teams as student managers."

The fastest, and largest, of the four was fullback Layden of Davenport, Iowa. The six-foot, 162-pound speedster was steered to South Bend by his high school coach, Walter Halas. Walter's brother George founded the Chicago Bears and is generally regarded as the father of the NFL.

"Even by 1924 standards, we were small," Layden wrote in 1969. "By today's standards, we were almost midgets. We'd probably have trouble getting on most of today's college teams as student managers."

Rockne, however, stressed that football is "a game of wit and intelligence, not brute strength." No wit was sharper than Crowley's. During Notre Dame's 13-0 win against Army in 1923 at Ebbets Field, "Sleepy Jim" called a time-out with Notre Dame facing a crucial third and 10. In front of thirty thousand spectators, Crowley calmly paced off the yardage to the first-down marker, then turned to his teammates and announced, "It's only 10 yards. A truck horse could run that far."

As a unit, the Four Horsemen were born on November 18, 1922. On that afternoon against Butler University in Indianapolis, senior fullback Paul Castner broke his hip. The following Monday at practice, Rockne shifted Layden, who had been sharing the left half-back spot with Crowley in the Notre Dame T set, to fullback.

"I can't play fullback," Layden protested. "I'm not heavy enough."

"That's where we're going to fool them, Elmer," replied Rockne, who was simply trying to find a way to get his fastest player on the field. "Everyone is accustomed to the big lumbering line plunger who packs a lot of power. But in you we're bringing a new type to the game. You are very fast, and we're going to make you into a slicing and quick-opening fullback."

From that moment up until the '24 Army contest, the Irish record was 12-2. Both losses had come at Nebraska. While the Irish were vastly undersized—none of the linemen, who later would garner their own nickname, "The Seven Mules," weighed more than 190 pounds—their speed was relentless. And feared. Consider the scouting report that Army's Pat Mahoney brought back to West Point after witnessing Notre Dame defeat Wabash on October 11:

"Now, that Crowley, he's like lightning. Better put two men on him! And that Layden makes yardage every time. Put two men on him! Then there is Miller. I don't have to tell you that I advise putting two men on him! Stuhldreher, the quarterback, is the most dangerous of them all. He can think! Have three men on him!"

The pregame handshake between Notre Dame captain Adam Walsh and Army captain Ed Garbisch, both of whom played center, illustrates how extraordinary the contest was. Garbisch was no stranger to the Irish, as he had been an All-American at Washington and

Jefferson (which played Notre Dame in 1917) before coming to West Point. In fact, this game would mark the fifth time that Garbisch would play all sixty minutes in a game against Notre Dame.

Walsh, meanwhile, shook his counterpart's hand using his left, since his right hand was broken. In the first half Garbisch would inadvertently jump on Walsh's left hand, breaking that one as well. Walsh, playing with two broken hands, would remain in the game.

Starting fullback Paul Castner broke his hip in 1922. In a move reminiscent of Wally Pipp to Lou Gehrig, Rockne moved the smaller and speedier Elmer Layden into Castner's spot, and the rest is history.

The other pregame injury concern was Stuhldreher. The senior quarterback had been complaining all week that he could barely lift his right arm. Shortly before game time Rockne informed the diminutive signal-caller that the trainers had acquired a miracle cure for his shoulder. Rockne had the trainers apply the magical ointment, which was just ordinary rubbing liniment. Stuhldreher would play without pain that afternoon.

> Shortly before game time Rockne informed the diminutive signal-caller that the trainers had acquired A MIRACLE CURE FOR HIS SHOULDER. Rockne had the trainers apply the magical ointment, which was just ordinary rubbing liniment. Stuhldreher would play without pain that afternoon.

Any keen-eyed observer at the Polo Grounds noticed something else unusual in the game's first quarter. Although, as reserve halfback Harry O'Boyle would later say, "the Holy Ghost couldn't have broken into that lineup," three of the four members of Notre Dame's brilliant backfield were not in the game. The second unit, with the exception of Crowley, was. Rockne was employing his "shock troops" innovation, which today might seem ludicrous but, in the era of one-platoon football, made perfect sense.

"The second team acts very much in the capacity of shock absorbers," Rockne often said. "We know by experience that two football teams generally hit the hardest in the first quarter."

The shock troops played the Cadets to a 0-0 standstill in the first quarter. In the second period the Irish, starting on their own twenty, went on an eight-play scoring drive in which each back carried or passed the ball. Crowley had runs of eight and 15 yards and caught a Stuhldreher pass for 12 more. Miller sped for gains of 10 and 20 yards. Layden scored on a run from one yard out. Crowley missed the point after, and at halftime the score was 6-0.

Upstairs in the press box, George Strickler, Notre Dame's student press assistant (a position created by Rockne that is now its own cottage industry in college athletics) was chatting with Rice and fellow sportswriters Davis Walsh and Damon Runyon. As Strickler later recalled, "The night before we left South Bend, a Wednesday, they had this [movie], *The Four Horsemen of the Apocalypse*, showing at Washington Hall, the recreational hall on campus. I went to see it for about the seventh time."

As the sportswriters talked about Notre Dame's backfield and the manner in which they were stampeding through the Army defense, Strickler recalled the celluloid images of Famine, Pestilence, Destruction, and Death, on horseback, charging through the clouds. "Yeah," Strickler commented, "just like the Four Horsemen."

The second half was a dead heat. After Layden intercepted an Army pass, Crowley scored on a 21-yard sweep in which he shed at least three Cadets. Notre Dame 13, Army 0, heading into the fourth quarter. Army's Chick Harding scored on a naked bootleg in the fourth quarter to bring the Cadets within six, 13-7. Army mounted one final drive, but Walsh, the Irish center with a pair of broken hands, leaped into the air and intercepted Cadet Tom Trapnell's pass. The game ended soon afterward, but the hype was only beginning.

That evening Strickler and most of the Notre Dame traveling party attended the Will Rogers Follies in New York. Rogers walked out onstage wearing a Notre Dame sweater. When the team returned to the Belmont Hotel later that evening, the early edition of the *New York Herald Tribune*, with Rice's story on page one, was waiting for them. The next morning, before the team boarded the train, Strickler wired his father in South Bend.

"I got the idea for the picture, for putting the Four Horsemen on horseback," Strickler, then a sophomore, would recall decades later. "I wired my father. I asked him to see if he could round up four horses. The next afternoon [Monday], as soon as my train got into the depot, I called my father. He had the horses lined up at a coal and ice house, which was about four doors away from [his] favorite saloon."

Strickler had hoped to get riding horses, but instead he got work horses. The mounts were in poor shape, but at least they were saddled. Somehow Strickler walked all four horses over to practice, where he interrupted Rockne's preparations for the following Saturday's Princeton contest in order to have the Four Horsemen sit tall in the saddle. If not comfortably.

"Next to flying, about which I remain a devout coward," Layden would later say, "I like riding a horse least."

Layden's coach, meanwhile, initially was not pleased with Strickler's publicity stunt. "Rockne gave me a little hell," Strickler remembered. "He said he only had a couple of days before the Princeton game and that I should have made other arrangements. I said, 'I didn't have a chance.' He kept giving me hell, but he wound up saying it was a good idea."

Within a week that photo had appeared in every major newspaper in the country. Strickler, who secured the copyrights, sold eight-by-elevens of the photo on campus and received royalties. "I made about ten thousand dollars that year as a publicity man for Rockne," he later said. "Most of it was on that picture."

The Four Horsemen, meanwhile, were sanguine about their newly found celebrity status. After one practice a female reporter, anxious to uncover an as-yet-untold anecdote about the quartet, bothered Crowley beyond the point of exasperation.

Center Adam Walsh started the game with a broken right hand, and by the end of the first quarter his left had suffered a similar fate. Walsh soldiered on, though, and played a key role in the emergence of the Four Horsemen.

"Who was she?" a teammate asked after the reporter had finally departed.

"That was the Second Horsewoman: Pestilence," Crowley replied.

Notre Dame would win its next six games and then defeat Stanford, 27-10, in the Rose Bowl to secure the school's first national championship. Generations later, the legend of the Four Horsemen eclipses everything about Rockne's 1924 squad. For example, the fact that the defense, which allowed just fifty-four points in ten games, was every bit as brilliant as the offense.

"I didn't realize the impact [Rice's story] would have," Crowley remembered years later. "At the time I thought it was just another well-written story." It was, but Rice's prose, combined with Strickler's photo, burnished a legend in South Bend. And there was one more not inconsequential factor. "I think if we had lost a game or two after that splurge by Granny Rice," said Crowley, "I don't think we would have been remembered."

But they are. Perhaps Rice was the first college football writer to demonstrate that words pack more punch than the most fearsome linebacker, that their power to mold perception far outweighs reality, whether the issue at stake is "Who's No. 1?" or "Who deserves the Heisman?"

If you do not believe that, think about this. On the same afternoon during which the Four Horsemen first rode to fame, William "Red" Grange of the University of Illinois ran for five touchdowns and passed for a sixth in the Illini's 39-14 whipping of Michigan. The Wolverines had not surrendered more than a touchdown in a game in almost three seasons, yet Grange (who would be christened "the Galloping Ghost" by—who else?—Rice) had four long touchdown runs in the first quarter. If only there had been a photo of Grange atop a galloping horse. At the end of the season Grange joined three of the Four Horsemen in comprising the consensus first team All-American backfield. The only one of the Four Horsemen who failed to crack the unit was Miller, Notre Dame's leading rusher and receiver in 1924.

All of the Four Horsemen coached football at the college level at some point in their lives. Stuhldreher became athletic director and head coach at the University of Wisconsin. He died in 1965 at age sixty-three.

Layden earned a law degree, then became head coach at his alma mater from 1934 to 1940, where he compiled a 47-13-3 record. He passed away in 1973 at age seventy.

Miller coached for four seasons at Georgia Tech and then practiced law. In 1941 President Franklin Delano Roosevelt appointed him U.S. district attorney for northern Ohio. Miller died in 1979 at age seventy-seven.

Finally, there was Crowley, who died in 1986 at age

Don Miller was the only one of the Four Horsemen not named a first team All-American, beaten out at his position by no less than the immortal Red Grange. Miller would still get his Hall of Fame due, as he does here years later at a Notre Dame Stadium ceremony that also included Rev. Edmund Joyce and Moose Krause.

eighty-three. In the 1930s he was the coach at Fordham University. One of his players was Vince Lombardi, who would later gain nearly equal fame as Rockne by coaching the NFL's Green Bay Packers to victory in Super Bowls I and II.

Lombardi coached the Packers, a team founded by Curly Lambeau, a man who had played a season for Rockne and then steered local boy Jim Crowley to Notre Dame.

Notre Dame 13, Army 7
Polo Grounds, New York, New York
October 18, 1924

SCORING SUMMARY							Team	Qtr.	Play	Score
	1	2	3	4			ND	2	Elmer Layden 1 run	ND 6-0
Notre Dame	0	6	7	0	13				(Jim Crowley kick failed)	
Army	0	0	0	7	7		ND	3	Crowley 21 run (Crowley kick)	ND 13-0
							A	4	Chick Harding 11 run	ND 13-7
Attendance: 55,000									(Ed Garbisch kick)	

MICHIGAN STATE Spartans
NOTRE DAME Fighting Irish

SPARTAN
GRIDIRON
NEWS 50¢

Souvenir Program

November 19, 1966
SPARTAN STADIUM
Kickoff 1:30 p.m.

NOTRE DAME 10, MICHIGAN STATE 10

NOVEMBER 19, 1966

IT WAS A YEAR OF CULTURAL TRANSFORMATION, A YEAR IN WHICH the Beach Boys released *Pet Sounds*, Texas Western (now the University of Texas–El Paso) became the first school to have an all-Black starting lineup in an NCAA basketball final, and two midwestern schools located 150 miles apart showed the world just how big college football could be.

Notre Dame–Michigan State was as highly anticipated as any matchup on a collegiate gridiron had ever been. Its legacy is that it provided the least-satisfying conclusion the sport would ever see.

Notre Dame was ranked No. 1 in the Associated Press (AP) poll. Michigan State was No. 2. Never since the AP poll began in 1936 had No. 1 met No. 2. This would be, as then ABC sports publicist Beano Cook described it, "the greatest battle since Hector fought Achilles."

Certainly it was the most anticipated meeting on the college gridiron since the Irish played Army twenty years earlier. The ballyhooed Notre Dame passing combo of sophomores Terry Hanratty and Jim Seymour, alias the "Baby Bombers," had already been featured on the covers of both *Time* and *Sports Illustrated* that season. Notre Dame, at 36.2 points per game, had the top scoring offense in the nation. The Irish, 8-0, had outscored their previous six opponents 240-7, Navy having scored the lone touchdown on a blocked punt.

> The ballyhooed Notre Dame passing combo of sophomores Terry Hanratty and Jim Seymour, alias the "BABY BOMBERS," had already been featured on the covers of both *Time* and *Sports Illustrated* that season.

Michigan State had the top scoring defense in the nation, led by All-Americans Bubba Smith, a six-foot-seven, 285-pound monster masquerading as a defensive end, and rover back George Webster. The Spartans also had the nation's longest regular-season win streak at the time, nineteen games. And Duffy Daugherty's squad was the defending national champion.

Talent? Combined, the two squads had twenty-five current or future All-Americans and thirty-one future pro football players.

Enmity? Two years earlier in East Lansing, the Irish had humiliated the Spartans, 34-7. Michigan State returned the favor in South Bend in 1965, holding Notre Dame to negative yardage on offense in a 12-3 Spartan win. "We hated MSU," said Notre Dame team captain Jim Lynch, "and they hated us."

Hype? The *Wall Street Journal* ran a front-page story on the game earlier in the week. The press box at Spartan Stadium would welcome 754 accredited journalists, a record at the time. All week long reporters descended on East Lansing and South Bend in droves, even phoning obscure offensive linemen in hopes of unearthing a fresh angle on one of the showdown's myriad subplots. How was Notre Dame backup quarterback Coley O'Brien dealing with having recently been diagnosed a diabetic? Was Michigan State's Bubba Smith, about whom Spartan fans had printed buttons reading "KILL, BUBBA, KILL," the scariest player in football? Did the Irish, losers of nine of their last ten to Michigan State, believe they could win in East Lansing for the first time since 1949?

Notre Dame students were ready for the Spartans, especially six-foot-seven, 285-pound "monster" Bubba Smith.

"We're putting out enough material," said ABC's Cook, now a college football analyst emeritus at ESPN, "to make *Gone With the Wind* look like a short story."

The game even changed the way network television aired college football. At the time the NCAA's deal with ABC stipulated that no team could appear on national television more than once per season. The Irish had already been on ABC for their season opener against Purdue and its All-American quarterback Bob Griese (a 26-14 Irish victory). ABC announced that this would be a regionally televised game, precipitating a flood of literally tens of thousands of letters to its New York headquarters. Roone Arledge, then an ABC vice president, heard from an inmate in a Texas jail, who wrote, "If I weren't here, I'd travel to see the game on television, but I won't be out by November 19."

On Wednesday ABC and the NCAA relented, overturning the rule. The game would be a national broadcast, and ABC would not be sorry. More than thirty-three million viewers, then a record for the sport, would tune in to watch the game live. In Hawaii, the home state of Spartan kicker Dick Kenney, the game would mark the first event of any kind to air live via satellite. In Vietnam soldiers in the jungle would listen in live on the Armed Forces Radio Network.

"There was more buildup to [this game]," Lynch, an All-American linebacker, would later say, "than the Super Bowl."

Lynch, a member of the Kansas City Chiefs for eleven seasons, said this after the Chiefs won Super Bowl IV.

> Roone Arledge, then an ABC vice president, heard from an inmate in a Texas jail, who wrote, "If I weren't here, I'd travel to see the game on television, but **I WON'T BE OUT BY NOVEMBER 19."**

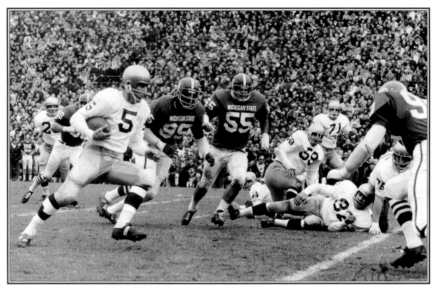

Irish quarterback Terry Hanratty wouldn't go far against the Spartans. A separated shoulder knocked him out of the game in the first quarter.

But then, this was the college game's super bowl in 1966. Michigan State, despite its 9-0 record and Big Ten championship, was not going to a bowl. The Big Ten at the time had a rule that no member school could play in the Rose Bowl two years in a row (the Spartans had lost to UCLA, 14-12, the previous New Year's Day). Notre Dame, due to a school policy, had not accepted an invitation to a bowl since 1925. This would be the Spartans' final game of the season, while the Irish would end their season one week later in Los Angeles versus Southern Cal.

Bubba Smith, the largest and reputedly meanest character on the field, agreed. "Man, those cats hit and stick to you," Smith said. "THAT GAME WAS ROUGH."

While the week had supplied more than its share of color—Notre Dame students hanging Bubba Smith in effigy at a pep rally; Michigan State students marching to Smith's window chanting that familiar refrain, "Kill, Bubba, kill!"—on Friday things got interesting. That afternoon in East Lansing, Smith was driving his Buick Riviera, known locally as the Bubbamobile, down Grand Avenue when he was pulled over by the police. It seemed that Smith had several outstanding traffic violations. Smith looked at his passenger, Spartan quarterback Jimmy Raye, and said, "Man, there ain't no way they're going to arrest Bubba Smith."

They did. "I was laughing," Smith later recalled, "right up until they put the handcuffs on."

Smith spent an hour in jail. Michigan State athletic director Biggie Munn arrived at the station, fuming. "Do you like your job?!" he asked the chief of police. Smith was released.

Notre Dame found trouble on the eve of the game by way of a railway, where along the route Michigan State fans held signs such as "Hail Mary, Mother of grace, Notre Dame's in second place." Upon arrival in East Lansing, All-American halfback Nick Eddy, the school's leading rusher in 1965 and 1966, slipped while disembarking from the train. "I had on a new pair of wing tips that night and it was cold and damp," recalled Eddy, who had injured his shoulder two weeks earlier against Pittsburgh. "I slipped on the metal steps and when I lost my balance, I grabbed a hold of something and pulled my shoulder again."

By the time the first quarter had ended, quarterback Terry Hanratty had joined center George Goeddeke and halfback Nick Eddy on the injured list. Hanratty's replacement was sophomore Coley O'Brien, handing off to fullback Larry Conjar.

Eddy would not play.

Also on Friday, the two schools' freshman football teams met (freshmen were not eligible to play varsity at the time) at East Lansing High School. Playing in front of ten thousand fans, Notre Dame won, 30-27, on a last-second field goal (Steve Garvey, the Dodgers' future first baseman, played defensive back for the Spartans that night). Would this thrilling finish be a harbinger of tomorrow's ending?

The official play-by-play lists the weather as "thirty-three degrees, mostly cloudy and cold." The Irish were four-and-a-half-point favorites, but how could the oddsmakers account for the adrenaline? "On the opening kickoff," said Notre Dame sophomore Bob Gladieux, who was pressed into a starting role after Eddy's injury, "I went to block a

Michigan State guy and he literally flew over my head, spread-eagled, screaming. I said to myself, 'Baby, these guys are high.'"

Midway through the first quarter, Notre Dame had a second and nine from the Spartan 36 when coach Ara Parseghian ordered a halfback draw. Hanratty, the Irish quarterback, thought Parseghian had called a quarterback draw. "I thought it was strange," he admitted. Hanratty took a four-step drop, then ran into the line. Linebacker Charlie "Mad Dog" Thornhill stood Hanratty up and Smith landed on top of him, separating his left shoulder.

Hanratty stayed in the game for one more play, tossing an incomplete pass to halfback Rocky Bleier. "He was in pain in the huddle," said Hanratty's classmate and cover-boy pal, Seymour, "and we tried to get him out, but he wouldn't go."

On the following play, a botched Notre Dame punt, Irish center George Goeddeke

On their only touchdown drive of the day, the Irish covered fifty-four yards, all of them through the air on what otherwise was a grind-it-out day for both teams. Here, Notre Dame's Bob Gladieux goes up to get a pass.

sprained his ankle. Like Hanratty, Goeddeke was done for the day. The first quarter was not even over and already the Irish offense had lost its starting center, quarterback, and halfback, each an All-American.

Pads were popping in the slate-gray chill. "The hitting in that game was tremendous," said the six-foot-four Seymour, who had caught a school-record thirteen passes in his debut versus Purdue. "If you had to characterize it, you'd call it brutal." Double-teamed all afternoon by Michigan State, he would be held without a reception.

Bubba Smith, the largest and reputedly meanest character on the field, agreed. "Man, those cats hit and stick to you," Smith said. "That game was rough."

Michigan State scored early in the second quarter on a four-yard run by Regis Cavender, capping a 73-yard drive. The key play in the drive was the first, a 42-yard pass from Raye to All-American split end Gene Washington, the Big Ten hurdles champion.

On Michigan State's next possession, Lynch intercepted a short pass by Raye. As he turned upfield with the ball, Lynch was hit by a thunderclap in the form of Spartan halfback Clinton Jones. Lynch, who would win the Maxwell Award as the nation's top collegiate football player in '66, was flipped onto his helmet, fumbling the ball. Six plays later the bare-footed Kenney booted a 47-yard field goal. Michigan State led, 10-0.

The Irish were in trouble. They now had five sophomores on offense. Their defense had already allowed more points in the first half than it had in any contest all season (one of Purdue's TDs in the 26-14 game had come on a fumble recovery). They had been allotted just eight hundred tickets for the 80,011-seat capacity crowd. And their backup quarterback, sophomore Coley O'Brien, had been diagnosed as a diabetic just a few weeks earlier.

Instead of wilting, O'Brien led the Irish right back into the game on the very next series. After an incomplete toss to Seymour, O'Brien hit Gladieux on an 11-yard pass, Bleier for nine yards, and then Gladieux on a 34-yard post pattern for a touchdown.

> Both coaches would risk it on fourth and one in their own territory and convert. History, however, has painted Michigan State's Daugherty heroic and Parseghian something less. **THAT IS NOT FAIR.**

Four plays, 54 yards, and all through the air. O'Brien, who required twice-daily insulin shots and ate candy bars on the sideline on this day to maintain his blood sugar, had made it 10-7.

Just before halftime Notre Dame downed a punt on the Michigan State one-yard line. The Spartans ran three straight quarterback sneaks, playing it safe. The Irish called time-outs, hoping to get the ball back or for a Spartan turnover, but neither happened. The clock ran out and, if the game had not ended the way it did, that series would have long ago been forgotten.

In the Notre Dame locker room at halftime, Parseghian surveyed his team. The Spartans had dominated the first half statistically, but the Irish only trailed by three. "You have thirty minutes out there to remember what you are and how hard you had to work to earn it," Parseghian, then forty-two and seeking his one hundredth career coaching victory, told them. "You can't let them take that away from you."

The third quarter was a scoreless stalemate, as the Irish defense clamped down on the Spartan attack. Michigan State in fact never advanced past the Notre Dame 45 in the second half. On the first play of the fourth quarter Irish kicker Joe Azzaro, celebrating his twenty-first birthday, connected on a 28-yard field goal.

The score was tied, 10-10. Few viewers, if any, among the record national TV audience had turned the channel. In Plainville, Connecticut, the priests at Our Lady of Mercy Church had moved the Saturday confession time from 4:00 P.M. to 5:00 P.M., in anticipation of an ending just like this one. The classic battle had thus far lived up to the hype. All this drama needed was a finish worthy of its combatants.

Midway through the fourth quarter, Irish safety Tom Schoen intercepted his second Raye pass of the period. Indicative of the Irish's surfeit of talent in 1966, Schoen had been the backup quarterback in 1965 but now was an All-American defensive back who led the Irish in interceptions (seven). Schoen returned Raye's pass 31 yards to the Michigan State 18, and it looked as if the Spartans had committed the fatal blunder.

On second down, though, Notre Dame halfback Dave Haley, subbing in for Gladieux, lost eight yards back to the 24. Gladieux had been knocked out on a clean hit by Spartan

The Irish defense pressured MSU quarterback Jimmy Raye much of the day, even picking off three of his passes. Pete Duranko goes after Raye here.

safety Jess Phillips, a shot that shattered Gladieux's shin pad. "That Haley play," Parseghian later fretted, "we leaked a guy through. Blew an assignment. Damn."

With 4:39 left, Azzaro's 41-yard field goal attempt into the wind sailed wide right by a foot or two.

Both teams would get the ball one more time. Both coaches would risk it on fourth and one in their own territory and convert. History, however, has painted Daugherty heroic and Parseghian something less. That is not fair.

Michigan State, facing fourth and four on its 36 with under two minutes left, punted. Schoen fielded the punt at his 30 and fumbled! The Irish recovered. First down on the 30-yard line with just under ninety seconds remaining.

On first down, O'Brien rushed for four yards. The Irish looked toward the bench, expecting a pass play, or at least a time-out. Instead, Parseghian called another run. Painfully, disbelievingly, the Michigan State defense began to realize what was happening.

"We couldn't believe it," said the rover, Webster. "When they came up for their first play, we kept hollering, 'Watch the pass, watch the pass.' But they ran. We knew the next one was a pass for sure. But they ran again. We were really stunned. Then it dawned on us. They were settling for a tie."

"Come on, you sissies," Bubba Smith sneered.

Webster yelled across the line of scrimmage. "You're going for the tie, aren't you? You're going for the tie?"

"And you know what?" Webster would recall years later. "They wouldn't even look us in the eyes."

"I'll admit, when the plays came in, we were all a little surprised," O'Brien said afterward, "because we knew we couldn't win on a belly series. I didn't have that speed."

PARSEGHIAN DID HAVE A TRICK UP HIS SLEEVE— until Gladieux's injury. The Irish had worked on a halfback option pass all week with the left-handed Gladieux tossing the ball.

The Irish ran four more plays. O'Brien did roll out to pass on the game's penultimate play, but Smith sacked him for a seven-yard loss. Michigan State, out of time-outs, was helpless. O'Brien took the final snap and kept it for a five-yard gain to the 39. The game ended in a 10-10 tie. Notre Dame left the field to a chorus of boos.

"Tears were running down my face when we left the field," said Bleier, who would earn a Purple Heart in Vietnam and four Super Bowl rings with the Pittsburgh Steelers. "It was a monumental disappointment, like we lost."

Parseghian would have none of it. In the locker room he told his players to keep their heads up. "Time will prove everything that has happened here today," he said.

With the media, the son of Armenian immigrants was defiant. "I wasn't going to blow it by throwing down there," Parseghian told reporters. "I know how good a place-kicker Kenney is (in fact, Kenney had barely missed a 57-yarder one week earlier). We were trying to get to midfield running and then throw. But I wasn't going to do a jackass thing like letting them get an interception on us and cost us the game after sixty minutes of football like our boys played."

Parseghian weighed the circumstances. He had five first-year players on offense, one of them a quarterback who had misfired on his last six passes. The Spartans had Kenney, the wind at their backs, and were in a prevent defense. Most persuasively, the Irish, with another game before them, could not lose in the rankings unless the Spartans won the game.

"If you looked at that game play-by-play," Lynch later said, "you'd understand Ara was guilty of playing intelligent football."

Parseghian did have a trick up his sleeve—until Gladieux's injury. The Irish had worked on a halfback option pass all week with the left-handed Gladieux tossing the ball. "Late in the game, Ara came to me and asked if there was any way I could get in there," said Gladieux, who was unable to do so. "I'm sure that's the play he had in mind."

The press criticized Parseghian for punctuating such an unforgettable, and savage, contest with such an effete strategy. "NOTRE DAME RUNS OUT THE CLOCK ON MICHIGAN STATE" proclaimed *Sports Illustrated* on its cover. Writer Dan Jenkins said, "Old Notre Dame will tie over all. . . . No one really expected a verdict in that last desperate moment. But they wanted someone to try."

Thousands of copies of that issue of *SI* were burned in South Bend that week.

Parseghian had chosen discretion as the better part of valor. And the move paid off. The following Saturday, despite all the injuries and what should have been an inevitable letdown, the Irish crushed USC in the Los Angeles Coliseum, 51-0. Both the final AP poll (voted on by the writers) and the United Press International (UPI) poll (voted on by the coaches) proclaimed Notre Dame national champions.

And even while Michigan State's coach later admitted that Parseghian's lack of daring at the end was the smart move, he could not resist getting in a friendly dig on his counterpart later that winter. At a National Football Foundation Hall of Fame dinner in New York, in which both schools were awarded the McArthur Bowl, representative of the Hall of Fame's national champion, Daugherty and Parseghian stood before a large audience. Daugherty stole a look at Parseghian's suit and then leaned into the microphone to speak.

"Nice tie, Ara," he said. The room erupted.

Notre Dame 10, Michigan State 10
Spartan Stadium, East Lansing, Michigan
November 19, 1966

SCORING SUMMARY

	1	2	3	4	
Notre Dame	0	7	0	3	10
Michigan St.	0	10	0	0	10

Team	Qtr.	Time Left	Play	Score
MS	2	13:20	Regis Cavender 4 run (Dick Kenney kick)	MS 7-0
MS	2	5:47	Kenney 47 FG	MS 10-0
ND	2	4:30	Bob Gladieux 34 pass from Coley O'Brien (Joe Azzaro kick)	MS 10-7
ND	4	14:57	Azzaro 28 FG	10-10

Attendance: 80,011

TEAM STATISTICS

	ND	MS
First Downs	10	13
Total Net Yards	219	284
Rushes-Yards	38-91	46-142
Passing	128	142
Punt Returns	2-5	3-(-8)
Kickoff Returns	3-64	3-63
Interceptions-Returns	3-38	1-0
Comp-Att-Int	8-24-1	7-20-3
Punts	8-42.0	8-38.0
Fumbles-Lost	3-1	2-1
Penalties-Yards	1-5	5-32

INDIVIDUAL STATISTICS

Rushing: ND: Bleier 13-53, Conjar 11-32, Hanratty 2-12, Gladieux 1-1, Haley 2-(-4), O'Brien 9-(-3). MS: Raye 21-75, Cavender 7-36, Lee 6-17, Jones 10-13, Apisa 2-1.

Passing: ND: O'Brien 7-19-1-102, Hanratty 1-4-0-26, Hardy 0-1-0-0. MS: Raye 7-20-3-142.

Receiving: ND: Gladieux 3-71, Bleier 3-16, Haley 1-23, Conjar 1-18. MS: Washington 5-123, Lee 1-11, Brenner 1-8.

40th Sugar Bowl Battle

Official Sugar Bowl Souvenir Brochure $1.00
Complete Schedule of Events for Football. Basketball, Tennis, and Regatta.

Fighting Irish of Notre Dame vs. Crimson Tide of Alabama

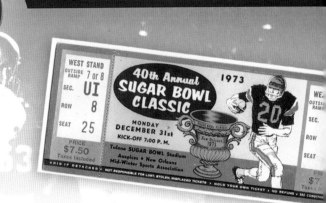

NOTRE DAME 24, ALABAMA 23
1973 SUGAR BOWL

DECEMBER 31, 1973

IN THE FINAL MOMENTS OF 1973, IN THE FINAL MINUTES OF THE fortieth annual Sugar Bowl contest, Notre Dame had the football and the lead. The pressure was squarely on coach Ara Parseghian's shoulders.

For, while the third-ranked Irish led top-ranked Alabama, 24-23, with 2:12 remaining, the football was on the Notre Dame five-yard line. The Irish were facing third and six, facing a stiff wind, when the Crimson Tide called time-out.

Quarterback Tom Clements approached Parseghian on the sideline. First, Parseghian told Clements to use a long count in hopes of pulling Alabama offsides. Then he called the play, "Power-I-Right, Tackle-Trap-Left," a play-action pass. A high-risk call.

"I nearly flipped when coach called for the pass," Clements would later say. "I do remember asking Coach Parseghian if he was sure he wanted that play."

Tom Pagna, Notre Dame offensive backfield coach, was just as startled. As Clements trotted back out onto the field, Pagna asked Parseghian, "Did you really call that play?"

"Hell, yes, I did," Parseghian replied. Perhaps that's when Parseghian knew it would work. If his quarterback and top assistant never expected him to call for a pass in the shadow of his own end zone, with nothing less than the national championship at stake, why should Alabama?

Clements stepped to the line of scrimmage. The Irish had taken out Clements's favorite target, split end Pete Demmerle, in favor of seldom-used tight end Robin Weber, who had caught only one pass all season. The two tight-end set, though, further sold the run to the Tide defense. Clements barked the signals. Someone jumped offsides. Unfortunately, it was All-American tight end Dave Casper, the primary receiver on the play.

> **CLEMENTS BARKED THE SIGNALS.** Someone jumped offsides. Unfortunately, it was All-American tight end Dave Casper, the primary receiver on the play.

Referee Gene Calhoun backed the Irish up half the distance to their own goal line. Now it was third and eight, the ball just shy of the three-yard line. Clements stared at the Notre Dame sideline, where Parseghian was signaling "repeat."

Again Clements stepped under center. The ball was snapped. Clements faked a hand-off to fullback Wayne "The Train" Bullock, then dropped back into his own end zone—a safety would give Alabama the lead—and cocked his right arm. His primary receiver was Casper. Weber was the secondary receiver.

"I'm just supposed to clear out an area for the other tight end," said Weber, whose lone catch of the season was in the opener against Northwestern, a 44-0 win. "But Alabama froze on [Casper] and I was wide open."

"Weber was so open, I didn't even look at Casper," Clements recalled.

Weber ran a diagonal fade route to Clements's left, toward the Alabama bench. Tide coach Bear Bryant, who was readying his punt-return unit for a block attempt on fourth down, had his back to the play. Clements lofted a spiral. It floated in the New Orleans night air, as a Sugar Bowl-record crowd of 85,161 and a national television audience of some forty million held their breath.

Oh, s---, thought the six-foot-five, 238-pound tight end from Dallas, *this is one I better not miss*.

"Please," whispered Parseghian, "don't drop it."

It was a gamble worthy of a game with national-championship implications. Ara Parseghian opted to have quarterback Tom Clements throw deep on third down out of his own end zone with the Irish ahead by one late in the game.

Parseghian was in his tenth season in South Bend, and though his record as Irish coach (84-15-4 before this game) rivaled those of his legendary predecessors Knute Rockne (105-12-5) and Frank Leahy (87-11-9), Parseghian did not yet belong in their company. Parseghian had led the Irish to a national championship in his third season (1966), but, unlike Rockne and Leahy, he had not achieved an unbeaten, untied season. A perfect season.

The Irish had surely come close. In 1964, Parseghian's first year under the Golden Dome, 9-0 Notre Dame lost the season finale at Southern Cal, a 20-17 nail-biter. In 1966 the infamous 10-10 tie at Michigan State, which hung like a yolk around Parseghian's neck, left the Irish 9-0-1. In 1970 USC was once more the spoiler, again sullying a 9-0 record with a 38-28 win at the Los Angeles Coliseum.

Not since 1949 had Notre Dame finished unbeaten and untied. Parseghian, an intense Armenian Presbyterian named after a ninth-century-B.C. Armenian king, drove himself to perfection. And exhaustion. He was in the office from 7:30 A.M. to 10:00 P.M. each day.

"When football starts," his wife, Katie, would say, "we know Ara won't be home for supper from September 1 until the end of the season."

This season, 1973, was as close as Parseghian had ever come to perfection. In October the Irish had upended USC, against whom they had gone 0-4-2 since 1967. The win also halted the Trojans' twenty-three-game win streak. On December 1 Parseghian led his team into the Orange Bowl against Miami for their last game of the regular season. The Irish pummeled the Hurricanes, 44-0, culminating a perfect 10-0 season. The Irish were infused with a renewed spirit, one certainly not dampened by the school's admitting females as students for only the second year since it opened its doors in 1842.

Parseghian, an intense Armenian Presbyterian named after a ninth century B.C. Armenian king, DROVE HIMSELF TO PERFECTION. And exhaustion. He was in the office from 7:30 A.M. to 10:00 P.M. each day.

Now all that remained was a bowl. Only five previous Notre Dame teams had ever played eleven games in a season. None had gone 11-0. Where would the Irish play? The Orange Bowl was offering a hundred thousand dollars more than the Sugar Bowl, but the latter already had secured top-ranked Alabama.

"We will select the competition first and the site second," Parseghian said. "It doesn't take too much intelligence on the part of anybody to figure what will happen."

Sugar. "Look at the possibilities," wrote *New Orleans Times-Picayune* columnist Dave Lagarde. "Alabama undefeated and untied; Notre Dame undefeated and untied; North against South; Catholic against Protestant; Parseghian against Bryant; the Pope against the Bear."

If Parseghian, fifty, had the most prominent coaching job in college football, Paul "Bear" Bryant, age sixty, was easily the most prominent college football coach. The Bear, with that legendary drawl, hound's-tooth hat, and inimitable visage, was practically the Alabama state seal. Bryant also had more victories at the time, 231 (231-69-16), than any other active coach.

Bryant, who had taken the Tide to fifteen straight bowl games but was winless in his last seven, had never faced Parseghian. Alabama (11-0) and Notre Dame (10-0), two of the sport's few, true leviathans, had never met. This was the game that everyone wanted. "It's

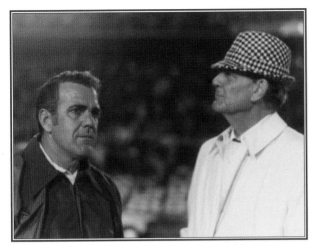

This would be the first of two bowl meetings between coaches Ara Parseghian of Notre Dame and Bear Bryant of Alabama with a national title at stake for at least one of the teams.

the kind of game," noted Bryant, "you can sink your teeth into."

The easy story line was Alabama's wishbone offense versus Notre Dame's defense. Alabama, in becoming only the eighth team in history to average seven-plus yards per play, had finished second in the nation in yards per game (480.7) and rushing yards per game (366.1). Their 41.3 points per contest was third-best nationally. Roll, Tide, indeed.

On the other side of the line of scrimmage, the Irish defense, bolstered by two outstanding freshmen, end Ross Browner and defensive back Luther Bradley, were second in the nation in total defense (201.2 yards per game) and third in scoring defense (6.6 points per game). Somewhat forgotten, though, was a Notre Dame rushing offense that, at 350.2 yards per game, was the most prolific in school history. Halfbacks Art Best and Eric Penick were both sprinters capable of covering a hundred yards in fewer than ten seconds. Bullock led the Irish in rushing with 752 yards.

Here were two offenses, then, that were adept at playing keep-away from the other team with their ground attacks. Who controlled the line of scrimmage would control the outcome.

The Tide were installed a six-point favorite. The usual pregame craziness surrounding a "game of the century" was not lacking, especially considering the location, New Orleans. For instance, a flash fire in the Alabama team hotel burned fifty-three steaks that were intended for the Tide's pregame meal. "You can't run against Notre Dame," one wag quipped, "on Rice Krispies."

THUNDERSHOWERS PELTED THE BIG EASY on the afternoon of the game, making Tulane Stadium's Poly-Turf surface slick.

Thundershowers pelted the Big Easy on the afternoon of the game, making Tulane Stadium's Poly-Turf surface slick. The rain, however, convinced Notre Dame equipment manager Gene O'Neill to borrow shorter cleats from Tulane. A blessing in disguise.

Lightning pierced the night sky shortly before the kickoff. The early moments of this game, which had been likened to, and would play out like, a heavyweight championship bout, featured each team trading jabs. Notre Dame, on its third possession, began to challenge the Tide secondary. Clements completed three passes, all to Demmerle, for 19, 26, and 14 yards. The last completion set the Irish up on the Tide three. Three plays later Bullock, following the block of left guard and tri-captain Frank Pomarico, scored from a yard out. The point-after failed, though, as holder Brian Doherty was unable to rein in a high snap. Notre Dame led, 6-0.

Offensively, the Tide was out. In the first quarter Alabama ran nine plays for a total of zero yards and no first downs. They had the ball for less than five minutes, as Notre Dame concentrated less on quarterback Gary Rutledge than they did on his pitchouts on the option.

"There may have been more coaching strategy in that game than any I've ever been in," Parseghian later said. "We had become familiar with the wishbone by playing Texas in the Cotton Bowl, but it was Alabama that had perfected it. We used about seven different defenses, including the mirror defense we had used in the [1971] Cotton Bowl."

In the second quarter the Tide came in, driving to the Notre Dame 17. Then Notre Dame linebacker Jim Stock put a vicious lick on Rutledge as he rolled out. The ball

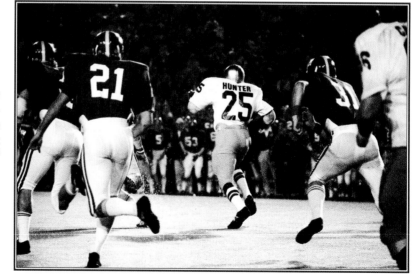

This is the kind of view most of the Alabama kick-coverage team had of Notre Dame's Al Hunter as he set sail on a 93-yard kickoff return for a touchdown.

bounced all the way back to the 36-yard line, where Stock recovered for the Irish. Notre Dame returned the favor a few plays later, though, as Bullock lost a fumble, one of three turnovers each side would commit in this imperfect, but unforgettably intense, thriller.

This time the Tide did roll, marching 48 yards in seven plays for the go-ahead touchdown. Randy Billingsley scored on a six-yard run. Alabama kicker Bill Davis, the third Davis brother to kick for the Tide in a Sugar Bowl (the first, Tim, had made four field goals in the 1964 game), made it 7-6.

Alabama's lead lasted for one play. Earlier in the week Pagna, with Parseghian's approval, had installed a new kickoff return. "It wouldn't have worked against an undisciplined team," said Pagna, "but Alabama was so disciplined about keeping in their lanes on kickoffs. What we basically did was have everyone but the ball carrier try to block their middle five men."

Freshman Al Hunter fielded Davis's kick on his own seven, near the left sideline. Following his wedge of blockers, Hunter raced 93 yards for a touchdown. No one had scored on a kickoff or punt return against Alabama all season. Clements found Demmerle in the end zone for the two-point conversion and the Irish led, 14-7.

Bryant replaced Rutledge with sophomore quarterback Richard Todd, the Tide's second-leading rusher. Todd led Alabama on a 60-yard drive that ended with a 39-yard field goal by Davis, narrowing the Irish lead to 14-10 with 0:39 left in the half. Notre Dame nearly responded in kind: Bob Thomas attempted a 48-yarder as the half ended, but it was short.

Inside the Notre Dame locker room, Parseghian exhorted his white-jersey-clad team. "We're one half away from the national championship!" he reminded.

Whatever Bryant said to his team was just as inspirational. Alabama took the second-half kickoff and, starting at their own seven-yard line, marched 93 yards in eleven plays for the go-ahead touchdown. Wilbur Jackson scored on a five-yard run and Alabama was again in the lead, 17-14.

After both kickers missed long field-goal tries (Davis from 45 and Thomas from 54), Notre Dame linebacker Greg Collins made the defensive play of the game. As Rutledge handed off the ball to Willie Shelby on the Tide 21, Collins knocked the ball loose. Another Notre Dame linebacker, Drew Mahalic, fielded the ball in midair and returned it eight yards to the Alabama 12. On the next play Penick, with the help of a crushing block by Casper, scampered in on a counter play. The Irish were back in front, 21-17, when the third quarter ended.

Early in the fourth quarter the offenses began trading errors instead of scores. Notre Dame's Best lost a fumble at the Tide 25. Rutledge drove Alabama downfield, but a pass intended for wide receiver Johnny Sharpless was intercepted by Notre Dame's Reggie Barnett at the Notre Dame 32. Bullock fumbled the ball right back to Alabama's David McMakin at the Irish 39.

Up in the ABC broadcast booth, Howard Cosell, who was much more familiar with the NFL, WONDERED ALOUD WHY BRYANT DECLINED THE PENALTY.

Alabama drove to the Irish 25 when Bryant again replaced Rutledge with the swifter Todd. The play was a sweep right to Mike Stock, an Elkhart, Indiana, native. Then Stock stopped and threw across the field to a wide-open Todd, who ran untouched into the end zone. Tulane Stadium was bedlam. Alabama had regained the lead, 23-21, but Davis, who had converted fifty-one of fifty-three extra points this season, missed. The Tide led by a precarious margin with 9:33 remaining.

On the ensuing drive, Notre Dame faced a third and one at the Tide 45. Clements rolled out right and lofted a pass deep to the hulking Casper, a converted tackle, in double coverage. The pass was anything but beautiful. "It was a 'quacker' all right," Casper said, "but the two defensive guys were playing me, not the ball. So I was able to come back for it."

Casper hauled it in at the 15-yard line for a first down. Six plays later, on fourth and goal from the two, Thomas, a five-foot-ten, 170-pound senior, jogged onto the field. He chipped in a 19-yarder that came within two feet of the crossbar.

"That was a little close, don't you think?" Parseghian asked as Thomas returned to the sideline.

"I was thinking on the way out," Thomas replied in earnest, "that if I stuck it right down the pipe nobody would ever remember it. This way they'll be talking about it for years."

Alabama went backward on its next drive. Rutledge lost four yards on first down and threw incomplete on second. Browner, a freshman who may have been the best player on the field, sacked Rutledge for a six-yard loss on third down. Facing fourth and 20 on their own 30, the Tide decided to punt.

Tide punter Greg Gantt let loose one of the great clutch punts of all time, a 69-yarder that was downed at the one. Gantt's boot was even more impressive considering that

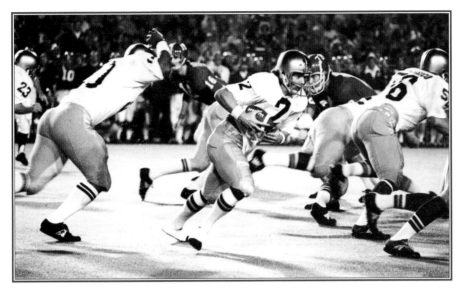

Quarterback Tom Clements wasn't a great passer or superb runner. However, he knew how to win, going 29-5 over three seasons as a starter.

Browner roughed him up on the play, a 15-yard penalty. However, in college at the time a roughing-the-kicker flag did not constitute an automatic first down. Up in the ABC broadcast booth, Howard Cosell, who was much more familiar with the NFL, wondered aloud why Bryant declined the penalty.

"I would have done the very same thing that Coach Bryant did," Parseghian said later. "I was surprised that none of the football people in the booth challenged Cosell's comments."

That potential controversy extinguished, the stage was set for Clements's third-down pass to Weber. If it fell incomplete, the Irish would be punting against the wind from their own end zone to the Tide with two minutes left. The little-used tight end hauled it in, of course, a 35-yard gain that allowed the Irish to run out the clock and finish the season a perfect 11-0.

"I would have bet my life we were going to win the game," said Bryant, who had won in his three previous Sugar Bowl appearances [1962, 1964, and 1967], "after we had them back against the goal line."

Tide offensive lineman Sylvester Croom was just as dumbstruck. "I didn't think they had the guts to do something like that," he mumbled.

Like Bryant, Clements never saw Weber's catch. "After I threw, my vision was obstructed," he said. "I held my breath for a minute, and then I saw our bench go wild, and I knew he'd caught it."

Weber held onto the ball, and so the Irish held on to their first perfect season in twenty-four years. Parseghian was as widely praised for his gutsy third-down call as he had been criticized seven years earlier for running out the clock against Michigan State. The play-calling may have been vastly different, but the strategy was the same: keep the ball out of the other team's hands at the end of the game.

> Parseghian was as widely praised for his gutsy third-down call as he had been criticized seven years earlier for running out the clock against Michigan State. The play-calling may have been vastly different, but **THE STRATEGY WAS THE SAME:** keep the ball out of the other team's hands at the end of the game.

If this finish was vindication for Parseghian, it was validation of Clements. A three-year starter, Clements is rarely mentioned in the same breath as Notre Dame's four Heisman Trophy-winning quarterbacks or other famous Irish passers such as George Gipp and Joe Montana.

Yet the laconic Clements, whose younger sister had died after being hit by a car in September of '73 (he learned of her death immediately after the season-opening win versus Northwestern), led the Irish to a 29-5 record as a starter. Rarely spectacular, Clements actually tossed more career interceptions (twenty-nine) than touchdowns (twenty-four). When it mattered, though, the McKees Rocks, Pennsylvania, native always seemed to deliver. Clements was more than a leader of these Irish; he was a symbol of them.

"This team had the enthusiasm of the 1964 club, my first at Notre Dame," Parseghian said, "and the skill and ability of the 1966 team, my only national champion, even though this was a young club."

Notre Dame 24, Alabama 23
Sugar Bowl
Tulane Stadium, New Orleans, Louisiana
December 31, 1973

SCORING SUMMARY

	1	2	3	4	
Notre Dame	6	8	7	3	24
Alabama	0	10	7	6	23

Team	Qtr.	Time Left	Play	Score
ND	1	3:19	Wayne Bullock 1 run (Bob Thomas kick failed)	ND 6-0
UA	2	7:30	Randy Billingsley 6 run (Bill Davis kick)	UA 7-6
ND	2	7:17	Al Hunter 93 kickoff return (Pete Demmerle pass from Tom Clements)	ND 14-7
UA	2	0:39	Davis 39 FG	ND 14-10
UA	3	11:02	Wilbur Jackson 5 run (Davis kick)	UA 17-14
ND	3	2:30	Eric Penick 12 run (Thomas kick)	ND 21-17
UA	4	9:33	Richard Todd 25 pass from Mike Stock (Davis kick failed)	UA 23-21
ND	4	4:26	Thomas 19 FG	ND 24-23

Attendance: 85,161

TEAM STATISTICS

	ND	UA
First Downs	20	23
Total Net Yards	421	317
Rushes-Yards	59-252	52-190
Passing	169	127
Punt Returns	1-3	2-6
Kickoff Returns	4-150	4-59
Interceptions-Returns	1-0	0-0
Comp-Att-Int	7-12-0	10-15-1
Punts	7-35.8	6-46.3
Fumbles-Lost	4-3	5-2
Penalties-Yards	5-45	3-32

INDIVIDUAL STATISTICS

Rushing: ND: Bullock 19-79, Clements 15-74, Best 12-45, Penick 9-28, Hunter 4-26.
UA: Jackson 11-62, Billingsley 7-54, Spivey 11-44, Todd 3-32, Stock 3-13, Beck 2-5, Culliver 2-5, Shelby 3-1, Rutledge 10-(-25).

Passing: ND: Clements 7-12-0-169.
UA: Rutledge 7-12-1-88, Todd 2-2-0-14, Stock 1-1-0-25.

Receiving: ND: Casper 3-75, Demmerle 3-59, Weber 1-35.
UA: Pugh 2-28, Jackson 2-22, Sharpless 2-22, Todd 1-25, Stock 1-15, Wheeler 1-13, Billingsley 1-2.

NOTRE DAME

OKLAHOMA

50th Anniversary
1907 - 1957

Statehood Day

NOVEMBER 16, 1957 - OWEN FIELD -

SOUVENIR PROGRAM 50¢

11

NOTRE DAME 7, OKLAHOMA 0

NOVEMBER 16, 1957

WHAT THOUGH THE ODDS BE GREAT OR SMALL? INDEED, NOTRE Dame never entered a stadium with the odds less in their favor than they did on November 16, 1957, in Norman, Oklahoma. The Fighting Irish ran onto Owen Field on an overcast, fifty-eight-degree afternoon against the University of Oklahoma as nineteen-point underdogs.

Yet the likelihood of victory seemed less hollow as a numerical quantity. There was a historic aspect to this mismatch, as one local periodical was inclined to report. "They (Notre Dame) have about as much chance as their Catholic forefathers did," wrote an Oklahoma City newspaper, "when the Romans chucked 'em to the lions."

The Sooners, led by forty-one-year-old head coach Bud Wilkinson, were equal to that analogy. All Oklahoma had done was win forty-seven consecutive games, an NCAA Division I record that has still not been matched. The Sooners had last lost on

September 26, 1953, to, of all schools, Notre Dame. The score that afternoon in Norman had been 28-21 in favor of Coach Frank Leahy's last squad. Oklahoma, which had already clinched a tenth straight conference title, had tied Pitt the following Saturday, then commenced their stultifying streak with a win against Texas.

Simply put Wilkinson, who had become head coach at Oklahoma in 1947 at age thirty-one, was the Sooners' Rockne. Before him, OU had no football tradition. Already the Minnesota native had coached the Sooners to a thirty-one-game win streak (1948–1950) and now this one. The Sooners entered this game as the two-time defending national champions, having won in 1955 and 1956. No school had ever won three straight, but why not Oklahoma?

A third straight Sooner title appeared, at this late juncture in the season, manifest destiny. In the week before the game *Sports Illustrated*, a magazine that at the time was not even as old (it debuted in August, 1954) as Oklahoma's forty-seven-game victory march, put the Sooners on its cover under the heading, "Why Oklahoma Is Unbeatable."

Even if this Sooner squad was not invincible, who were the Irish to prove otherwise? The mid-fifties was among the most fallow periods in Notre Dame gridiron history. Under fourth-year head coach Terry Brennan, who was only twenty-nine, the Irish came to Norman having lost ten of their last sixteen contests. Brennan's 1956 squad had, despite the presence of Heisman Trophy winner Paul Hornung, finished 2-8. It marked the school's first losing season in twenty-four years. No loss was more ignominious that year than the 40-0 beating administered by Oklahoma, the worst home shutout defeat in school history.

> Brennan's 1956 squad had, despite the presence of Heisman trophy winner Paul Hornung, finished 2-8. It marked the school's first losing season in twenty-four years. No loss was more ignominious that year than the 40-0 BEATING administered by Oklahoma, the WORST HOME SHUTOUT DEFEAT IN SCHOOL HISTORY.

In 1957 Brennan, a halfback hero from some of Leahy's 1940s squads, silenced the hordes calling for his job with a 4-0 start and number five ranking. But then the Irish lost 20-6 to Navy and were embarrassed at Michigan State, 34-6. Notre Dame's upcoming trip to Norman was suddenly looming ominously as Brennan's own Little Big Horn.

On top of Oklahoma's imposing dominance, on top of Notre Dame's slide toward mediocrity, there was also this: Saturday, November 16, 1957, was Oklahoma's fiftieth birthday. Oklahoma had entered the Union on November 16, 1907. Statehood Day would be the culmination of a weeklong festival of events—President Dwight Eisenhower had visited Oklahoma City four days earlier—and the Sooners could think of no better birthday present than a forty-eighth straight victory, this time against the Catholics from Indiana.

Notre Dame center Bob Scholtz, a Tulsa native and the heaviest Irish player at 225 pounds, was dating his future wife, an OU student at the time. "The teasing she took inspired me," Scholtz said. "Bill Krisher (an All-American guard for the Sooners) asked her how many of my teeth she wanted him to bring back. I had the impression the Oklahoma players were very confident."

There hadn't been much for Notre Dame students to cheer about over the last year or two. So another shot at the mighty Sooners offered a rallying point.

Back in South Bend, the Notre Dame student body was, if not confident, definitely plucky. The student council had declared it "Beat Oklahoma Week." Each day in the cold November rain between four hundred and five hundred students would trudge across campus to watch the Irish practice and cheer them on, using a most popular song as inspiration.

"Happy birthday to you, happy birthday to you, happy birthday, Oklahoma, happy birthday to you!"

"It started Monday with the whole school," Brennan would say afterward. "A lot of them came down to practice, and got themselves all keyed up. When you get the whole school fired up, some of it rubs off on the team."

Unlike other worthy rivals Notre Dame had met in the past, such as Army, the Sooners and their environs meant a culture clash. Oklahoma was just 3 percent Catholic, and many from that minority were not white. To avoid undo distractions, Brennan quartered the Irish in an "old, dumpy hotel" in the tiny town of Chickasha. "There was an awful lot of animosity against Catholics in that state," recalled Notre Dame end Monty Stickles. "We went to our game mass that Saturday morning, and there were these little Mexican kids just begging for us to win so they wouldn't have to take all that crap for so long. If we beat Oklahoma, maybe that would make it easier on the Catholics in the state."

By 2:00 P.M. that Saturday the Irish, the Sooners, some 350 reporters (more than had been on hand to cover the president's visit earlier in the week), A CROWD OF 63,170, and a national NBC television audience were at last ready.

How much of the hostility was based in prejudice and how much in good old-fashioned sports fanaticism is difficult to say when looking back on the game years later. To be sure, many of the eight thousand Irish fans who ventured to the Sooner state for the contest were treated hospitably. Notre Dame athletic director Edward "Moose" Krause and business manager Herb Jones were unable to get hotel reservations, for example. John Rinehart, an OU alumnus and the executive vice president of Oklahoma City's Biltmore hotel (the same hotel in which the Sooners stayed on the eve of the game) opened his office to Krause and Jones and let them sleep there.

By 2:00 P.M. that Saturday the Irish, the Sooners, some 350 reporters (more than had been on hand to cover the president's visit earlier in the week), a crowd of 63,170, and a national NBC television audience were at last ready. The big question was whether Notre Dame would be able to stop Oklahoma's top-ranked offense (300 rushing yards per game) and Sooner speedster Clendon Thomas. While most observers doubted the Irish would be equal to that task, others pointed out that in '56 the Irish, despite the 40-0 score, had held the Sooners to 147 net rushing yards. That total had been Oklahoma's lowest in four years.

The team in the red jerseys dominated the first quarter, which was played almost entirely in the Notre Dame half of the field. After the Irish failed to move the ball on their opening possession, Oklahoma marched down the field. Quarterback Carl Dodd

As it turned out, quarterback Bob Williams didn't have to throw much for the Irish to have a chance to beat Oklahoma. All it would take would be one run-oriented touchdown drive.

completed a short pass to fullback Dennit Morris for a first down to the Irish 41. Then Notre Dame was called for defensive holding. The crowd was rabid, but on fourth down with the ball on the 13-yard line, the Irish stopped the Sooners on a pass attempt that fell incomplete. No one watching knew it, or would have guessed it, but the team with the forty-seven-game winning streak had just gotten as close to scoring as it would all afternoon.

Notre Dame, using eight- and sometimes even nine-man lines, were daring the Sooners to pass the ball. "Notre Dame *knew* Clendon Thomas was the one big Sooner threat," one prominent coach (who wished to remain anonymous) said at the time. "Stop Clendon Thomas and you can beat Oklahoma."

The Irish were the beneficiaries of a superb scouting job done by assistant coach Bernie Crimmins. "It was tremendous," Notre Dame right halfback Dick Lynch would say afterward. "It was the most tremendous job of scouting I ever saw. We really had 'em tabbed."

Still in the first quarter, Notre Dame halfback Pat Doyle fumbled on his own 34. Oklahoma recovered, only to lose five yards on three plays and then punt. Early in the second period the Sooners threatened again, advancing to the Irish 23-yard line when quarterback Dodd lost the ball on a fumble. By the time the pigskin stopped bouncing, the Irish had recovered on the Oklahoma 49-yard line.

The Irish, featuring the passing of quarterback Bob Williams, then mounted their first offensive drive of the day. Williams completed four of seven passes for 38 yards as the Irish advanced the ball to the Sooner three-yard line. On fourth down just inches away, right halfback Jim Just got the call. The Irish thought he scored. Referee Eddie Herbert ruled the ball dead six inches from the goal line. "We were certain he scored," center Scholtz said later, "and we started worrying about the officiating."

Herbert, in fact, was conscientious about his call. At halftime he would visit Brennan in the Notre Dame locker room and inform him that while the ball crossed the goal line, Just's knee had touched the ground before that.

The Irish would have another scoring opportunity on their next possession. On fourth down at the Sooner 16, Notre Dame faked a field goal, with Williams completing a pass to Just to the Sooner six for a first down. Two plays later their momentum was stopped, as Williams threw an errant pass into the arms of OU's David Baker in the end zone.

The first half ended 0-0. The Irish might have been dismayed that they were not ahead 14-0, but they had to be pleased with their defensive effort. The mighty Sooner ground attack had gained just 41 yards, or 1.5 yards per carry. Moreover, Oklahoma, which had not been shut out since the final game of the 1945 season, a span of 123 games, was preparing itself for a stalemate. Later Wilkinson, whose team entered the contest averaging 28.5 points per game, would admit, "I was ready to settle for a scoreless tie."

The third quarter was a punting duel, more like a punting bombardment from a suddenly defensive-minded Oklahoma squad. OU's Baker and Thomas, with two kicks each, consistently pinned the Irish down in the shadow of their own goalposts. Notre Dame drives began at the 15-, four-, three- and seven-yard lines. Then again, that Oklahoma punted four times in one quarter indicated that both offenses were effete at this point. It was trench warfare.

The Irish finally got a break early in the fourth quarter, as a Sooner punt rolled just beyond the Notre Dame goal line for a touchback. The Irish would start at their own 20. The clock showed 12:51 remaining. Thus began a drive for the ages. Williams, who shared the same name and position with a Notre Dame two-time All-American from 1949 and 1950, was about to forge his own legend by calling every play on this epic march.

> The Irish might have been dismayed that they were not ahead 14-0, but they had to be **PLEASED WITH THEIR DEFENSIVE EFFORT.** The mighty Sooner ground attack had gained just 41 yards, or 1.5 yards per carry.

On a fourth-down sweep right, Notre Dame's Dick Lynch took it the last three yards for the game's only touchdown.

Nick Pietrosante, a tough 205-pounder, gained eight. Then Lynch ran for five and a first down at the 33. Pietrosante was stopped cold, and Frank Reynolds raced for 11 and another first down. Lynch for one. Reynolds rushed for four. Pietrosante, getting the call again on the "Tank 75" play, gained eight, to the Oklahoma 43. First down.

Two plays gained four yards. Third down and six. In the huddle Williams looked at his ten teammates. "That '75' is working so well that they'll be stacked up to meet it this time," he said. "But that's what we'll call anyway."

Pietrosante took the hand-off and gained exactly six. First down at the Sooner 32.

Two more plays created another critical third down, this time on the 29. On the thirteenth play Williams called the lone pass of the drive, a jump pass to Dick Royer that was good for 10 yards and another first down. Then Pietrosante gained seven, but on the next play Williams fumbled—the ball squirted back to the 16, but the quarterback recovered. Third and seven. Lynch gained eight.

First and goal from the eight. Pietrosante gained four on the Tank 75. Lynch was stopped at the line of scrimmage. Williams, on a keeper, gained one. Fourth down at the Sooner three. Would the Irish kick a field goal? Brennan decided not to, and the Irish lined up needing three yards on what would be, for better or worse, the final play of this drive.

Williams took the snap and immediately pitched the ball to Lynch, who was sweeping right. Pietrosante burst through the line, and took out OU's Dodd with a cut block.

Lynch was never touched as he dashed into the end zone. Notre Dame, 7-0. Twenty plays, nineteen of them runs, that took 9:01 off the clock. Pietrosante, who would be the game's leading rusher with 56 yards on seventeen carries, ran for 35 of Notre Dame's 80 yards on the game-winning drive.

Wilkinson inserted well-rested reserves and abandoned the running game. The Sooners, who until this point had completed two passes for 16 yards, took to the air. Quarterback Bennett Watts completed a pair of passes for 31 yards down to the Irish 36. The fans at Owen Field smelled, if not victory, at least a tie. But on the next play Dale Sherrod threw the ball into the end zone and Notre Dame's Williams intercepted. Seconds later the clock ran out and, at 4:17 P.M., the Sooner streak was dead. The Irish had just spoiled the biggest birthday bash Oklahoma had ever seen.

Afterward, talk centered on the end of the Sooner streak and Notre Dame's game-winning drive. "It was a great drive," said Sooner fullback Morris. "They did not big-play us, but they seemed to make three yards on every play."

Brennan, aware that the Sooners had entered the game having surrendered just two rushing touchdowns in 1957, was particularly proud of the scoring play. "It was the first time all year we used that play on the goal line," the embattled coach said, "and I think it fooled Oklahoma. They were sucked in to stop us in the middle."

Coach Terry Brennan, just twenty-nine years old, didn't have much to smile about in 1956 or 1957, but ending Oklahoma's forty-seven-game winning streak was a nice consolation prize.

Wilkinson took no solace in knowing that the pressure of maintaining the streak was over. His players, after all, had never lost a game in college. Still, the OU coach was more than gracious. "If we had to lose, I couldn't have picked any better team to lose to," he said. "Some of the people from Notre Dame told me that the boys came into the game knowing that if they got beat nobody would ever remember the 1957 Irish. But if they beat us . . . they sure are going down in history."

Back in South Bend, the largest welcoming party in school history, some four thousand students, awaited the Irish. As a bus ferried the victors from Norman to the airport, Brennan smiled in deep satisfaction. "Looks as if the Catechumens," he said, "ate up the lions!"

Notre Dame 7, Oklahoma 0
Owen Field, Norman, Oklahoma
November 16, 1957

SCORING SUMMARY

	1	2	3	4	
Notre Dame	0	0	0	7	7
Oklahoma	0	0	0	0	0

Team	Qtr.	Time Left	Play	Score
ND	4	3:50	Dick Lynch 3 run	ND 7-0
			(Monty Stickles kick)	

TEAM STATISTICS

	ND	OU
First Downs	17	9
Total Net Yards	247	145
Rushes-Yards	64-168	47-98
Passing	79	47
Punt Returns	2-10	6-49
Kickoff Returns	1-19	2-40
Interceptions-Returns	1-0	1-0
Comp-Att-Int	9-20-1	4-11-1
Punts	8-39.0	10-37.0
Fumbles-Lost	4-1	2-1
Penalties-Yards	5-45	5-35

INDIVIDUAL STATISTICS

Rushing: ND: Pietrosante 17-56, Lynch 17-54, Reynolds 7-29, Doyle 4-26, Just 6-17, Izo 2-(-10), Lima 3-(-3), Williams 8-(-1). OU: Thomas 10-36, Morris 6-17, Boyd 4-17, Baker 7-14, Carpenter 3-5, Dodd 8-3, Sandefer 8-3, Rolle 1-3.

Passing: ND: Williams 8-19-1-70, Izo 1-1-0-9. OU: Watts 2-3-0-31, Dodd 2-3-0-16, Sherrod 0-1-1-0, Carpenter 0-1-0-0, Sandefer 0-1-0-0, Thomas 0-1-0-0, Hobby 0-1-0-0.

Receiving: ND: Colosimo 3-30, Royer 2-19, Pietrosante 1-10, Just 1-10, Wetoska 1-9, Lynch 1-1. OU: Pellow 2-31, Morris 1-11, Rector 1-5.

Attendance: 63,170

12

NOTRE DAME 31, MICHIGAN STATE 8

SEPTEMBER 19, 1987

DOES TIM BROWN DESERVE TO WIN THE HEISMAN TROPHY? IN early December of 1987, no issue in sports aroused more spirited debate. The Notre Dame senior flanker had been the front-runner for the award since appearing on the cover of *Sports Illustrated*'s college football preview issue that August. Brown's highlight-reel touchdowns, along with the resurgence of the Fighting Irish in general, had galvanized the nation in September and October.

Then in November both Brown and the Irish faltered. Consecutive losses at Penn State and Miami, in which Brown had had little impact, dropped Notre Dame out of the national championship picture and soured many on the six-foot, 195-pound Dallas native. By season's end his detractors were pointing out that, statistically, Brown led the nation in no offensive categories. He may have been Notre Dame's best player, but so what? The Cotton Bowl–bound Irish were 8-3 and ranked twelfth in the nation. Fans and pundits were not the only ones openly questioning Brown's bona fides. His peers were doing so as well.

"He's not worthy," University of Miami defensive back Bennie Blades bluntly stated.

"If you want to base the trophy on stats and ability to make the big play, I look at myself and [Syracuse quarterback] Don McPherson," said Pittsburgh running back Craig Heyward, who finished second in the nation in rushing with 1,655 yards. "If you want to base it on publicity then give it to Tim Brown."

While Brown certainly benefited from the *SI* cover and the five-page story inside the magazine, his "Heisman campaign" was less a result of hype than hysteria. In fact, Notre Dame never spent a penny in order to publicize Brown as a Heisman candidate—unlike UCLA, which earmarked ten thousand dollars toward promoting running back Gaston Green that season.

Brown staged his Heisman campaign on the gridiron. And, were it not for a two-minute span in the season's second game, he may not have won the award. On this warm, breezy September evening, Brown created bedlam in Notre Dame Stadium before the usual sellout crowd of 59,075. Under the glare of the temporary Musco lights as well as a national television audience on ESPN, the shy, shifty-hipped senior returned consecutive first-quarter punts for touchdowns of 71 and 66 yards against Michigan State.

After this evening, the Heisman Trophy would be Brown's to lose. And though he would not do anything the rest of the season to exceed this evening's performance, the question facing Heisman voters at season's end was whether any other Heisman hopefuls had closed the gap.

Michigan State was 1-0 following an impressive nationally televised, 27-13 home win against USC on Labor Day evening. The Spartans, ranked seventeenth in the nation,

> After this evening, **THE HEISMAN TROPHY WOULD BE BROWN'S TO LOSE.** And though he would not do anything the rest of the season to exceed this evening's performance, the question facing Heisman voters at season's end was whether any other Heisman hopefuls had closed the gap.

would be the fifth consecutive top-twenty team the Irish had faced. Notre Dame had ended the 1986 season, head coach Lou Holtz's first in South Bend, with a 24-19 home loss to No. 3 Penn State; a 21-19 road loss to No. 8 LSU; a 38-37 road win at No. 17 USC; and then opened the 1987 season with a 26-7 victory at No. 9 Michigan.

The 1986 come-from-behind victory at Southern Cal, after the Irish had lost five games by a combined total of fourteen points, provided a sweet coda to Holtz's frustrating, inaugural 5-6 autumn in South Bend. "I think the USC game was a great stepping-stone going into this season," linebacker Wes Pritchett noted before the Michigan State tussle. "Everybody realized that what Coach Holtz had been talking about, that it takes a little extra to win, was really true."

That Southern Cal game, during which Notre Dame trailed, 30-12, with 3:52 remaining in the third quarter, also was Brown's national coming-out party. Though the Dallas native had already returned three kickoffs for touchdowns during the season, Notre Dame's 4-6 record had negated his impact. Then, against the Trojans, Brown made a trio of spectacular plays to catalyze three of the Irish's last four scoring drives. Brown:

▧ returned a kickoff 57 yards, and soon after the Irish trailed, 30-20.

▧ caught a 49-yard pass before Notre Dame closed the gap to 37-35.

▧ returned a punt 56 yards to the Trojan 16 with 2:15 to play.

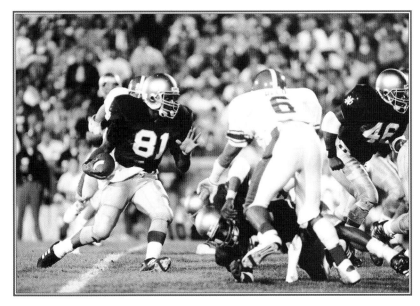

After getting the ball, Tim Brown heads into a crowd looking for a lane to speed through.

Shortly thereafter, John Carney kicked the game-winning field goal as time ran out. After the Southern Cal game, Brown's talent was no longer even a poorly kept secret.

Brown had led all Division I-A players in all-purpose yardage in 1986 (176.1 yards per game), averaging 14.8 yards each time he touched the ball, Holtz was of a similar mind. "The only way to keep Tim Brown from getting the ball

Farther upfield, Brown heads for open ground and looks to juke by another would-be tackler.

next season," Holtz warned opposing defenses, "is to intercept the snap from center."

In the 1987 opening-season victory at Michigan, Brown had made an acrobatic touchdown catch in the corner of the end zone. Now Michigan State loomed. The 59,075 fans comprising the seventy-second consecutive sellout crowd at Notre Dame Stadium wondered whether the Irish could begin the season 2-0 for the first time in five years.

The night began ignominiously for the team from East Lansing. Sophomore Blake Ezor, the Spartans' starting fullback, fielded Ted Gradel's opening kickoff at his two-yard line. Seeing the Notre Dame kick team converging toward him, Ezor took a step backward into the end zone and dropped to one knee for a touchback. Referee John Soffey put his palms together over his head to rule a safety. Notre Dame led, 2-0.

> Seeing the Notre Dame kick team converging toward him, Ezor took a step backward into the end zone and dropped to one knee for a touchback. Referee John Soffey put his palms together over his head TO RULE A SAFETY.

Later in the first quarter, Notre Dame started at its own 14 after a 52-yard punt by the Spartans' Greg Montgomery, who led the nation with a 52.8-yard average. The Spartan defense, which had limited USC to 61 rushing yards in their win over the Trojans two weeks earlier, was poised to stop Irish tailback Mark Green. Instead, quarterback Terry Andrysiak, in his first season as the starter, converted a trio of third-down passes to move the Irish 76 yards. The drive stalled at the MSU 11. Gradel, a walk-on who had converted only two PATs in his college career, made a 27-yard field goal with 4:08 remaining in the first quarter. The Irish now led, 5-0.

The Spartan offense, which featured big-play weapons such as Heisman candidate Lorenzo White at tailback and future NFL All-Pro Andre Rison at wide receiver, was feckless against the Irish defense. On the next series, fourth down and 17 from the Spartan 30, Montgomery trotted onto the field to punt. That's when the magic began.

Montgomery's punt of 41 yards was relatively short. Brown fielded it at the Notre Dame 29-yard line, then cut to his right,

> Brown always caused a buzz whenever he carried the ball. As Holtz was fond of saying, "IF I WAS BLIND, I COULD STILL TELL WHEN TIM BROWN HAS THE FOOTBALL."

breaking two tackles from white-jerseyed Spartan defenders. At that point Brown appeared to shift into a higher gear as he approached Michigan State linebacker Todd Krumm. It was Krumm who the year before had intercepted two Irish passes, returning one for a touchdown, in the Spartans' 20-15 upset of the Irish.

Using a swivel-hipped juke, Brown left Krumm, arguably MSU's top open-field tackler, flatfooted near midfield. Notre Dame's Rod West had already taken punter Montgomery out of the play with a downfield block, allowing Brown to race into the north end zone for a 71-yard touchdown with 2:14 remaining in the first period. The Saturday-night crowd erupted at the sight of Notre Dame's first punt return for a touchdown since Tim Simon had done so against Army in 1973.

Brown always caused a buzz whenever he carried the ball—Holtz was fond of saying, "If I was blind, I could still tell when Tim Brown has the football"—but now the stadium was erupting.

After going fourteen years without a punt return for a touchdown, the Irish needed just four plays to accomplish the feat again. Brown's second punt return touchdown, a 66-yard effort in the last seconds of the first quarter, outshone his first score for a variety of reasons. First, the Irish had the punt-block on, meaning that if they failed to block Montgomery's punt (and they did fail), Brown would have no blockers. Second, and because of that, Brown was under orders to call for a fair catch. He did not.

"I was supposed to fair catch the ball, but I saw that I had a cushion," Brown said. "I

Brown's big payoff comes in reaching the end zone, something he did twice on dramatic punt returns of 71 and 66 yards.

figured I was going to get chewed out when I got to the sidelines, so I better make it good."

Montgomery, to Michigan State coach George Perles's chagrin, finally booted a punt worthy of his prodigious leg. He outkicked his coverage. When Brown fielded the punt at his own 34, he saw a wall of seven Spartan tacklers racing toward him—but they were still more than 10 yards away.

"Our seven guys were flying down there," said Perles, who two seasons earlier on this field had witnessed Brown return a kickoff 93 yards for a touchdown against his Spartans. "They were trying so hard, some just ran by him. And Brown is a great, great football player."

Three different Spartans laid a hand on the elusive senior with the 4.31 speed in the 40, but nobody slowed him down. Brown slipped past that gauntlet, and then headed into open pasture. The only defender left was Montgomery, who was waiting for him near the Spartan 20.

"I had to beat the punter," Brown grinned. "If I got tackled by the punter, I knew I'd hear it from my teammates."

Brown put an ankle-breaker of a fake on Montgomery, who swooned to the ground without touching him. A second or two later he crossed the goal line, tying a then-NCAA record (held by several players) for punt return touchdowns in one game. Moreover, he became the first Irish gridder to return two punts for touchdowns in a game since 1926, when Vince McNally had done so against Beloit.

"I don't know where a dance is being held tonight," said Holtz. "That's the only place you might see another move like that."

The Irish led, 19-0, and there were still thirteen seconds left in the first quarter. Brown's heroics had incited mass histrionics around the stadium. The repercussions were being felt across the country, by anyone who was watching ESPN. "Tim Brown. Boom! Boom!" declared ESPN analyst Beano Cook. "He did the impossible."

Three more quarters remained to be played, but the contest was anticlimactic following Brown's second return. With 3:37 remaining in the first half, senior defensive tackle Jeff Kunz sacked Bobby McAllister for another safety that extended the Irish lead to 21-0. In Notre Dame's one hundred previous seasons, the Irish had never recorded two safeties in the same *year*.

Kunz's safety was the product of an Irish squad that played with much more confidence and determination under Holtz than it had under his predecessor, Gerry Faust. For example: punter Vince Phelan, a first-year starter as a senior, had boomed a kick 53

It was a big day for the Irish defense as well, with Notre Dame defensive tackle Jeff Kunz exulting after another big stop. Kunz's sack of Michigan State quarterback Bobby McAllister produced one of Notre Dame's two safeties on the day.

yards which Tim Grunhard, the long-snapper on the play, had downed at the Spartan two-yard line.

"We've paid our dues," said senior co-captain Chuck Lanza, the center. "This isn't luck. We know we're so well-prepared for each game so we have an air of confidence. That's why we feel so good when we step on the field."

The Irish still played with hunger. Andrysiak, on third and seven, escaped three tacklers in the backfield and lunged just past the first-down marker, to keep a drive alive. Nine plays later Gradel kicked a 37-yard field goal resulting in Notre Dame leading at halftime, 24-0.

Early in the third quarter, McAllister fumbled at his own 13 after being sandwiched by Notre Dame linebacker Cedric Figaro and lineman Tom Gorman. Four plays later running back Anthony Johnson scored on a three-yard run to complete the Irish scoring. Michigan State would at last spoil the Irish shutout bid with sixty-six seconds left in the game on a 57-yard McAllister-to-Rison heave. It was simply a blemish, as the Irish won convincingly, 31-8.

Besides recording eight sacks and forcing four turnovers, Notre Dame's "No Name" defense, led by coordinator Foge Fazio, had held Lorenzo White to 51 net rushing yards in nineteen carries, a 2.7-yard average. "They seemed to know just what we were doing," White said. "They adjusted very well to every move we made. And they blitzed more often than we thought they would."

Seven different Irish defenders had sacks, while the leading tackler on the evening, linebacker Ned Bolcar, had just seven tackles. Defensively, it was a team effort. Offensively? Just the opposite, as Brown accounted for 275 all-purpose yards. Seventy-seven days later at the Downtown Athletic Club in New York City, his name was called when they announced the winner of the Heisman Trophy.

"Tim Brown makes runs like you used to see thirty years ago," Holtz said. "You just don't see people make as many things happen by themselves anymore. It would have been interesting to see what Grantland Rice would have written about him."

Brown's resounding Heisman victory (he received 1,442 points while runner-up McPherson of Syracuse had 831) was a happy ending to a four-year saga. On his first collegiate play, on the opening kickoff of the 1984 season-opener versus Purdue at the Hoosier Dome in Indianapolis, Brown, a true freshman, had fumbled the kickoff. The Boilermakers recovered and kicked a field goal, which proved to be the margin of victory in a 23-21 win.

"If I could have," the future Hall of Famer with the Oakland Raiders said, " I would have packed my bags right then and gone back to Dallas."

Instead, Tim Brown, perhaps the shiftiest open-field runner ever to play at Notre Dame, stayed put. Four years later, he became the school's record-setting seventh Heisman Trophy winner.

Notre Dame 31, Michigan State 8
Notre Dame Stadium, South Bend, Indiana
September 19, 1987

SCORING SUMMARY

	1	2	3	4	
Michigan State	0	0	0	8	8
Notre Dame	19	5	7	0	31

Team	Qtr.	Time Left	Play	Score
ND	1	15:00	Safety, Blake Ezor backs into end zone and downs the ball	ND 2-0
ND	1	4:08	Ted Gradel 27 FG	ND 5-0
ND	1	2:14	Tim Brown 71 punt return (Gradel kick)	ND 12-0
ND	1	0:13	Brown 66 punt return (Gradel kick)	ND 19-0
ND	2	3:37	Safety, Bobby McAllister tackled in end zone by Jeff Kunz	ND 21-0
ND	2	0:08	Gradel 37 FG	ND 24-0
ND	3	10:40	Anthony Johnson 3 run (Gradel kick)	ND 31-0
MS	4	1:06	Andre Rison 57 pass from McAllister (Bernard Wilson pass from McAllister)	ND 31-8

Attendance: 59,075

TEAM STATISTICS

	MS	ND
First Downs	13	15
Total Net Yards	229	252
Rushes-Yards	36-21	50-140
Passing	208	112
Punt Returns	5-43	6-150
Kickoff Returns	5-58	3-55
Interceptions-Returns	0-0	2-17
Comp-Att-Int	10-18-2	10-19-0
Sacked By-Yards Lost	2-17	8-59
Punts	7-43.1	8-47.0
Fumbles-Lost	4-2	1-0
Penalties-Yards	4-24	5-45
Time of Possession	26:45	33:15

INDIVIDUAL STATISTICS

Rushing: ND: Green 17-46, Rice 2-28, Andrysiak 9-22, Johnson 5-13, Brooks 6-12, Robb 1-11, Watters 5-9, Jefferson 2-2, Belles 1-1, Brown 2-(-4). MS: White 19-51, Wilson 1-4, Moore 1-3, Ezor 1-2, McAllister 14-(-39).

Passing: ND: Andrysiak 9-17-0-105, Rice 1-2-0-7. MS: McAllister 10-18-2-208.

Receiving: ND: Brown 4-72, Green 3-30, Watters 2-10, Jacobs 1-0. MS: Rison 5-137, Bouyer 2-28, Jacobs 1-19, White 1-15, Gicewicz 1-9.

Notre Dame
vs.
Penn State

November 14, 1992
Notre Dame Stadium

$4

13

NOTRE DAME 17, PENN STATE 16

NOVEMBER 14, 1992

"I love to get out there to catch a pass."

—Reggie Brooks, from bio page, 1992 Notre Dame media guide

REGGIE BROOKS'S AFFINITY FOR PASS RECEIVING MUST HAVE come as a surprise to the Notre Dame coaching staff. The five-foot-eight, 200-pound fire-plug from Tulsa, Oklahoma, entered his senior season in 1992 with two career catches—one on offense and one on defense. At his height, Brooks, who had finally cracked the starting lineup at tailback after sitting behind his older and bigger brother Tony (six-foot-two, 223 pounds) among others for three seasons, did not present an inviting target. And, if quarterback Rick Mirer was able to locate number forty flaring out of the backfield . . .

"Let's put it this way," said coach Lou Holtz. "Reggie Brooks is not the first guy I would want to throw to."

Reggie Brooks ran like a bull. That is why he was named the starter at tailback after playing mostly on special teams (and, as a sophomore, in the defensive secondary) before his senior season. By season's end, Brooks would run for 1,343 yards on 167 carries, an incredible average of 8.04 yards per carry. Only two Irish runners ever gained more yards in a season (Vagas Ferguson, 1,437 yards in 1979, and Allen Pinkett, 1,394 yards in 1983). Only the legendary George Gipp averaged more yards per carry (8.10), a number Brooks came within 10 yards of eclipsing.

MIRER DROPPED BACK TO PASS, but his primary, secondary, and even tertiary receivers were covered. Having exhausted his options, Mirer rolled right as Penn State linebacker Rich McKenzie bore down upon him.

Yes, Brooks ran like a bull. And caught like one. He had that four-yard reception in 1991 and, entering the tenth game of the season in 1992, had added one more to that total, i.e., doubling it. He was not the first guy you would want to throw to on a day when a blizzard hit and the turf had the traction of an ice rink, or if he had to dive in order to make the reception, or if the entire ballgame was riding on that one catch. When Rick Mirer dropped back to pass, Brooks was his last option.

Catch the ball? "He doesn't seem to be able to do that," Mirer said, "on Tuesday, Wednesday, or Thursday."

On this particular Saturday, however, Brooks saw the football flying his way. Twenty seconds remained in eighth-ranked Notre Dame's snowy contest against No. 22 Penn State. The Irish had just scored to cut the visiting Nittany Lions' lead to 16-15. Opting for the two-point conversion—and the win—Lou Holtz called a play that the Irish had never run in a game.

Mirer dropped back to pass, but his primary, secondary, and even tertiary receivers were covered. Having exhausted his options, Mirer rolled right as Penn State linebacker Rich McKenzie bore down upon him. Brooks, who had lined up as a flanker on Mirer's left, was now skating/running across the end zone toward the right corner. Mirer spotted him.

"We've run that play a hundred times [in practice]," Mirer said, "but I'd never gotten to the point where I had to look for Reggie."

"I don't think Rick saw me until the last minute," said Brooks. "I was in a situation, do-or-die. I was accountable to what happened on that play. I was accountable to every one of these guys."

■ ■ ■

One week earlier the Fighting Irish had pummeled ninth-ranked Boston College, 54-7, in what was the most impressively dominant performance of the Holtz era. On another campus, or perhaps in another year, beating the ninth-ranked team in the nation by forty-seven points would have been the highlight of the football season. Not this time. To a man, the players on the Fighting Irish roster had yearned all year to play twenty-second-ranked Penn State.

"I've been thinking about this game for a long, long time," said senior linebacker and co-captain Demetrius DuBose. "It's circled on my calendar in red. I did that at the start of the season. I think about it every day."

"We all have that date circled," seconded Mirer, DuBose's fellow senior and co-captain.

Since 1981, when Notre Dame and Penn State began playing one another each November, the Nittany Lions were 8-3

> On another campus, or perhaps in another year, beating the ninth-ranked team in the nation by forty-seven points would have been the highlight of the football season. **NOT THIS TIME.**

against the Irish (8-7-1 all-time). The schools had met five times between 1913 and 1976 with Notre Dame going 4-0-1 in those matchups. The only other school that had an all-time winning record against the Irish was Michigan.

The games were almost always played in bitter weather, which mirrored the manner of defeat to which Notre Dame often succumbed. A cursory review:

■ 1981: Nittany Lion quarterback Todd Blackledge scored on a one-yard keeper with 3:48 left as Penn State won, 24-21, in the first regular-season meeting between the two schools in fifty-three years.

■ 1982: A week after the Irish upset Dan Marino and top-ranked Pittsburgh, Penn State beat them, 24-14.

▓ 1983: On what is described as a "cold and woolly day" in Happy Valley, the Nittany Lions drove 50 yards in the final minute for the game-winning touchdown in a 34-30 win.

▓ 1986: The Lions entered South Bend at 9-0 in what was Holtz's first season at the Notre Dame helm. The 4-4 Irish hung tough, however, in the subfreezing temperatures. Trailing 24-19, Notre Dame drove 79 yards for a first and goal on the Penn State six in the final minutes. The Nittany Lions stopped the Irish on downs (one of them a dropped pass in the end zone), then went on to win the national title. "It was a great football game if you didn't care who won," Holtz said. "Unfortunately, we did [care]."

▓ 1987: The 8-1 Irish entered Beaver Stadium with a faint hope for a national championship against unranked Penn State. The wind-chill factor was minus-one degree. Notre Dame scored with 0:31 remaining to trail, 21-20, but quarterback Tony Rice was tackled behind the line of scrimmage on the two-point conversion attempt. "We went out," said Nittany Lion quarterback Matt Knizner, "and really ruined their season."

▓ 1990: DuBose and Mirer were sophomores, and the Nittany Lions did it again. The Irish were ranked No. 1 nationally and jumped out to a 14-0 lead against the Lions. Penn State scored the final seventeen points, however, punctuated by a Craig Fayak 34-yard field goal with 0:04 left to shock the Irish, 24-21. Mirer's interception with 0:59 left set up Fayak's game-winner that quashed Notre Dame's national-championship dreams.

"You can't blame anybody but myself," Mirer said after that loss.

Two Novembers later, Mirer approached the final home game of his college career with mixed emotions. In his first start in the 1990 season opener, televised by ABC in prime time, Mirer had led the top-ranked Irish to a late touchdown against No. 4 Michigan. Notre Dame won, 28-24 (Brooks, playing cornerback, clinched the victory with the lone interception of his career). Mirer was pictured on the cover of the next week's *Sports Illustrated* under the headline "Golden Boy."

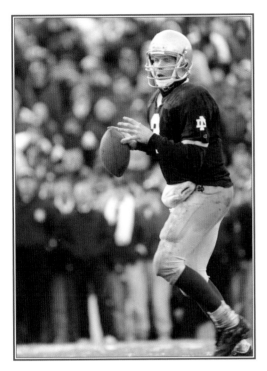

Rick Mirer gets ready to deliver the winning two-point conversion toss.

Now, nearly three full seasons later, Mirer was on the cusp of becoming the school's all-time leader in total offense and touchdown passes. A sure-fire first-round NFL draft pick, Mirer had returned for his senior season expressly to win a national championship. The Irish, 7-1-1, would not do that. They had never come closer than when the Irish led the Nittany Lions by two touchdowns at halftime in 1990.

"I'm mad," Mirer now admitted. "This game means a little more."

The Irish scored first on the game's opening drive. Mirer completed four of five passes, but Notre Dame could get no closer than the Penn State nine-yard line. The Irish settled for a 26-yard field goal from senior Craig Hentrich.

Shortly thereafter, Notre Dame Stadium transformed into the snow bowl. A winter squall hit the stadium, blanketing the turf in a thin layer of snow for the remainder of the

first half. It was the first snow game the Irish had been involved in since 1974 (a 48-0 home defeat of Army). If the old-fashioned uniforms and Penn State's old-fashioned head coach, Joe Paterno, had not already lent the game a timeless and classic ambiance, certainly the weather now did.

"THE FOOTING WAS TERRIBLE," said Irish All-American left guard Aaron Taylor. "One play, I went to pull and fell flat on my face."

Viewers at home found the scene enchanting. The players, especially on offense, were not as delighted. "The footing was terrible," said Irish All-American left guard Aaron Taylor. "One play, I went to pull and fell flat on my face."

Mirer calls signals over center while an early winter squall turns Notre Dame Stadium into the Snow Bowl.

Mirer's counterpart, Penn State quarterback Kerry Collins, accounted for all of his first-half passing yards on one throw: a 46-yarder to Tisen Thomas. Irish safety Jeff Burris was flagged for a late hit on the play, moving the ball to the Notre Dame 7. Five downs later Nittany Lion tailback Richie Anderson leaped over the scrum to score, barely avoiding a bare-armed DuBose in midair.

On the ensuing point-after another airborne battle of sorts took place. Notre Dame freshman free safety Bobby Taylor, a six-foot-four, 190-pound physical specimen with a thirty-six-inch vertical leap, blocked Penn State kicker V. J. Muscillo's extra-point attempt.

"The defensive line got a big surge and I just jumped as high as I could," Taylor said. "It's just one of those little things."

It was just one of those little things that would turn out to be huge. "What a difference one point makes," Holtz said afterward.

With 8:15 to play in the second quarter, Notre Dame linebacker Brian Ratigan recovered a fumble by Collins at the Nittany Lion 14. The Irish failed to score, however. On fourth and one from the five, Holtz, assessing the blowing snow and the absence of his regular long-snapper, Lance Johnson, due to a torn arch support, eschewed a field-goal try.

Mirer's pass intended for tight end Irv Smith in the end zone fell incomplete.

Later in the quarter, the snow stopped and the Irish again were in field-goal position. With 0:09 on the clock, Hentrich booted a 31-yard field goal to even the score at six apiece.

By the third quarter the playing conditions had improved. The Irish drove within 20 yards of pay dirt for the fourth time, but again Penn State's defense held. Hentrich's 37-yard field goal made it 9-6, Irish. With 8:35 left in the game the

Notre Dame freshman free safety Bobby Taylor (No. 21) was a special-teams phenom against the Nittany Lions, blocking an extra point that proved to be the difference.

Nittany Lions tied the game on a 22-yard Muscillo field goal, setting the stage for an unforgettable finish.

Notre Dame blinked first. On the very next series, facing third and seven from the Irish 35, Mirer dumped a pass to his tight end, Smith, beyond the first-down marker. Struggling for extra yardage, Smith had the football jarred loose by Nittany Lion linebacker Reggie Givens. Penn State linebacker Brian Gelzheiser recovered at the Irish 44 with 7:11 left.

Notre Dame defensive tackle Bryant Young was one of a number of Irish defenders putting pressure on Penn State quarterback Kerry Collins.

A few plays later flanker O. J. McDuffie beat Taylor on a slant pattern that was good for 15 yards down to the Irish 15. On the sixth play of the drive Brian O'Neal scored on a 13-yard burst up the middle, Penn State's longest rushing gain of the game. DuBose a moment too early had vacated the hole through which O'Neal ran.

"I couldn't find the ball," DuBose said. "I saw the flow of the play going left, so I followed the flow. When I picked up the ball, it was too late." Muscillo's extra point gave Penn State a 16-9 lead with 4:25 remaining. As DuBose trotted off the field he was met by his fellow co-captain. "Don't worry about it," Mirer said. "We're going to win this thing."

"And I believed him," DuBose said.

Notre Dame's twelve-play, 64-yard victory march almost ended before it began. On first down at the Irish 36, with 4:19 remaining, Mirer's pass was deflected and nearly intercepted. Then the senior quarterback and his two classmates in the backfield, Brooks and Jerome Bettis, embarked upon the defining drive of their college careers. Mirer completed a 21-yard pass to Bettis that moved the ball to the Penn State 43.

Bettis, nursing a sore ankle, probably should not have even been on the field. "I knew I had to be in there," said Bettis, who rushed for 68 yards on fourteen carries. "After the day our defense had, the offense owed it to the defense to win the game. So I had to suck it up and be in there."

> As DuBose trotted off the field he was met by his fellow co-captain. "Don't worry about it," Mirer said. "WE'RE GOING TO WIN THIS THING." "And I believed him," DuBose said.

The Irish lost six yards on first down, but Mirer scrambled for a gain of 15 on second down. Two plays later he calmly completed a 17-yard pass to another classmate, flanker Ray Griggs, advancing the ball to the Lion 21. After a five-yard gain by Brooks, followed by Mirer's seven-yard keeper, the Irish had a first and goal on the nine-yard line.

"It was so calm in the huddle," recalled Brooks, who then on first down moved the ball halfway to the goal line with a four-yard run. Mirer gained one yard on an option keeper, then threw a pass that bounced in front of Brooks on third down. Facing fourth and goal from the three with 0:25 left, the Irish called time-out.

Holtz called for a play that the Irish ordinarily would have saved for a two-point conversion. Mirer & Co. had never run the play in a game before. Mirer dropped back looking for his intended target, Smith, but could not find him.

"Go!" Mirer yelled, which was Bettis's cue to run out of the backfield and underneath the Nittany Lion coverage in the middle of the field. Mirer lofted a soft pass that Bettis caught with one foot in the south end zone as the stadium erupted. "I was the last option," Bettis said. "But the last option turned out to be the best option."

Penn State 16, Notre Dame 15. The Irish had tied Michigan, 17-17, in the home opener two months earlier. Holtz had drawn much criticism for having his offense play conservatively in that game's final drive. This time there was no doubt that the Irish were going for two. They had just used the play that they would normally save for such a situation, so Holtz called a pass pattern that his offense knew very well.

In the huddle Mirer looked at his teammates. "If they get through and I'm in trouble," Mirer said, "I'm throwing it straight up in the air. We're going to fight for it. I'm not going down with the ball in my hands." Three receivers, including Brooks, lined up to

It was a big day for Irish tailback Reggie Brooks, ending spectacularly with his diving catch of a two-point conversion pass from Mirer that gave Notre Dame the victory, 17-16.

Mirer's left. One receiver lined up wide right. Bettis stayed in the backfield. Mirer took the snap and dropped back, looking to his left. Nothing.

"Usually, we hit one of the two wideouts from the left that are crossing," Mirer explained. "Lake [Dawson] was open but I was slow getting there, so I worked my way across, looked at Irv [Smith], but couldn't get it to him."

Feeling pressure, Mirer scrambled to his right. McKenzie was closing in on him. Brooks raced across the end zone, mirroring his quarterback. "I saw Rick scrambling," said Brooks, "and I just took off for the sideline."

"Reggie just kept moving and got to the corner," said Mirer. "I just laid it out and let him go and get it."

Brooks stretched all sixty-eight inches of his body and hauled in the pass, then fell across the sideline and out of bounds. It was ugly, but Brooks's third collegiate reception incited mass euphoria in the southwest corner of the stadium.

> "Irv [Smith] plopped all over me right after I caught the ball," Brooks said. "I said, 'Get off of me, I can't breathe.' They just kept piling on. IT WAS THE GREATEST FEELING I EVER HAD."

The steamrolling senior had at last stepped out of his big brother's shadow (although the *New York Times*, in its game recap, referred to him as "Tony"), but in so doing he was instantly buried beneath a mountain of blue jerseys.

"Irv [Smith] plopped all over me right after I caught the ball," Brooks said. "I said, 'Get off of me, I can't breathe.' They just kept piling on. It was the greatest feeling I ever had."

Said Mirer, "That's pressure right there. Win or lose was on the line and if you don't come through there's all the critics and if you do, there's all the people praising you. That's kind of how my job is."

The Irish were penalized 15 yards for excessive celebration, but the penalty would be of no consequence. Three Collins passes later, the game was over. Notre Dame 17, Penn State 16.

"I can't say much," Holtz said in response to the celebration penalty. "I saw some coaches in that celebration."

The Notre Dame seniors, in their final home game, had found some redemption. The all-time series record with Penn State was now tied, 8-8-1. The Nittany Lions would move to the Big Ten the following season and the two teams would discontinue the series (they will next meet in 2006).

"This was the perfect football game," said DuBose, who had a team-high twelve tackles.

Mirer, who finished 12-of-23 passing for 164 yards, was giddy. "Reggie sometimes does not catch the ball on weekdays," he said, "but he makes it count on Saturdays."

The second pick in the following April's NFL draft, Mirer would be starting his twelfth professional season in autumn of 2004. Yet Mirer has never forgotten the thrill of that snowy Saturday in South Bend. "I've never had a better feeling playing football," he said, "than what I had when Reggie caught that pass."

Notre Dame 17, Penn State 16
Notre Dame Stadium, South Bend, Indiana
November 14, 1992

SCORING SUMMARY

	1	2	3	4	
Penn State	6	0	0	10	16
Notre Dame	3	3	3	8	17

Team	Qtr.	Time Left	Play	Score
ND	1	9:57	Craig Hentrich 26 FG	ND 3-0
PS	1	1:26	Richie Anderson 1 run (V. J. Muscillo kick blocked)	PS 6-3
ND	2	0:09	Hentrich 31 FG	6-6
ND	3	5:27	Hentrich 37 FG	ND 9-6
PS	4	8:35	Muscillo 22 FG	9-9
PS	4	4:25	Brian O'Neal 13 run (Muscillo kick)	PS 16-9
ND	4	0:20	Jerome Bettis 3 pass from Rick Mirer (Reggie Brooks pass from Mirer)	ND 17-16

Attendance: 59,075

TEAM STATISTICS

	PS	ND
First Downs	14	17
Total Net Yards	238	344
Rushes-Yards	40-107	53-180
Passing	131	164
Punt Returns	0-0	0-0
Kickoff Returns	5-100	2-21
Interceptions-Returns	1-13	1-0
Comp-Att-Int	7-28-1	12-24-1
Sacked By-Yards Lost	3-29	2-13
Punts	6-36.0	4-39.0
Fumbles-Lost	1-1	3-2
Penalties-Yards	2-10	4-32
Time of Possession	26:18	33:42

INDIVIDUAL STATISTICS

Rushing: ND: Brooks 23-78, Bettis 14-68, Lytle 3-35, Becton 2-5, Zellars 1-3, Mirer 10-(-9).
PS: Anderson 26-73, O'Neal 6-30, McDuffie 1-12, Archie 2-1, Collins 5-(-9).

Passing: ND: Mirer 12-23-1-164, Hentrich 0-1-0-0.
PS: Collins 7-28-1-131.

Receiving: ND: I. Smith 4-59, Dawson 2-39, Bettis 2-24, Jarrell 2-13, Griggs 1-17, Mayes 1-12.
PS: McDuffie 3-46, Drayton 2-29, T. Thomas 1-46, O'Neal 1-10.

The Squad 1913

NOTRE DAME 35, ARMY 13

NOVEMBER 1, 1913

WHEN THE DAY BEGAN ON NOVEMBER 1, 1913, THE UNIVERSITY of Notre Dame and the forward pass had one thing in common: both were afterthoughts to the college football establishment. By the end of the day, thanks to an innovative coach, the first great passing tandem in the sport's history, and the center stage of West Point's Cullum Field, that would all change. Never again would anyone consider the forward pass or Notre Dame as anything but signature landmarks on the sport's landscape.

Neither the forward pass nor Notre Dame was brand-new, or even unheard of, in 1913. The forward pass had been legalized in 1906—laterals had been around since the 1876 Yale-Princeton contest—with coaches such as the University of Chicago's Amos Alonzo Stagg and St. Louis University's Eddie Cochems taking full advantage of it. Still, the pass was in its infancy. Teams rarely used it, except in desperation, and the concept of pass patterns was as yet undeveloped. Instead, an end would run to a spot and wait for the quarterback to toss him the ball.

Notre Dame was entering its twenty-fifth season of football in 1913. Yes, the "Catholics," as they were then known (along with "Hoosiers" and "Westerners"), played in relative obscurity as far as the eastern football establishment was concerned. One East Coast writer described the school's location as "South Bend, Illinois."

Still, Notre Dame had already put together five undefeated seasons (for seasons greater than two games in length). In 1909, when they had gone 7-0-1, Notre Dame knocked off former two-time national champion Michigan, 11-3. The small Catholic institution from north central Indiana had not lost more than one game in a season since 1905.

Notre Dame's success was also its worst enemy heading into the fall of 1913. The powerhouse conference of the Midwest, the Western Conference, refused to allow Notre Dame to join. Worse, the Western Conference, the precursor of the Big Ten, was waging an unofficial boycott of Notre Dame. Unable to draw major opponents close to home, the Catholics were obliged to play—and annihilate—smaller schools in their neighborhood. Notre Dame was winning on the scoreboard (they outscored the opposition, 389-27, in 1912) but losing money. After the 1912 season, coach John Marks, despite a two-year record of 13-0-2, was let go for that very reason.

Meanwhile, the coach at Wabash College (Indiana) was speaking one day to an attorney, who happened to be a Notre Dame alumnus. The coach, Jesse Harper, commented that "football should be made to pay for itself." Harper's remark was passed on to the Notre Dame president, who said, "I want to see that man." Harper was hired.

Notre Dame dressed out for the big game, dapper, and ready, for the Cadets.

Harper's first challenge at Notre Dame was not to assemble a quality lineup. Seven of the regulars (and remember, this was single-platoon football) were returning. Instead, Harper had to find worthy opponents. Notre Dame, which had never traveled farther east than Pittsburgh or farther west than Kansas, was about to go on a crusade.

On December 18, 1912, Harper wrote to Army's student manager of athletics, Harold Loomis, to request a space on their schedule. Harper was in luck. Army traditionally played Yale on the Saturday nearest to November 1 each season, but the Elis had opted to discontinue the series. In truth, Army had become a pariah to many East Coast teams due to its practice of accepting players who had already graduated from—and played four years for—another university. Loomis sent word by telegraph that Army would place Notre Dame on its schedule and agreed to Notre Dame's request for a thousand-dollar visitors' guarantee. The folks at West Point had never paid a visiting opponent even half that sum before.

When the 1913 fall semester arrived, the new Notre Dame football coach was at the Lake Central Station in South Bend to meet his players whenever they embarked from the train. Mal Elward, a backup end, recalled, "The first thing [Jesse Harper] said was, 'I've got great news for you fellows. We're going to play Army at West Point!'"

Harper's hiring was good fortune. A former quarterback at Chicago under Stagg, Harper was a proponent of the forward pass. "I used the forward pass a great deal at Wabash before going to Notre Dame," he later recalled. "In fact, Wabash was the first team to use intentional grounding."

When this early architect of the aerial met his senior quarterback, Gus Dorais, and Dorais's roommate, senior end and team captain Knute Rockne, he must have been pleased. Although only five-foot-seven, 145 pounds, Dorais was a magical passer and a spry athlete. "As agile as a cat," the *New York Times* would soon describe Dorais, "and as restless as a jumping jack."

Rockne, who had not matriculated at Notre Dame until he was twenty-two, was bigger at five-foot-eight, 165 pounds. Though not the athlete that Dorais was, the Norwegian native by way of Chicago possessed a shrewd football mind.

The pair had roomed together as freshmen at Corby Hall. While Dorais was an instant success—the school's only four-year starter until Blair Kiel seventy years later—Rockne had failed his freshman tryout. "I played as if my fingers were frozen," Rockne recalled. "I did everything wrong."

"I really liked him at first sight," Dorais, five years younger than Rockne, would say years later. "There was something about Rock, a kind of smartness, quick, bright eyes, that made you forget his battered face."

After distinguishing himself in track, Rockne was invited back to the football team later in his freshman year. By the summer of 1913, Dorais and Rockne were fast friends. "Dorais and I spent a whole summer vacation at Cedar Point on Lake Erie," Rockne wrote just two months before his death in 1931. "We worked our way as restaurant checkers and what not, but played on the beach with a football, practicing forward passing."

In a 1930 article for *Collier's*, Rockne wrote, "Perfection of the forward pass came to us only through daily, tedious practice. I'd run along the beach, Dorais would throw from all angles. People who didn't know we were two college seniors making painstaking preparations for our final football season probably thought we were crazy."

Knute Rockne already was twenty-two years old when he arrived at Notre Dame.

The story of Dorais and Rockne and the summer at Cedar Point would come to life on celluloid twenty-seven years later with the release of *Knute Rockne: All-American*. In one apocryphal scene, the two roommates discuss their squad's chances against the mighty Army team the following autumn:

> DORAIS: "Don't be a sap, Rock. The Army will outweigh us twenty pounds
> to the man. We couldn't lick 'em if we took a shotgun along."
> ROCKNE: "All right—we'll take a shotgun. . . . We're going to pass the
> Army, Gus—we're going to pass 'em dizzy!"
> DORAIS: "Rock—if that works it'll make history!"

Much of *Knute Rockne: All-American* is sentimental blarney interwoven with a grain of fact. Take the title, for example. Rockne was an All-American . . . a third-team All-American. Likewise, Dorais and Rockne did not formulate the game plan to beat Army on the banks of

Lake Erie. "They took a football with them," Harper would write in 1954, "to teach Rock to catch the ball in his hands instead of his stomach, the way many coaches taught at that time."

On Thursday, October 30, eighteen Notre Dame football players, toting their own equipment, sandwiches, and just fourteen pairs of football shoes, boarded a train headed east. After a stop in Buffalo, they moved into sleeping car accommodations. The regulars slept in the lower bunks; the reserves in the higher ones.

Arriving at West Point on Friday afternoon, Halloween, the Notre Dame squad held a light practice. Omar Bradley, a Cadet gridder who would go on to lead World War II campaigns in North Africa and Normandy, noticed the Notre Dame players doing a strange type of running and juggling with the football. Bradley failed to report his information to Army coach Charlie Daly. Even if he had, who knows how Daly would have reacted?

Both squads entered the contest with 3-0 records. Notre Dame's victories had come against Ohio Northern (87-0), South Dakota (20-7), and Alma (62-0), the last of which was where Harper had started out as a coach in 1906. On game day approximately five thousand people, including the army chief of staff, Maj. Gen. Leonard Wood and former Princeton coach Bill Roper (who helped officiate), were in attendance at Cullum Field (which today serves as the Academy's parade grounds). Injured Army back Dwight D. Eisenhower, who would not play this season, was on the sidelines.

Notre Dame won the coin toss and elected to receive (a bold move in that era). On the opening series, fullback Ray Eichenlaub fumbled, and the largely pro-Cadet crowd cheered as Army recovered on the Notre Dame 27. The Cadets, who outweighed the visitors by fifteen pounds per man at the line of scrimmage, gained only one yard on four downs. The crowd sensed that these "westerners" were not patsies.

Both sides parried in the first quarter, but neither drew blood. Dorais's first pass of the afternoon fell incomplete. Notre Dame punted. Then Army punted the ball back to

> Dorais and Rockne did not formulate the game plan to beat Army on the banks of Lake Erie. "THEY TOOK A FOOTBALL WITH THEM," Harper would write in 1954, "to teach Rock to catch the ball in his hands instead of his stomach, the way many coaches taught at that time."

Dorais, who was hit hard on the return and fumbled. Army again recovered, yet still had no success advancing the "yellow leather egg," as the *Times* referred to the football. Dorais attempted another pass, and it, too, failed.

Early in the second quarter Dorais said to his teammates, "Let's open up." With swiftness and stunning precision, Notre Dame unleashed its passing attack. Dorais tossed an 11-yard completion to right halfback Joe Pliska for a first down. A few line plunges by bruising six-foot, 210-pound Eichenlaub, mixed with two more completions to Pliska, gained two more first downs. Meanwhile, it appeared as if Rockne, who had torn rib cartilage in the season opener, had again been injured.

On each pass play during the drive, Rockne limped downfield. "After the third play the Army halfback covering me figured I wasn't worth watching," Rockne later said.

Now, with the ball on the Army 25-yard line, Dorais dropped to pass. Rockne started limping downfield, then suddenly burst into a full-speed sprint. Before the Cadet defender was able to recover, Rockne ran under the pass, caught it, and crossed the goal line. Dorais kicked the extra point.

"At the moment when I touched the ball," Rockne later said of this reception, "life for me was complete. We proceeded to make it more than complete."

This photo of Rockne scoring a touchdown is the only known action photo from the game.

Not immediately, however. The Army offense, using the forward pass as well, marched downfield for two scores in succession. On the first one, fullback Paul Hodgson scored on a one-yard run. The score was tied, 7-7.

Soon after, a Vernon Prichard pass moved the ball down to the Notre Dame five-yard line. First and goal. Three times the Cadet backs Hodgson and Leland Hobbs smashed into the line, only to gain four yards. A Notre Dame holding penalty, however, gave the Cadets a first down from the one-yard line. Two more Army plunges failed. Finally, on third down, the home team's sixth play since reaching the five, Prichard took it in himself for the score. The extra point was missed. Army led, 13-7.

Still in the first half, Notre Dame responded as Dorais put on an aerial exhibition. He lofted a 25-yard pass to Rockne. Pliska was his next target and Dorais hit him for a 35-yard completion. For a moment the partisan Army crowd, having just witnessed the longest completion in college football history to that point, forgot its allegiance and cheered the play. Another pass completion set up Pliska's five-yard touchdown scamper. Notre Dame led, 14-13.

> On the last play of the first half, DORAIS AND ROCKNE TRIED SOME TRICKERY.

On the last play of the first half, Dorais and Rockne tried some trickery. Ten of the Irish lined up on one side of the field with the ball, while Rockne split wide to the other. Dorais took the snap and attempted a long crossfield pass to Rockne, but it was intercepted.

Army attempted to regroup at halftime. As the visitors huddled under blankets, Army coach Daly adjusted to a five-man front, instead of an eight- or nine-man front. The third quarter, as Dorais later put it, was a "ding-dong scrap." Notre Dame handed off to Eichenlaub more often, but could not mount a consistent drive. Army, substituting liberally (the Cadets would play ten subs, Notre Dame just one), advanced to a first and goal at the Notre Dame two-yard line.

Here is where the game turned for good. Prichard handed the ball to Hodgson on an end sweep. Rockne met Hodgson, lifted him up, and hurled him back to the five-yard line. Then Prichard attempted a pass into the end zone for Lou Merrillat, but Dorais intercepted it.

Having broken Army's spirit, Notre Dame proceeded to break the game open in the fourth quarter. Dorais passed—at one point completing at least ten straight passes—when Army crowded the line of scrimmage. When the Cadets guessed pass, he handed off to Eichenlaub, who was nearly impossible to tackle one-on-one. Eichenlaub rushed for two touchdowns, of one and eight yards in the fourth quarter. To top it all off, Dorais kicked his fifth extra point. Final score: Notre Dame 35, Army 13.

Until the fourth quarter, the game was close. Not that there weren't moments of comedy. At one point Sam Finegan broke a shoelace, and Harper ordered benchwarmer Art "Bunny" Larkin to give the starter one of his shoelaces. "I didn't come all this way," Larkin said defiantly, "to sit on the bench." Harper relented, allowing Larkin to replace Finegan—but not before Larkin borrowed Finegan's helmet!

The headline in the next day's *New York Times* read "NOTRE DAME OPEN PLAY AMAZES ARMY." Reporter Howard Cross was agog at Dorais's passing statistics: 13-of-17, 243 yards, two touchdown passes, one interception. "The Eastern gridiron has not seen such a master of the forward pass as Charley [sic] Dorais, the Notre Dame quarterback," Cross wrote. "The yellow leather egg was in the air half the time, with the Notre Dame team spread out in all directions over the field waiting for it. The Army players were hopelessly confused. . . . "

Roper, the former Princeton coach, was one of many observers who were stunned by what they had witnessed. He said that he always believed that such playing was possible under the new rules, but that he had never seen the forward pass developed to such a state of perfection.

The *New York Evening Telegram* was genuinely prophetic in its account of the contest. "It would not be surprising," the paper wrote, "if the majority of the college and university football teams adopted the wide-open style of attack next season that Notre Dame showed to such advantage."

It was a landmark game for college football. It was a landmark victory for Notre Dame. The Catholics' 35-13 win on the Plains at West Point was also, according to one historian, "the greatest single miracle in the history of Catholic higher education." Why? Because after All Saint's Day 1913, Notre Dame was "a household word."

The game was also a resounding watershed moment in offensive strategy. No longer did the eleven with more brute

Fullback Ray Eichenlaub did his part to bring balance to the offense that day, pounding out plenty of yardage on the ground and scoring two touchdowns that helped break the game open for the Irish.

strength possess the advantage. Notre Dame's win proved that speed could be just as viable a weapon as power. Rockne, ironically, would never as a coach be a major proponent of the play that first gained him, as well as Notre Dame, national renown. "The pass is like a lot of dangerous things in life," Rockne would say. "If it cannot be controlled, it's wisest to stay away from it before it ruins you."

On the first day of November 1913, Notre Dame was foolish enough not to be prudent, and the result rocked the firmament of eastern football. Years later, long after Harper had retired to his family's ranch in Kansas, he enjoyed telling the tale of the ramifications of the school's victory. "I was out on the West Coast and was introduced to a naval submarine commander," Harper said. "As soon as he heard my name he started cussing. 'You ----!' he yelled. 'I've been looking for you for a long time. I'm Babe Brown and I was captain of the 1913 Navy team that lost to Army, and it was your fault because you're the one who showed 'em how to use those passes.'"

> The Catholics' 35-13 win on the Plains at West Point was also, according to one historian, "THE GREATEST SINGLE MIRACLE IN THE HISTORY OF CATHOLIC HIGHER EDUCATION."

Notre Dame 35, Army 13
Cullum Field, West Point, New York
November 1, 1913

SCORING SUMMARY

	1	2	3	4	
Notre Dame	7	7	0	21	35
Army	6	7	0	0	13

Attendance: 5,000

Team	Qtr.	Play	Score
ND	1	Knute Rockne 25 pass from Gus Dorais (Dorais kick)	ND 7-0
A	1	Paul Hodgson 1 run (Roscoe Woodruff kick failed)	ND 7-6
A	2	Vernon Prichard 1 run (Benjamin Hoge kick)	A 13-7
ND	2	Joe Pliska 5 run (Dorais kick)	ND 14-13
ND	4	Ray Eichenlaub 1 run (Dorais kick)	ND 21-13
ND	4	Pliska 5 pass from Dorais (Dorais kick)	ND 28-13
ND	4	Eichenlaub 8 run (Dorais kick)	ND 35-13

FIFTY CENTS

ARMY ★ NOTRE DAME ★ 1946

15

NOTRE DAME 0, ARMY 0

NOVEMBER 9, 1946

WORLD WAR II WAS OVER, AND AMERICA YEARNED TO RETURN to its merry distractions. The war had snuffed out a great many lives, however, and interrupted countless others. As for college football, the war had created a unique set of circumstances that may never again appear. If any one game could demonstrate the bizarre effect the worldwide conflict had on the sport, it was the 1946 meeting between the United States Military Academy and Notre Dame.

Consider the following:

■ Army had defeated Notre Dame, 59-0, in 1944 and 48-0, in 1945, yet the Cadets had not scored a point off Irish coach Frank Leahy in three previous meetings against Notre Dame from 1941 through 1943.

▨ Between the two squads that suited up at Yankee Stadium on this day in 1946 were four former or future Heisman Trophy winners, a record for one game. Army had Felix "Doc"Blanchard (1945 Heisman winner) and Glenn Davis (1946), while Notre Dame had Johnny Lujack (1947) and Leon Hart (1949), a freshman reserve end who did not get into the game.

▨ Notre Dame fullback Jim Mello had actually played for a military squad, Great Lakes Naval Training Station, which had beaten the Irish twice during the war (Notre Dame's five losses between 1943 and 1945 all were to military outfits: twice each to Army and Great Lakes, and once to Navy).

▨ Finally, because the war had interrupted so many college careers, the 1946 edition of the Fighting Irish had players who were as much as eight years apart in age vying for positions. At center, for example, eighteen-year-old Bill Walsh was battling for a spot against twenty-two-year-old George Strohmeyer and twenty-six-year-old Bill Vangen.

Notre Dame coach Frank Leahy was thirty-eight years old. He had played under Rockne as a tackle and had sat in on the "Win One for the Gipper" speech in 1928. Leahy had been an assistant coach at Fordham in the mid-1930s and shepherded the famed "Seven Blocks of Granite" line, one of whom was future NFL coaching legend Vince Lombardi. Hired in 1941 by Notre Dame at the age of thirty-two, Leahy already was a legend in South Bend. In his inaugural campaign the Irish went undefeated. Two years later, in 1943, they were national champions, finishing 9-1, and had their first Heisman Trophy winner, quarterback Angelo Bertelli.

The war took Leahy away for two seasons, however. On May 19, 1944, he was commissioned into the navy and spent eighteen months in the service. Assigned to the Pacific, Leahy's primary duty was to organize and supervise athletic recreation activities for submarine crews returning from combat at places such as

> Assigned to the Pacific, Leahy's primary duty was to ORGANIZE AND SUPERVISE athletic recreation activities for submarine crews returning from combat at places such as Midway and Tarawa.

Midway and Tarawa. Leahy was discharged on November 15, 1945. Two weeks later he signed a ten-year contract with Notre Dame, spurning offers from the pro ranks for as much as half a million dollars.

In the absence of Leahy and many of his players, the gridders from West Point had filled the college football void. The Cadets not only had great talent, but, as an institution that prepared men to become officers in the U.S. Army, they suffered no defections from the ranks during the years of the conflict. Army was simply a juggernaut at this time, winning national titles in 1944 and 1945. The Cadets entered the 1946 contest against the Irish with a twenty-five-game win streak.

Before the season even began, this was the most anticipated game of the year. Tickets went on sale to the public on August 1, but in truth the game had been sold out since June. Notre Dame wound up refunding more than four hundred thousand dollars in checks from

Coach Frank Leahy missed two college football seasons while serving an eighteen-month stint in the navy during World War II.

hopeful ticket-seekers, a figure that was actually greater than what the gross from ticket sales would be from the 74,121 fans who would witness the game in person. Financially, this thirty-third meeting between the two gridiron superpowers was a far cry from the first, in 1913. Then, admission had been free for the five thousand or so souls who showed up.

Interest in the contest at Notre Dame, where many of the forty-five hundred students were returning war veterans, was at a fever pitch. As far back as springtime they had begun

West Point's terrific trio included head coach Earl "Red" Blaik and a couple of running backs who would win Heismans, Doc Blanchard (No. 35) and Glenn Davis (No. 41).

inundating Army coach Earl "Red" Blaik with postcards warning of Army's doom. All were cryptically signed, "SPATNC." Only later would Blaik learn that the signature was actually an acronym for "Society for the Prevention of Army's Third National Championship."

The Notre Dame players were no less enthused. During practice that week, the Irish would break their huddle by chanting, "Fifty-nine and forty-eight, this is the year we retaliate."

Both squads were flush with talent. Army's arsenal included the Touchdown Twins, Blanchard and Davis. They were known, respectively, as Mr. Inside and Mr. Outside, an allusion to where each player's running talent was most dangerous. The Cadets also had a pair of imposing ends in Hank Foldberg and Barney Poole, as well as a young quarterback named Arnold Tucker who would win the Sullivan Award as the nation's top amateur athlete in 1946.

> Both squads were flush with talent. Army's arsenal included the Touchdown Twins, Blanchard and Davis. They were known, respectively, as MR. INSIDE AND MR. OUTSIDE, an allusion to where each player's running talent was most dangerous.

As for the Fighting Irish? Leahy had assembled what may be the deepest pool of talent any one coach has ever been fortunate enough to lead. Besides the two future Heisman winners, Lujack and Hart, Notre Dame had two future Outland Trophy winners, an award that debuted in 1946 and was given to the nation's top interior lineman. George Connor, a transfer from Holy Cross, would win the award in its inaugural year. Two years later Bill Fischer would earn the honor. In all, the Irish had ten future All-Americans on its roster.

Just how deep were Leahy's "lads," as he often referred to them? The Irish would lead the nation in rushing offense in 1946 (3,061 yards) despite having no player gain more than 350 yards. Instead, thirteen different players rushed for at least 100 yards that season. As one wag noted, "Leahy got a little thin when he reached down to the sixth and seventh string."

Leahy's lads were battle tested in a sense that renders any current use of the term among athletes ridiculous. End Jim Martin was an ex-Marine who had swum ashore on the Pacific island of Tinian on a reconnaissance mission in advance of the invasion. Tinian was one of many gruesome and bloody battles in the Pacific theater. Guard Bob McBride had survived 122 days in a German prison camp. Lujack, who had thrown for two touchdowns and run for another in Notre Dame's 26-0 blanking of Army in 1943, had spent eleven months on a submarine chaser in the Atlantic with the navy. Like many of his teammates, one-third of whom were at least twenty-three years old, Lujack had returned to South Bend more mature physically and emotionally.

Mature, but not somber. Quarterback George Ratterman, a better passer than Lujack, once called time-out during the Navy game to remind his teammates of a party later that evening. Tackle Ziggy Czarobski, a future All-American, was the team clown. Before the Iowa game, which preceded the Army tilt by two weeks, Czarobski asked Leahy if he might address the team's freshmen. After impressing upon the first-year players the importance of not letting down against

Army quarterback Arnold Tucker (No. 17) could not only throw the ball, he could catch it. On defense, he picked off three Johnny Lujack passes.

an underdog foe, Czarobski concluded his pep talk by saying, "The point I wish to make is that soon we are going to New York to play Army, a great team, in Yankee Stadium. Army hasn't lost in two years. Think of the price we'll be able to get for our Army tickets if we go to New York unbeaten!"

Both sides scouted one another extensively. Irish alumnus Jack Lavelle, a scout for the New York Giants, had watched every Army game of the past three seasons and delivered an extensive report to Leahy. The Cadet coaching staff, meanwhile, sent a dozen people to watch Notre Dame play Pittsburgh (one for each player and "a twelfth for Leahy," someone joked). On the Saturday prior to the epic clash, Blaik skipped his own squad's game against West Virginia in order to see the Irish knock off Navy in person.

Leahy, a pessimist in public, told the press that he foresaw a 27-14 Army win. Lujack, who had turned down an appointment to West Point, was more candid. "I never walked on a field with a Notre Dame team expecting to lose."

Then, three days before the game and with some of the nation's most renowned sportswriters such as Red Smith and Jimmy Cannon looking on, Lujack collided with teammate Frank Kosikowski in practice and sprained his right ankle. Would Lujack even

Notre Dame's Johnny Lujack made the game-winning tackle on Army's Doc Blanchard.

walk onto the field on Saturday? Trainer Hugh Burns worked overtime on Lujack's ankle, while issuing nearly hourly updates to the media. Leahy, mindful that the media found his chronically grim disposition disingenuous, could only say, "If it happened without the writers around, no one would have believed me."

By Saturday, though, Lujack, his ankle taped up, was well enough to play. The Irish, along with thirteen hundred students (more than one-third of the enrollment), had made the pilgrimage to New York for what some were calling "the most publicized football game of all time." Not a man in Army's black jerseys or Notre Dame's green ones needed a pep talk for this confrontation. In the Irish locker room, Leahy was silent. His only words to his team before they took the field were, "Army is waiting out there."

Perhaps because neither coach wanted to be responsible for losing the game, neither team won. In fact, neither team scored. Both had opportunities, though.

In the first quarter Notre Dame halfback Emil Sitko, who would lead Notre Dame in rushing for four straight seasons beginning in 1946, fumbled on his own 24-yard line. Army recovered, but the drive stalled and the Irish took over on their own 14.

Notre Dame's best scoring chance came in the second quarter, when Lujack led the Irish on an 85-yard drive. However, on fourth and one from the Army three, the Cadets snuffed a pitchout to Bill Gompers, as Foldberg drove him out of bounds inches shy of a first down.

The game's most memorable play occurred in the third quarter and pitted two Heisman winners, Lujack and Blanchard. On the preceding play, Tucker, who would intercept three Lujack passes, had returned a pick 32 yards to the Army 42. On the next play Blanchard burst through the line, then cut to his left and sprinted up the sideline. Lujack was the only man with a chance to stop Blanchard before he would reach the end zone. But nobody could recall the powerful, 205-pound Mr. Inside being tackled in the open field one-on-one.

Lujack measured his angle as Blanchard measured his defender. The kid from Connellsville, Pennsylvania, who had taken out four teeth of a teammate with a tackle in his first day of practice as a freshman, hung on and tackled Blanchard by the ankles at the Notre Dame 37. Two plays later Notre Dame's Terry Brennan intercepted a Tucker pass at the Irish five. For the afternoon, Lujack would recover two fumbles inside the Notre Dame 20 and also pick off a pass.

Neither team would seriously threaten again. When the clock finally ran out, nothing had changed. Neither the scoreboard, nor either team's won-loss record. Notre Dame had turned the ball over six times, Army four. Statistically, the teams were identical in passing yardage (52) and nearly the same in total first downs. In short, the most antici-pated game of, certainly, the decade, had ended in a standoff, 0-0. As one writer noted, "It was much ado about nothing to nothing."

On fourth and one from the Army three, Notre Dame's Bill Gompers was driven out of bounds inches short of a first down.

Lujack, who had played all sixty minutes, entered the Notre Dame locker room as if in shell shock. "Gee, that was tough," he said.

Everyone wanted to discuss his third-quarter tackle of Blanchard. "They said Blanchard couldn't be stopped, one-on-one, in the open field, yet I did it," Lujack said matter-of-factly. "I really can't understand all the fuss. I simply pinned him against the sideline and dropped him with a routine tackle."

Lujack was anything but the boastful sort. "Tell me, John," Leahy asked Lujack, who was 6-of-17 passing, "how did you happen to throw so many of them to Tucker?"

"Well, it was this way, Coach," Lujack replied. "He was the only man I could find open."

"You played your hearts out, but you were not quite good enough today," Leahy told his players. As successful as Leahy's tenure in South Bend would be—four national titles and six undefeated teams in eleven seasons, an all-time win percentage that is second in all of college football only to Rockne—the tie may have been mostly Leahy's fault.

Blessed with such a deep squad, Leahy normally platooned his first and second strings by quarters. In fact, backup quarterback Ratterman was on the field for 49 percent of Notre Dame's touchdowns in 1946. Against this foe, Leahy stuck with his starters throughout. "It was the only game in the four-year span that he was undefeated that he didn't go with that system of his," recalled Frank Tripucka, a third-string quarterback at the time, "and that day, as a matter of fact, he only used about eighteen players. If he had stayed with that system, I felt we would have worn them down. He even told us afterwards that he made a mistake by doing that."

Blaik was just as contrite. Years later he told Terry Brennan, a future Notre Dame coach who was an Irish freshman that afternoon, "We [he and Leahy] both choked in that game."

Nobody realized it that afternoon, but this contest was both a crossroads for two storied programs and the end, of sorts, to their relationship. Both teams would go unbeaten the rest of the way. Army, however, would lose the national championship on the final

> Blaik was just as contrite. Years later he told Terry Brennan, a future Notre Dame coach who was an Irish freshman that afternoon, "We [he and Leahy] BOTH CHOKED IN THAT GAME."

day of the season by barely beating Navy, 21-18, a team that had lost seven straight. When the game had ended, the Midshipmen had the ball on the Army three-yard line. At season's end, Notre Dame ascended to No. 1 and was awarded the national championship.

The following season, 1947, Army's unbeaten streak would be halted at thirty-two games by Columbia. Two weeks later in South Bend the Irish, in the midst of their own thirty-nine-game unbeaten streak, would upend the Cadets, 27-7. Notre Dame wasted no time in erasing the sour taste of 1946's scoreless tie, as Terry Brennan ran the opening kickoff back for a touchdown.

Then the series was halted. Officials from both schools felt that, as evidenced by $4.80 tickets being scalped for as much as $200, this friendly feud had grown out of proportion. The two most storied programs of the 1940s, who between them accounted for four Heisman Trophy winners and six national titles in this decade, would not meet again until 1957.

Notre Dame 0, Army 0
Yankee Stadium, Bronx, New York
November 9, 1946

SCORING SUMMARY

	1	2	3	4	
Army	0	0	0	0	0
Notre Dame	0	0	0	0	0

TEAM STATISTICS

	A	ND
First Downs	9	11
Total Net Yards	190	225
Rushes-Yards	50-138	48-173
Passing	52	52
Punt Returns	6-84	4-46
Kickoff Returns	1-24	1-22
Interceptions-Returns	3-39	2-5
Comp-Att-Int	4-16-2	6-17-3
Punts	7-40.0	8-40.0
Fumbles-Lost	4-2	5-3
Penalties-Yards	2-30	1-5

INDIVIDUAL STATISTICS

Rushing: ND: Brennan 14-69, Cowhig 7-37, Sitko 5-24, Gompers 10-26, Lujack 8-9, Slovak 3-6, Mello 1-2. A: Blanchard 18-50, Davis 17-30, Tucker 9-37, Rowan 3-11, West 3-10.

Passing: ND: Lujack 6-17-3-52. A: Tucker 2-10-0-22, Davis 2-6-2-30.

Receiving: ND: Skoglund 1-25, Brennan 1-8, Martin 1-7, Sitko 1-6, Gompers 1-4, Cowhig 1-2. A: Blanchard 1-23, Foldberg 1-13, Davis 1-9, Poole 1-7.

Attendance: 74,121

TEXAS
NOTRE DAME

THE 1978 COTTON BOWL CLASSIC ▣ DALLAS, TEXAS   JANUARY 2

#16

NOTRE DAME 38, TEXAS 10 1978 COTTON BOWL

JANUARY 2, 1978

SOME FOLKS NEVER LEARN. WHEN NOTRE DAME ARRIVED IN Dallas in December of 1977 to play the University of Texas in the Cotton Bowl, the Fighting Irish were six-and-a-half-point underdogs. The Longhorns, the last unbeaten team left in the nation, were No. 1 according to the Associated Press (AP), which also declared that the game would be "a one-sided mismatch."

For good measure, Texas also had Heisman Trophy-winning rusher Earl Campbell, who had set the NCAA single-season scoring record that year. With the odds so stacked in the Longhorns' favor, one wonders why anyone would have bet against Notre Dame.

The Fighting Irish had seamlessly been playing the role of plucky underdog in big games for more than six decades. And now, in the 1970s, they had added a new wrinkle to that role: spoiler. Since reversing eight years earlier a forty-five-year old university policy to not appear in bowl games, the Irish already had accepted invitations to bowls matching them against top-ranked and undefeated teams. The results had been uniform:

- 1971 Cotton Bowl: Notre Dame 24, Texas 11
- 1973 Sugar Bowl: Notre Dame 24, Alabama 23
- 1975 Orange Bowl: Notre Dame 13, Alabama 11

But that was the past. Besides, those three Irish outfits were coached by Ara Parseghian. This edition was coached by Dan Devine, who in his third season had yet to exorcise the ghost of his predecessor. Before the game Devine joked that some alumni from Chicago had presented him with "moccasins for Christmas. Water moccasins."

> Before the game Devine joked that some alumni from Chicago had presented him with "MOCCASINS FOR CHRISTMAS. WATER MOCCASINS."

Despite leading the Irish to a 10-1 regular-season record, Devine was a beleaguered man. "If I would get the ax from Notre Dame . . . " he began one sentence during his final pre–Cotton Bowl press conference.

The heat had been on Devine and his staff ever since the 20-13 loss at unranked Mississippi in their second game. The Irish roster was flush with talent, including a defense that had eight future NFL players. Devine had acknowledged as much during spring practice, saying, "If we don't win with these players, we're all in trouble."

And so they were in September. But then Joe Montana emerged from third-string on the depth chart at quarterback to lead the Irish back from a ten-point, fourth-quarter deficit at Purdue to a 31-24 victory. Then in October, Notre Dame unveiled new green jerseys and a renewed spirit in a 49-19 upset of fifth-ranked Southern Cal. On that same day Michigan, the only other unbeaten team besides Texas, lost, 16-0, to Minnesota. In the bowels of Notre Dame Stadium, Trojan coach John Robinson told Devine, "It's wide open now."

And so here were the fifth-ranked Irish in Dallas. The Longhorns, under first-year coach Fred Akers, had come through the front door. Texas, 11-0, averaged 300 yards per game rushing as the six-foot-one, 224-pound Campbell steamrolled opponents for 1,744 yards. The defense, led up front by Outland Trophy-winning defensive tackle Brad Shearer, had not yielded a touchdown in slapping Oklahoma and Arkansas with their only defeats of the season. So dominant were the Longhorns that Campbell scored more points (119) than the defense allowed (114).

Earl Campbell of Texas won the 1977 Heisman Trophy and would rush for 116 yards against the Irish. But he was not the dominant force he had been that season—his longest run against the Irish was 18 yards.

Devine, cognizant that the eyes and ears of Texas were upon him, paid the Longhorns homage. "Although they are number one, I still feel they are underrated," he told the media. "This could be the best football team that's come along in the last ten, twenty years."

Senior middle guard/linebacker Bob Golic, however, refused to play the humility card. "I think we are going to beat them soundly," Notre Dame's leading tackler said. "In my opinion, it won't be a squeaker."

Devine was not amused, especially since the Irish practices were less than crisp. "If you play like you're practicing," he told his team five days before the January 2 showdown, "Texas will blow your butts out of the Cotton Bowl. The day is gone when people lay down for Notre Dame. Play like this and you'll wake up in the second quarter and it'll be twenty-one-zip."

Four days later, Devine, whose personal bowl win streak (he had coached at Missouri and Arizona State) stood at five, was eerily calm. He scrapped a talk that he'd planned to give the Irish about how they'd been slighted since their December 23 arrival in the Lone Star State. "It's not necessary," he said, putting his notepad down. "We're going to win."

On January 1 the Irish moved out of their hotel in Dallas to spend the night at Holy Trinity Seminary in nearby Irving. Afterward, Devine would say, "I never felt better in my life and slept as well as I have before any game."

January 2 dawned sunny and cold, with a brisk wind making it feel colder than thirty-five degrees. After each Notre Dame player downed a twelve-ounce T-bone steak, four eggs, and toast in silence ("The breakfast was almost a religious experience," said one observer), the Irish made their way to the Texas state fairgrounds. There, a partisan Cotton Bowl–record crowd of 76,701 fans was waiting to witness what they hoped would be a coronation. The Longhorns were sixty minutes of football away from their third unbeaten national-championship season in fifteen years.

Instead, the burnt-orange-clad fans witnessed a near repeat of the 1971 Cotton Bowl debacle. In that loss Texas had turned the ball over to the Irish six times as Notre Dame raced out to a 21-3 lead in the second quarter en route to a 24-11 victory. Today the Longhorns would again commit six turnovers (three fumbles followed by three interceptions), and the Irish would roar out to a 24-10 lead at the half.

The Longhorns' daylong case of the yips started early in the first quarter. Quarterback Randy McEachern, who, like Montana, had begun the season third on the depth chart, rolled out to his right, where he was met by Ross Browner, Notre Dame's two-time All-American defensive end. "He was beginning to make a pitchout, so I reached for the ball—I try to stay close to that ball—and deflected it," said the six-foot-three, 248-pound senior who had finished fifth in the Heisman Trophy balloting. "Then I pounced on the fumble."

Four plays later a Dave Reeve 47-yard field goal gave the Irish a 3-0 lead. The Longhorns tied the score with a 42-yard field goal from Russell Erxleben, their All-American kicker and punter. Erxleben, who had 65-yard range (he still has the ten longest field goals in Longhorn history, using the

> A partisan Cotton Bowl–record crowd of 76,701 fans was waiting to witness what they hoped WOULD BE A CORONATION. The Longhorns were sixty minutes of football away from their third unbeaten national-championship season in fifteen years.

since-outlawed tee), was not a factor on this day. Texas habitually surrendered the ball by other means than his bare and talented right foot.

Late in the first quarter, McEachern tossed a screen pass to fullback Johnny "Ham" Jones. Defensive tackle Mike Calhoun and linebackers Doug Becker and Golic converged on Jones, forcing a fumble. Ross Browner's "little" brother, six-foot-three, 204-pound strong safety Jim Browner, recovered at the Longhorn 27. Four plays later halfback Terry Eurick, following a kick-out block by left guard Ted Horansky, scored without being hit from six yards out.

McEachern fumbled on the Longhorns' very next possession. Defensive tackle Ken Dike stripped the scrambling quarterback of the ball, and All-American defensive end Willie Fry recovered on the Longhorn 35. The Irish scored on their fifth play of the drive. Eurick, on his second carry of the game, scampered in for his second touchdown, this time on a 10-yard run on the left side.

> "I just stuck up my hands and WATCHED THE BALL COMING," Ferguson recalled, "but then I just shut my eyes as it hit me. I laid there awhile after I fell, not really sure if I had caught it or not."

"I'm normally put in there as a blocker," the senior tri-captain said later with a smile. "Maybe that's what they were expecting me to do."

The Texas Turnover Massacre was far from over. Two Texas possessions later, Becker intercepted McEachern and returned the ball to the Longhorn 20. Texas dug in, however, forcing the Irish into a third-and-seven situation. Montana rolled out, eluded two tacklers, and tossed a pass toward sophomore halfback Vagas Ferguson in the end zone. Montana's pass was underthrown and Ferguson, coming back for it, had to reach around Longhorn defender Mark Matignoni.

"I just stuck up my hands and watched the ball coming," Ferguson recalled, "but then I just shut my eyes as it hit me. I laid there awhile after I fell, not really sure if I had caught it or not."

Ferguson's teammate, All-American tight end Ken MacAfee, recalled the play vividly. "I was the first one to get to [Vagas] and he was just sitting there saying, 'I can't believe I caught that,'" said MacAfee, who finished third in the Heisman balloting that season. "I think that summed up how we all felt about the whole game."

Vagas Ferguson takes off on another run on his way to reaching the 100-yard mark for Notre Dame. He also caught a touchdown pass that gave the Irish a three-touchdown lead late in the first half.

Notre Dame now had a 24-3 lead. There was still 7:28 remaining in the first half, but the No. 1 team in the nation looked like Texas toast. After Golic stormed right past the Longhorn center to block an Erxleben 39-yard field-goal attempt, only the most resilient Texas fans flashed a "Hook 'em Horns" hand signal with any vigor.

Then, with just 0:22 remaining in the first half and the ball at the Texas 32, the Longhorn offense revived itself. Campbell rumbled 10 yards for a first down. McEachern completed a 34-yard pass to flanker Johnny "Lam" Jones, an Olympic sprinter, down to the Irish 25. After an incomplete pass, two seconds remained in the half. McEachern threw toward the end zone but misfired, his pass sailing high over the head of flanker Ronnie Miksch. Irish safety Browner, overzealous, shoved him from behind. Because the half cannot end on a penalty, the ball was moved half the distance to the goal line and the Longhorns had one more play with 0:00 on the clock.

This time McEachern made the Irish secondary pay, finding Mike Lockett for a 13-yard touchdown strike. The Longhorns headed into the locker room with their heads up. A score of 24-10 was a lot better than 24-3. The Irish, especially the seniors, could not help sensing déjà vu.

"It came to my mind as soon as Texas got its touchdown," said right guard Ernie Hughes. "I was in Los Angeles in 1974 when we thought we had that game put away at the half."

Hughes, like many of the first-stringers on this 1977 Irish team, had been a freshman when Southern Cal, down 24-0 late in the first half, had scored fifty-five straight points to rout the Irish, 55-24. Devine, who had not been the coach then, did tell his white-shirted squad that "this third quarter will be the most important quarter of the season."

"As soon as we got in the locker room at halftime," said Fry, "lots of players were saying we better make sure there wasn't another Los Angeles catastrophe. So we went back in the third quarter and showed everyone what the world should have known all along . . . that Notre Dame is the best football team in the country."

After a touchback on the kickoff, the Irish mounted their most important march of the day. They failed to score, but Montana led the Irish on a drive that consumed more than five minutes and 58 yards. Ferguson and fullback Jerome Heavens, each of whom would reach the 100-yard mark on this day, ground out the yardage. The drive stalled at the Longhorn 22. Reeve, who in his four seasons converted forty-two field goals, doubling the school record, missed the final attempt of his career, a 39-yarder.

Notre Dame's Jerome Heavens would rush for 101 yards.

"It didn't deflate us that Dave missed," Devine said later. "We came right back with a turnover on [linebacker Steve] Heimkreiter's interception and set up Vagas Ferguson's three-yard touchdown run."

The lead again was twenty-one points, with 6:49 left in the third quarter. "There was

Notre Dame rushed for 243 yards against the Longhorns and was especially effective in steering away from Texas's Outland Trophy winner, defensive tackle Brad Shearer (No. 77).

an occasional exchange of adjectives and words when we lined up," MacAfee said, "but when our thirty-first point went on the board, I could read it in their eyes. The enthusiasm was gone."

Notre Dame's last score came with 9:41 left in the game, when Ferguson scored his third touchdown of the day on a 26-yard run. Notre Dame 38, Texas 10. The five-play drive, covering 50 yards, was the longest of Notre Dame's five touchdown drives. The other four, each a result of a Texas miscue, were 27, 35, 20, and 29 yards.

When the final gun went off, more than a few Alamo references were tossed about. Notre Dame flanker Tom Domin was the first to trot into the Irish locker room. On his towel was a stenciled inscription: "Texas 11-1."

"We had a bad day," said Akers, whose sublime first season in Austin came to a sour end. "Didn't you ever have a bad day?"

McEachern had thrown three interceptions. The Longhorns were held to 131 yards on the ground, less than half of what their prolific wishbone offense averaged. While Campbell, known as the Tyler Rose, did gain 116 yards, he needed twenty-nine carries to do so. His longest run of the day was 18 yards. He left the game with a bruised ankle in the third quarter.

"Campbell is a great ballplayer, but we were set to get a hand on him or stick a helmet into his stomach every time he had the ball. We were psyched up," Ross Browner said.

Added Devine: "We pinched our ends to get to the heart of their offense. That's how we were able to slow down their running game. We forced them inside."

No Longhorn had a worse day than Shearer, the Outland Trophy winner who, in the week before the game, had aspired to be the most-quoted Texan since Lyndon B. Johnson. Shearer called MacAfee "an average blocker" and infuriated the six-foot-three, 253-pound Hughes by saying that he had faced two linemen during the season who were "easily as good" as the second-team All-American.

"My wife showed me the newspaper," Hughes said, referring to Shearer's quote. "She said, 'Look what this joker said about you.' It's been eating away at me all week."

While Campbell, KNOWN AS THE TYLER ROSE, did gain 116 yards, he needed twenty-nine carries to do so. His longest run of the day was 18 yards. He left the game with a bruised ankle in the third quarter.

Hughes's teammates tended the flame Shearer had lit, razzing him frequently during Notre Dame's practices. "You couldn't talk to Ernie all week," MacAfee said.

"Ernie was so psyched," center Dave Huffman added, "I thought he was gonna bite Shearer's head off."

Hughes, known to his teammates as "The Enforcer," limited Shearer to one solo tackle all afternoon. "Shearer's a good player," said Huffman, "but Ernie put a hurtin' on his head he isn't going to forget for a long time. Ernie ate his lunch." Hughes, a red-headed giant from Idaho, was the embodiment of this Irish squad on the second day of 1978. Underestimated, ornery, and ultimately victorious. Said Ross Browner, "Texas just underestimated me, and Fry, and others."

When the day began, there was one undefeated team in the nation. When it ended there were five 11-1 teams: the Irish and Longhorns, Arkansas, Alabama, and Penn State. While such a neck-and-neck finish would stir controversy today, in this pre–Bowl Championship Series era, it did not. The two major polls, the AP and UPI, placed the Irish No. 1. The National Football Foundation and the Football Writers Association of America also put the Irish atop the rankings.

Devine's national championship, while something few would have predicted after the

Unanimous across the board—national champions.

Ole Miss loss in September, was, in a manner of speaking, divine. This was his third season with the Irish. Knute Rockne had an undefeated team in his second season, 1920. Frank Leahy and Ara Parseghian both won their first national championships in their third seasons, 1943 and 1966, respectively. And now Devine had joined that legendary trio.

Devine, a great burden lifted from his shoulders, was candid and forthright. "There wasn't a football team in the country that could have stayed with us today," he said. "I don't know how this will come out in black and white and on television, but I firmly believe today we could have defeated any team in the country."

> Devine, a great burden lifted from his shoulders, was candid and forthright. "THERE WASN'T A FOOTBALL TEAM IN THE COUNTRY THAT COULD HAVE STAYED WITH US TODAY," he said.

The Irish didn't have to defeat any team in the country, just the best one. They did just that, on the grand stage provided by a bowl game, for the fourth time in eight years. Why was anyone surprised?

Notre Dame 38, Texas 10
Cotton Bowl, Dallas, Texas
January 2, 1978

SCORING SUMMARY

	1	2	3	4	
Notre Dame	3	21	7	7	38
Texas	3	7	0	0	10

Team	Qtr.	Time Left	Play	Score
ND	1	11:35	Dave Reeve 47 FG	ND 3-0
UT	1	6:07	Russell Erxleben 42 FG	3-3
ND	2	14:56	Terry Eurick 6 run (Reeve kick)	ND 10-3
ND	2	11:37	Eurick 10 run (Reeve kick)	ND 17-3
ND	2	7:28	Vagas Ferguson 17 pass from Joe Montana (Reeve kick)	ND 24-3
UT	2	0:00	Mike Lockett 13 pass from Randy McEachern (Erxleben kick)	ND 24-10
ND	3	6:49	Ferguson 3 run (Reeve kick)	ND 31-10
ND	4	9:41	Ferguson 26 run (Reeve kick)	ND 38-10

Attendance: 76,701

TEAM STATISTICS

	ND	UT
First Downs	26	16
Total Net Yards	399	291
Rushes-Yards	53-243	50-131
Passing	156	160
Punt Returns	0-0	1-1
Kickoff Returns	1-17	6-86
Interceptions-Returns	3-20	1-0
Comp-Att-Int	14-32-1	11-24-3
Punts	5-30.4	3-40.0
Fumbles-Lost	1-0	3-3
Penalties-Yards	4-37	1-5

INDIVIDUAL STATISTICS

Rushing: ND: Heavens 22-101, Ferguson 21-100, Eurick 4-16, Lisch 2-16, Stone 2-4, Mitchell 1-3, Montana 1-3. UT: Campbell 29-116, J. H. Jones 11-63, Thompson 1-2, Johnson 1-2, McEachern 8-(-52).

Passing: ND: Montana 10-25-1-111, Lisch 4-7-0-45. UT: McEachern 11-24-3-160.

Receiving: ND: MacAfee 4-45, Waymer 3-38, Ferguson 3-23, Haines 2-29, Eurick 1-12, Pallas 1-9. UT: Harris 4-57, Jackson 3-33, J. L. Jones 1-34, Miksch 1-18, Lockett 1-13, J. H. Jones 1-5.

S U N K I S[T]
FIESTA BOW[L]
EIGHTEENTH ANNUAL FOOTBALL CLA[SSIC]

WEST VIRGINIA

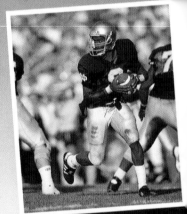

NOTRE DAME

JANUARY 2, 1989 • TEMPE, ARIZONA

NOTRE DAME 34, WEST VIRGINIA 21 1989 FIESTA BOWL

JANUARY 2, 1989

IF THERE IS SUCH A THING AS AN ANSWERED PRAYER FOR A NOTRE Dame football fan, its name was "Lou Holtz."

On November 30, 1985, the Fighting Irish were humiliated on national television by the Miami Hurricanes, 58-7, in head coach Gerry Faust's final game. Near the conclusion of the debacle former Notre Dame coach Ara Parseghian, who was an analyst for the CBS telecast, prophesied that the Fighting Irish would one day rise from the ashes of this annihilation like the phoenix of ancient mythology.

In fact, the Irish regeneration had already begun. Three days earlier the school had hired Holtz, then the coach at the University of Minnesota, to succeed Faust. Though, at first sight, the sandy-haired forty-eight-year-old, who had once been a guest on *The Tonight Show* and entertained host Johnny Carson with magic tricks, might not have inspired complete confidence.

"Look at me," said Holtz. "I'm five-foot-ten, I weigh 150 pounds, I talk with a lisp, I look like I have scurvy and beriberi, I'm not very smart, I was a terrible football player, and I graduated 234th in a high school class of 278. What do you think it feels like to be named head coach at Notre Dame?"

The players might have thought that they were getting the humorously glib coach who, while at Arkansas, opened his television show after a loss by saying, "Welcome to *The Lou Holtz Show*. Unfortunately, I'm Lou Holtz."

> Holtz handed out T-shirts. On the front, in big letters, was the word TEAM. Below that, in tiny letters, was the word ME. The entire squad wore those shirts to the thrice-weekly 6:15 A.M. conditioning workouts in the winter of 1986. "Puke-fests," the players referred to them.

Instead, they got discipline. Holtz walked into his first team meeting in December 1985 in the football meeting room inside the Athletic and Convocation Center and verbally cracked the whip. He admonished the players who were slouching or wearing baseball caps—those who in appearance or disposition looked lethargic. "The first thing he said," recalls tailback Mark Green, then a freshman, "was, 'Sit up in your seats and pay attention.'"

Holtz handed out T-shirts. On the front, in big letters, was the word *TEAM*. Below that, in tiny letters, was the word *me*. The entire squad wore those shirts to the thrice-weekly 6:15 A.M. conditioning workouts in the winter of 1986. "Puke-fests," the players referred to them.

The public, as well as Notre Dame nation, got the witty Holtz. When people asked him how come the Fighting Irish wore the old-fashioned-looking black Adidas shoes, he'd answer, "I didn't think the players would like brown ones."

The players saw that side, but they also saw the disciplinarian that Holtz rarely trotted out in public. During a late August scrimmage in 1988, Holtz basically had his coaches swallow their whistles. "I don't know if there has ever been a practice like that at Notre Dame," Holtz wrote in his memoir of the 1988 season, *The Fighting Spirit*. "It bordered on being brutal."

The public laughed with the coach who, disgusted with the passing of his quarterback Tony Rice early in the season, suggested that he practice throwing darts in his room. Said Rice, the most amiable player on the roster, "That man gets on my nerves."

The players knew the coach who, on the eve of their No. 1-versus-No. 2 showdown with rival Southern Cal in Los Angeles in the regular-season finale, suspended his leading rusher (sophomore Tony Brooks) and leading receiver (classmate Ricky Watters) for having been late to team dinners on consecutive days. Brooks and Watters were on a plane back to South Bend before the kickoff.

"Was he fatherly?" Brooks would later be asked, referring to Holtz's mood that day. "Was he steamed?"

"He was," replied Brooks, "a steamed father."

The Irish beat USC, by the way, 27-10.

By the end of the 1988 regular season, the Fighting Irish were 11-0 and had provided their fans with victories over No. 1 Miami, No. 2 USC, and No. 9 Michigan. In the process Holtz had restored the luster to the Fighting Irish legacy and given fans more thrills in one season than any fan who had sat on the wooden benches in Notre Dame Stadium could remember.

In September's season-opening win, 19-17, versus Michigan, played in prime time before a national TV audience, the Irish failed to score a touchdown from scrimmage. But, thanks to a Watters punt return for a touchdown and four field goals by five-foot-five, 135-pound walk-on Reggie Ho (a senior premed major with a 3.77 grade-point average), the Irish prevailed. In October had come the Miami victory. In November, a resolute Irish squad pummeled the Trojans and their Heisman-candidate quarterback Rodney Peete. In all three games the Irish had been, according to the point spread, the underdogs.

The final hurdle to the school's first national championship in eleven seasons, and to its first 12-0 season ever, would come on January 2, 1989, at the Fiesta Bowl in Tempe, Arizona. The opponent? Upstart West Virginia,

> "Half of the people in the country didn't think we belonged in the Fiesta Bowl," Nehlen said before the contest, "and now Holtz is calling us the greatest team in football. Well, he's the GREATEST CON MAN IN AMERICA."

also 11-0 and ranked No. 3 in the nation. By the time the Irish arrived in the desert—or as Richard Hoffer of the *Los Angeles Times* called it, "the mystique in the mesquite"—many alums considered the game little more than a coronation. Surely Miami, USC, and Michigan had presented tougher challenges than the Mountaineers would. Holtz, of course, confided that he was "scared to death of West Virginia."

"The Gipper" gets to meet the Notre Dame players. With less than a month to go in his second term as president, Ronald Reagan managed to take time to congratulate the Irish at the White House after their national-championship victory.

Mountaineer coach Don Nehlen was not buying it. "Half of the people in the country didn't think we belonged in the Fiesta Bowl," Nehlen said before the contest, "and now Holtz is calling us the greatest team in football. Well, he's the greatest con man in America."

Holtz *was* peddling a con. "I told (my) players a long time ago that it's not in their best interest for me to say they're invincible," Holtz wrote in his book. And, regarding "the psychology of a major game," Holtz added, "You don't go around saying how great you are."

You do, according to Holtz, go around saying how great your opponent is. And West Virginia was an easy sell. Led by their lightning-footed sophomore quarterback Major Harris (who had finished fifth in the Heisman Trophy voting), the Mountaineers averaged 482.6 yards of total offense (second in the nation) and 42.9 points per game. West Virginia had scored fifty or more points in five of their eleven games and their average margin of victory was nearly four touchdowns (twenty-seven points). The Mountaineers started sixteen seniors, including an offensive line comprised entirely of fifth-year seniors about whom *USA Today* carried a large story in the days leading up to the game (the Irish, by contrast, had an O-line made up of entirely first-year starters).

"I may be prejudiced," said Mountaineer guard John Stroia, "but I think we have the best line in the country."

Holtz as much agreed, of course. "West Virginia has completely dominated the offensive line against everyone they've played." Meanwhile, he had the *USA Today* article photocopied and posted in the room of every defensive player.

The Irish said little in the days approaching the game, but they were loose and confident. "In our minds we knew we were going to win the game when we first got to Tempe," junior quarterback Tony Rice said. "We never said that publicly, though."

Holtz reminded his players, if not the eight hundred or so credentialed journalists visiting the Valley of the Sun, that only two of the Mountaineers' opponents had finished the season with winning records. None had been in the top ten in the AP poll. Holtz also reminded them that while the game's biggest star was Major Harris, the other uniformed number nine playing quarterback, Rice, had actually rushed for more yards (700 to 583) on fewer carries against tougher defenses. In fact, Rice led the Irish in rushing in 1988, the first Notre Dame quarterback to do so since Paul Hornung in 1956. That year Hornung won the Heisman Trophy, rushing for 420 yards on only ninety-four carries.

On the eve of the game, after the entire team and coaching staff watched *Patton,* Holtz's favorite movie, the coach addressed his troops. "I don't know if West Virginia really and truly expects to win," Holtz told them. "I know they want to win. But deep down inside, I don't know if they truly believe they will win. But I do know for a fact that we believe we will win and we expect to win."

> "I don't know if West Virginia really and truly expects to win," Holtz told them. "I know they want to win. But deep down inside, I don't know if they truly believe they will win. But I do know for a fact that we believe we will win and WE EXPECT TO WIN."

The following day was overcast and unseasonably cool (fifty-five degrees) with intermittent drizzling. Holtz awoke early, turned on the TV, and was shocked to see ESPN showing *Wake Up the Echoes,* a documentary about the history of Fighting Irish football. "I was ready to play right then," he said.

A Fiesta Bowl—record 74,911 fans filled Sun Devil Stadium. The Irish chose not to wear the bowl's logo on their dark blue jerseys. "Our approach to the game," Holtz wrote, "had been, 'It's just another game.'" The Irish in fact wore the very same home jerseys that they had worn all season. In the locker room, Holtz implored his players to "dominate" this contest.

"He said he wanted to dominate the game so much," said six-foot-seven freshman tight end Derek Brown, "that whenever [West Virginia] gets a first down, he wants them to start playing their fight song and tearing down the goal posts."

Even Holtz might have been surprised how closely the Irish, especially his third-ranked defense (12.3 points per game allowed), followed his instructions. By the time West Virginia made its first first down, there was only 9:22 remaining in the first half and the Irish led, 16-0. The Mountaineers had gone three-and-out on their first four series (gaining a total of 27 yards) and the initial first down was actually the product of a late-hit penalty against Notre Dame linebacker Wes Pritchett.

The Irish were beating, as well as beating up, the Mountaineers. Already tailback Undra Johnson had been knocked out of the game with a knee injury, as had offensive guard John Stroia and nose guard Jim Gray with concussions. On the game's third play Harris became a human whisker to the twin blades of Notre Dame linebacker Michael Stonebreaker and six-foot-seven, 248-pound defensive end Jeff Alm, who buried him. Harris injured his left shoulder and, though he bravely remained in the game, was only a shadow of himself.

"I feel the injury affected the whole team," said Harris, who averaged nearly two yards less against the Irish defense than his normal five yards per carry. "Our timing wasn't on. I think on certain plays, I was thinking about my shoulder. Every time I landed on it, I could feel the pain. It affected my performance. We weren't pumped up at the beginning of the game like we usually are."

All season Notre Dame quarterback Tony Rice had been more of a running threat than a passing threat, although he would pass for a career high of 213 yards against the Mountaineers.

Added Nehlen, "We probably would have run ten or twelve more option plays and two or three more quarterback draws."

The Irish, meanwhile, suckered the West Virginia defense. Of Notre Dame's first seventeen plays, sixteen were runs. Among them was a 31-yard scramble by Rice on third and seven from the Irish 38, at the time the longest run from scrimmage in a bowl game in Notre Dame history. That drive ended with a career-long 45-yard field goal by Billy Hackett.

Rice passed just once on Notre Dame's next drive, but by then the Mountaineer linebackers were inching up to the line of scrimmage. In other words, they were vulnerable. Rice, rolling right, found Brown, his tight end, for a 23-yard gain. On fourth and goal from the one-yard line, the Irish gave the ball to fullback Anthony Johnson, who scored. Holder Pete Graham mishandled the snap on the extra-point attempt, so the Irish lead was only 9-0.

The next Irish touchdown, on an eleven-play, 84-yard drive, came in the second quarter. Rice, who would throw only eleven passes all afternoon for a career-best 213 yards (along with a game-high 75 rushing), faced third and 11 at the Irish 48. Again he found his tight end, Brown, this time for a 47-yard gain. Brown caught the ball near the West Virginia 25 and was finally pulled down from behind by Mountaineer safety Bo Orlando at the five. On the next play freshman fullback Rodney Culver scored to make it 16-0.

West Virginia would convert two Charlie Baumann field goals, of 29 and 31 yards, in the first half, but the Irish would score yet another touchdown. Rice found fullback Johnson on a 19-yard toss. Then he hit freshman burner Raghib "Rocket" Ismail on a crossing pattern at about the 11-yard line. Ismail, whose 4.28 speed made him the fastest player on the field, zoomed into the end zone virtually untouched for a 29-yard score. The Mountaineers, who had not trailed at halftime in any game all season, were down, 23-6, at the intermission.

Rice, 5-for-21 passing in Notre Dame's first three wins and failing to eclipse 100 yards passing in any of those games, was putting on an aerial show. "We can't throw the football," Holtz would say afterward, repeating a theme he'd been selling all week. "Although I did tell you guys that Tony was throwing the ball better this week."

After a 32-yard Reggie Ho field goal made the score 26-6, West Virginia scored its first touchdown on a 17-yard Harris-to-Grantis Bell pass with 3:32 remaining in the third quarter. On the very next series Rice was intercepted by Willie Edwards, who returned the ball 14 yards to the Irish 26. Suddenly, the capacity crowd at Sun Devil

The Irish defense put the heat on Mountaineers quarterback Major Harris all day.

Stadium as well as living rooms across the nation were abuzz. If the Mountaineers could score a touchdown, they'd enter the fourth quarter down only six points.

On first down, Notre Dame defensive end Darrell "Flash" Gordon tackled Harris on an option run for a two-yard loss. On second down Harris rolled out right. With Alm bearing down on him, Harris failed to spot tight end Keith Winn all alone in the middle of the field at the 10-yard line. Instead, Harris heaved a pass toward Bell in the end zone, but cornerback Stan Smagala deflected it to the turf. On third down Harris, backpedaling to pass, was sacked by Stams and freshman defensive end Arnold Ale for a 12-yard loss. It would prove to be the key play of the game. West Virginia, facing fourth and 24 from the Irish 40, punted. "That was disaster," Nehlen said. "Had we put something on the board, we would have been in business."

Instead, after a punt that resulted in a touchback, the Irish began a coup de grace scoring drive from their own 20. After a running play on third down gave the Irish a first and 10 at their 38, Rice tossed his longest completion of the afternoon, a 57-yarder to flanker Watters near the Mountaineer sideline. Only a shoestring tackle by West Virginia safety Lawrence Drumgoole at the five-yard line prevented Watters from scoring. Three plays later, Rice faked a hand-off to fullback Braxston Banks and jump-tossed a three-yard TD pass to tight end Frank Jacobs, who had sneaked behind the linebackers (a favorite Holtz play).

The Irish would go on to win, 34-21, and only a spate of late-hit and personal foul calls against the Irish marred what was otherwise a banner day. Notre Dame would be flagged for several unsportsmanlike conduct calls in the fourth quarter. Holtz received one after he ran onto the field to inquire as to the reason for his defense's miscreant behavior.

"When I went out on the field at the end of the game," Holtz said, "there were SO MANY FLAGS on the ground that I couldn't see the color of the grass."

"When I went out on the field at the end of the game," Holtz said, "there were so many flags on the ground that I couldn't see the color of the grass."

While Irish defenders Pritchett and cornerback Todd Lyght had been guilty of undisciplined late hits earlier, most of the fourth-quarter flags were a result of the Irish defense's mouthing off to the officials. They felt that they had been held all game and that the officials were ignoring it. Nevertheless, Holtz made no excuses afterward. "Our players were completely in the wrong," he said.

The Irish had the game well in hand in the fourth quarter before some on-field antics and penalties brought out some late-game frustration from Notre Dame coach Lou Holtz.

Coach Holtz addresses the jubilant locker room, a national championship soon to be theirs.

The Mountaineers sounded a lot like the Michigan, Miami, and Southern Cal squads that Notre Dame had vanquished. No one aspect of the Irish seemed especially impressive, but somehow the Mountaineers had played their worst game of the season against them. Said Stroia, "It was a real bad day to have a bad day."

With the perfect season, as well as the national championship, assured, Holtz was finally able to summon some candor for the media. "I think I underestimated his team," said Holtz, who then pointed out that the Irish's march to an eighth national title included wins over a No. 1 (Miami), a No. 2 (USC), and a No. 3 (West Virginia). "Is this a great team?" Holtz said, posing the question without prompting. "Yes, because nobody proved otherwise."

Rice, a junior who had started at Notre Dame the same autumn Holtz had arrived (1986), was named the Fiesta Bowl MVP, as well as the team MVP for 1988. Rice may have been the most valuable member of the team in pads and a helmet, but the seniors who had endured the 58-7 drubbing in the Orange Bowl knew better.

"We wouldn't be national champions today," tailback Mark Green said, "if it weren't for Coach Holtz."

Holtz was an answered prayer at Notre Dame and yet would also be a cipher. Despite his self-deprecation, for example, he had inserted a clause into his previous contract at Minnesota that allowed him to leave should Notre Dame offer him a head-coaching job. That was more than wishful thinking on Holtz's behalf. That was ambition.

Not that success would change Lou Holtz, nor his predilection for seeing the cloud in every silver lining. "I would be very surprised," he told the media after the game, "if we have a good team next year."

Notre Dame 34, West Virginia 21
Fiesta Bowl
Sun Devil Stadium, Tempe, Arizona
January 2, 1989

SCORING SUMMARY

	1	2	3	4	
Notre Dame	9	14	3	8	34
West Virginia	0	6	7	8	21

Team	Qtr.	Time Left	Play	Score
ND	1	10:25	Billy Hackett 45 FG	ND 3-0
ND	1	4:34	Anthony Johnson 1 run (Kent Graham run failed)	ND 9-0
ND	2	9:41	Rodney Culver 5 run (Reggie Ho kick)	ND 16-0
WV	2	6:18	Charlie Baumann 29 FG	ND 16-3
ND	2	1:48	Raghib Ismail 29 pass from Tony Rice (Ho kick)	ND 23-3
WV	2	0:00	Baumann 31 FG	ND 23-6
ND	3	5:34	Ho 32 FG	ND 26-6
WV	3	3:32	Grantis Bell 17 pass from Major Harris (Baumann kick)	ND 26-13
ND	4	13:05	Frank Jacobs 3 pass from Rice (Rice run)	ND 34-13
WV	4	1:14	Reggie Rembert 3 run (Rembert pass from Harris)	ND 34-21

Attendance: 74,911

TEAM STATISTICS

	ND	WV
First Downs	19	19
Total Net Yards	455	282
Rushes-Yards	59-242	37-108
Passing	213	174
Punt Returns	3-28	2-35
Kickoff Returns	2-36	6-107
Interceptions-Returns	1-0	1-14
Comp-Att-Int	7-11-1	14-30-1
Sacked By-Yards Lost	3-28	0-0
Punts	4-36.8	7-45.1
Fumbles-Lost	2-0	0-0
Penalties-Yards	11-102	3-38
Time of Possession	36:43	23:17

INDIVIDUAL STATISTICS

Rushing: ND: Rice 13-75, Green 13-61, Brooks 11-35, A. Johnson 5-20, Culver 4-20, Banks 5-12, Belles 3-10, Watters 3-5, Eilers 1-2, Mihalko 1-2.
WV: A. B. Brown 11-49, Tyler 2-21, C. Taylor 6-12, Harris 13-11, Napoleon 3-7, U. Johnson 1-5, Rembert 1-3.

Passing: ND: Rice 7-11-1-213.
WV: Harris 13-26-1-166, Jones 1-4-0-8.

Receiving: ND: D. Brown 2-70, Watters 1-57, Green 1-35, Ismail 1-29, A. Johnson 1-19, Jacobs 1-3.
WV: Bell 4-44, C. Taylor 3-34, Winn 3-31, Rembert 2-40, A. B. Brown 1-17, Tyler 1-8.

NOTRE DAME 13, ALABAMA 11
1975 ORANGE BOWL

JANUARY 1, 1975

ARA PARSEGHIAN WAS THE FIRST LEGENDARY NOTRE DAME coach to leave on his own terms. Knute Rockne died in a plane crash on March 31, 1931, after thirteen seasons and three national championships. Frank Leahy, who guided the Fighting Irish to four national titles in eleven seasons, resigned on January 31, 1954. Leahy's doctors had given him a choice: "Give up coaching or die."

Parseghian, in the midst of his eleventh season as the Notre Dame coach, understood full well why Leahy's health had so deteriorated on the job. "I've been exhausted for two years," he said. "The pressure is terrific. I remember what those pressures did to Frank Leahy."

On December 14, 1974, Parseghian announced his resignation. The Irish had a date in the Orange Bowl in seventeen days against the last undefeated team left in the nation, top-ranked Alabama. Parseghian, only fifty-one years old, would make that game his last as the Irish head coach.

"[Ara] was taking pills for high blood pressure, pills to sleep at night, and tranquilizers," said inveterate Notre Dame sports information director Roger Valdiserri. "Here was a guy who [ordinarily] wouldn't take an aspirin for a headache. He said, 'This is no way to live.'"

The year 1974 had begun euphorically, both for Parseghian and Notre Dame. The charismatic coach awoke on New Year's Day having just beaten undefeated and top-ranked Alabama, 24-23, in the Sugar Bowl in a thriller for the ages. The victory completed an undefeated, untied season for the Irish. Unlike 1966, Parseghian's team was the incontrovertible national champion. The win also vaulted Parseghian into the ethereal ranks of Rockne and Leahy for having won multiple national titles with the Irish.

On the sports front, the school seemed blessed. Eighteen days after the football team knocked off No. 1 Alabama, the Notre Dame hockey team toppled top-ranked Michigan Tech. One day after that the men's basketball team, on the heels of a game-ending 12-0 run, ended UCLA's NCAA-record eighty-eight-game win streak, 71-70. The luck of the Irish would soon change, though.

Injuries and suspensions riddled Parseghian's squad before their 1974 season opener. The worst blow came during the summer: six players were suspended by the university for having a female in their dormitory, Stanford Hall, after parietals.

The Irish also lost two games, each in individually stunning fashion. On September 28 a mediocre but inspired Purdue squad entered Notre Dame Stadium as decided underdogs. By the second quarter the Boilermakers led, 24-0, en route to a 31-20 victory. That, as Notre Dame fans know, was nothing compared to what happened on November 30 in Los Angeles. On that afternoon the 9-1 Irish took a 24-0, second-quarter lead of their own against 9-1 Southern Cal.

Then, in perhaps the most incredible turnabout in college football history, the Trojans humiliated the Irish, scoring fifty-five unanswered points in a shocking 55-24 debacle. The Notre Dame players had watched the film *Earthquake* the night before. The following afternoon in the Los Angeles Coliseum they lived it. Afterward, in the locker room, Notre Dame's leading tackler, linebacker Greg Collins, sat on a stool and stared disbelievingly at his shoes. "Say," he asked, looking up, "what was the final score, anyway?"

Parseghian's resignation followed two weeks later. "If I had been able to take a few months off after the Orange Bowl," Parseghian would say years later, "I might have gone back to Notre Dame. But it doesn't work that way. I needed a few months off. But that won't fit in with the recruiting."

For the second straight year, Ara Parseghian and Bear Bryant met in a bowl game. For Ara, it would be the last game he would ever coach.

The press corps in Miami had a plethora of angles with which to frame their stories leading up to the Orange Bowl: There was the "Win One for Ara" subplot, of course. The X-and-O intrigue of the Tide's wishbone offense, which averaged 299 yards per game on the ground and twenty-nine points per game, versus Notre Dame's top-rated rushing defense. The matter of the Crimson Tide's being the lone undefeated team in the country. The revenge angle: the Irish had spoiled the Crimson Tide's national title hopes a year ago. A year and a day later the Tide would have the opportunity for vengeance as well as a national championship all in one game.

"Ever since it sunk in what happened at New Orleans, we wanted another shot at Notre Dame," said Alabama senior center Sylvester Croom just days before the clash. "We could only hope we both had another good year so it would happen."

Then, finally, there was the matter of Alabama coach Paul "Bear" Bryant having gone 0-7-1 in his last eight bowl games with the Tide. "It looks as if I will go down as the losingest bowl coach in history," said Bryant. "I would like to keep that from happening."

The Tide had sequestered themselves on campus in Tuscaloosa until just a few days before the contest in Miami. Notre Dame escaped the Arctic climes of South Bend early and stayed on Marco Island, Florida. The Irish escaped the cold, but not the heat. In the week leading up to the game, *San Francisco Chronicle* columnist Wells Twombley wrote a piece alleging that racial dissension was rampant on the Notre Dame squad. It was easy to see how such a story would gain credence. The university had suspended half of the team's black players relating to the summer dorm incident. That, and USC's second-half blitz, suggested

The press corps in Miami had a plethora of angles with which to frame their stories leading up to the Orange Bowl: There was the "WIN ONE FOR ARA" subplot, of course.

that something had gone awry in the Irish locker room at halftime of their regular-season finale.

Notre Dame's remaining black players rejected the story outright. "I didn't spend four hours on an airplane to go to Los Angeles to lose on purpose," said halfback Eric Penick.

Those storm clouds of controversy soon abated, replaced by an injury front with potentially more dire consequences. First, fullback Wayne Bullock, the team's leading rusher with 855 yards, contracted the flu. He did not practice for three days. Four days before the game, linebacker Collins, who had set a school record with 144 tackles in 1974, crashed on a motorcycle, gashing both knees. Collins required fourteen stitches. Both men would play, as would center Mark Brenneman, who had fractured his right foot in the USC loss.

> Notre Dame's remaining black players rejected the story outright. "I didn't spend four hours on an airplane to go to Los Angeles **TO LOSE ON PURPOSE**," said halfback Eric Penick.

Alabama, which had entered the week as nine-point favorites, were eleven-point favorites on game day. A crowd of 71,801 filled the Orange Bowl on a beautiful seventy-degree evening. Inside the Notre Dame locker room, Parseghian, dressed in his customary navy blue pullover emblazoned with the words NOTRE DAME in gold, wasted no words on sentimentality.

"I want you to go out there and win—win not for me but for yourselves," he told the Irish before leading them onto the field for the 116th and final time. "You have won like men and lost like men. All I ask is that you play another like men. You owe me nothing. You owe one to yourselves."

As was the case the year before in the Sugar Bowl, the Irish wore white jerseys and the Tide donned crimson. As was also the case in New Orleans, the Tide offense stalled in the first quarter while the Irish drew first blood. Midway through the period Notre Dame punter Tony Brantley booted the ball deep into Alabama territory. The Tide's Willie Shelby called for a fair catch near his 15-yard line. Shelby muffed the catch and Notre Dame's Al Samuel recovered at the Tide 16.

"I called for a fair catch, but I was in bad position," said Shelby. "I didn't get a good hold of it and somebody hit me. If I had to do it over again, I would have let the ball bounce."

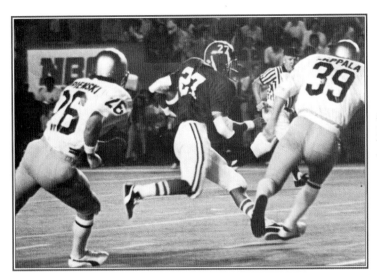

A pair of tough defenses kept big plays to a mininum. Notre Dame's Tom Lopienski (No. 26) and Tony Zappala (No. 39) give chase.

Three plays later the Irish had gained nine yards. Fourth and one from the Tide seven. Parseghian elected to go for it, sending Bullock behind All-American left guard Gerry DiNardo. Bullock gained three yards. On the next play Bullock carried it into the end zone. Dave Reeve added the point-after, and with 6:41 left in the first period, the Irish led, 7-0.

Late in the first quarter, with fifty seconds to play, the Irish began a series at their own 23. Senior quarterback Tom Clements, the MVP of the '73 Sugar Bowl, led the Irish on a time-consuming, seventeen-play march. Clements threw only one pass, a nine-yard completion to Mark McLane, on the seven-and-a-half-minute touchdown drive.

The key play occurred on fourth and four at the Tide 28. Parseghian elected to have Reeve attempt a 45-yard field goal. Alabama All-American defensive back Mark Washington blocked Reeve's kick, but was whistled for being offside on the play. The referee marched off five yards, which gave the Irish another first down. McLane took a pitchout and raced 12 yards two plays later. Then, on second and seven from the Alabama nine, McLane lined up at wingback on the right side.

Clements faked the inside hand-off to Bullock, then tossed a shovel pass to McLane, who was moving from right to left. McLane followed lead blocks by DiNardo and tackle Steve Sylvester around left end for a nine-yard touchdown run. Reeve missed the extra-point. With 8:29 left in the first half, Notre Dame was up, 13-0.

On the other side of the ball, the Irish stymied the 'Bama wishbone. Notre Dame used a seven-man front, anchored by All-American linemen Steve Niehaus (266 pounds) and

Mike Fanning (253). Those were gaudy figures in that era. Of Niehaus, USC coach John McKay had said, "He looks as big as a whale and moves like a porpoise."

Besides the seven-man line, the Irish would often blitz two defensive backs. Sophomore strong safety John Dubenetzky would blitz twelve times this night. The Irish were daring Alabama's two-headed quarterback, junior Richard Todd and senior Gary Rutledge, to pass. The Tide did just that, attempting twenty-nine passes—and completing fifteen—this evening. Alabama had averaged eleven passes per game during the season.

"I thought we could pass on them the whole damn day," Todd would say afterward. "They had ten, eleven men up on the line. They had the best front four we've seen this year [and that without future Outland and Lombardi Trophy winner Ross Browner, who had been suspended], but their secondary wasn't that good."

The Irish ran the ball sixty-six times and put it in the air only eight times. Al Samuel (No. 24) had 39 yards on ten carries.

With 5:46 left in the first half, Alabama at last benefited from a Notre Dame error. Bullock coughed up the ball at his own 40. Todd went to the air, completing passes to All-American end Ozzie Newsome for 11 yards and Jerry Brown for 12. On third down from the Notre Dame four, Todd's pass hit Newsome in the hands on the goal line. Newsome, arguably the best receiver ever to play for Bryant, dropped the ball. Alabama settled for a 21-yard Danny Ridgeway field goal and trailed at intermission, 13-3.

The score did not change in the third quarter. Alabama drove to the Irish 18, only to toss two errant pitchouts. The Tide kept possession, but lost 17 yards on the plays. Buck Berrey's 44-yard field-goal attempt sailed wide left.

Alabama, which had attempted eight first-half throws while alternating quarterbacks, now put all its faith in its aerial attack and Todd. "Me and Rooster [Rutledge] said the same thing," said Todd, who completed ten of seventeen second-half throws. "Leave one of us in and let him get something going."

Trailing, 13-3, midway through the fourth quarter, Todd's passes cut a swath through the Irish defense. Four plays netted four straight first downs all the way to the Notre Dame 12. Todd's next pass was intercepted by Dubenetzky at the 10. The Irish strong safety returned the interception 16 yards to the 26.

Alabama would not quit. With 4:29 remaining Alabama got the ball back on its own 47. Three plays and five yards later, Todd faced a fourth and five at the Irish 48. If Notre Dame got a stop here, it would be the ballgame. Todd threw a quick out to split end Russ Schamun, who eluded an Irish tackler and sprinted up the sideline. Touchdown, Bama! A two-point conversion pass to a diving George Pugh narrowed the Irish lead to two points, 13-11. There was still 3:13 remaining.

> Clements had also been knocked out of the game after a nine-yard run. "I got a helmet in the fanny," he said. "My leg tightened and swelled up, and I COULDN'T RUN."

"I thought we would pull it out at that point," Todd said.

He was not alone in that opinion. Notre Dame's conservative offense (the Irish would run sixty-six times and pass only eight) had mounted just one long drive all evening. Clements had been knocked out of the game after a nine-yard run. "I got a helmet in the fanny," he said. "My leg tightened and swelled up, and I couldn't run."

Alabama stopped Notre Dame and began its final drive from its 38 with 1:39 left to play. On first down Todd completed a pass to Schamun for 16 yards. Todd

By now, players from both teams were familiar with one another. The respect was mutual as the Irish downed the Tide for a second straight time.

stepped back into the pocket again and hit Randy Billingsley for an eight-yard gain to the Irish 38. The Tide, in need only of a field goal to win, were perhaps only one more pass away from being within range.

Again, Todd called a pass. Newsome did an out route to the right side, while Billingsley circled underneath. Notre Dame senior cornerback Reggie Barnett stood between the two. Todd fired a line drive to Newsome, where a lofted pass was needed. Barnett intercepted.

"We had just switched into a zone on that play," Barnett said. "I saw a guy in the flat and just went after the ball. I had visions of tucking the ball under my arm and sailing downfield for a touchdown, but when I saw those crimson shirts coming my way, I was glad to just step out of bounds."

Notre Dame ran out the clock. For the second straight season, the Irish had spoiled Alabama's perfect season and national title hopes. Parseghian went out a winner and also was carried out on the shoulders of his burly linemen.

Todd, who had a career passing night (13-of-24, 194 yards), was his own harshest critic. The first thing he said to the press gathered around his locker was, "I blew the game."

"I thought we had a good chance at the end," he said. "I felt confident. Then I just tried to throw the ball too hard and it got picked off. It was stupid, just stupid."

Across the field, inside the Notre Dame locker room, Parseghian was in tears. Although it was his final game, and although the Irish had not won a national championship, there was not a hint of melancholy in his expression. There was pride. And relief. And, knowing that he had gone out a winner, there was satisfaction. He spoke privately to his squad for ten minutes, after which one player said, "I've never seen him so happy."

"Half of us were crying after the game," said Collins, who played the whole game with his stitched-up knees. Bullock, still suffering from the flu, was the game's leading rusher with 83 yards on twenty-four carries.

> Parseghian was in tears. Although it was his final game, and although the Irish had not won a national championship, there was not a hint of melancholy in his expression. There was pride. And relief. And, knowing that he had GONE OUT A WINNER, there was satisfaction.

Having completed an imperfect season with such a rewarding victory, this Irish team seemed to savor it just as much, if not more, than the previous year's Sugar Bowl.

"After the game, I came into the locker room," Parseghian said, "and I wanted to say a lot of things to the team. It all hit me at that moment. This was my last game. I could not find the words to say what I was really feeling. What I said was so inadequate. I just told them I was proud of them, and that I appreciated their effort and I was pleased to go out a winner."

Notre Dame 13, Alabama 11
Orange Bowl, Miami, Florida
January 1, 1975

SCORING SUMMARY

	1	2	3	4	
Alabama	0	3	0	8	11
Notre Dame	7	6	0	0	13

Team	Qtr.	Time Left	Play	Score
ND	1	6:41	Wayne Bullock 4 run (Dave Reeve kick)	ND 7-0
ND	2	8:29	Mark McLane 9 run (Reeve kick failed)	ND 13-0
UA	2	1:45	Danny Ridgeway 21 FG	ND 13-3
UA	4	3:13	Russ Schamun 48 pass from Richard Todd (George Pugh pass from Todd)	ND 13-11

Attendance: 71,801

TEAM STATISTICS

	UA	ND
First Downs	14	15
Total Net Yards	285	204
Rushes-Yards	33-62	66-185
Passing	223	19
Punt Returns	5-34	0-0
Kickoff Returns	2-32	3-54
Interceptions-Returns	2-0	2-26
Comp-Att-Int	15-29-2	4-8-2
Punts	7-40.0	6-38.0
Fumbles-Lost	5-2	1-1
Penalties-Yards	1-5	1-15

INDIVIDUAL STATISTICS

Rushing: ND: Bullock 24-83, Samuel 10-39, McLane 8-30, Clements 11-26, Penick 6-15, Parise 3-4, Goodman 1-2, Allocco 3-(-14). UA: Culliver 11-60, Shelby 5-25, Todd 9-4, Randy Billingsley 2-3, Taylor 1-1, Pugh 1-(8), Stock 1-(-9), Rutledge 3-(-14).

Passing: ND: Clements 4-7-1-19, Goodman 0-1-1-0. UA: Todd 13-24-2-194, Rutledge 2-5-0-29.

Receiving: ND: Demmerle 2-12, McLane 1-9, Goodman 1-(-2). UA: Newsome 6-68, Schamun 5-126, Billingsley 3-17, Brown 1-12.

MICHIGAN · NOTRE DAME

September 20, 1980 • Notre Dame Stadium

SPECIAL COLLECTOR'S ISSUE $2.00

FULL-COLOR INSERT

NOTRE DAME 29, MICHIGAN 27

SEPTEMBER 20, 1980

HARRY OLIVER STOOD NEXT TO COACH DAN DEVINE ON THE Notre Dame sideline, listening for the magic words. The Irish trailed Michigan by one point, 27-26, with only four seconds remaining on this hot, blustery September afternoon in Notre Dame Stadium.

"Field goal," Devine said.

Oliver trotted onto the field to where holder Tim Koegel, a former high school teammate of his at Cincinnati Moeller, knelt at the 41-yard line. Oliver, a five-foot-eleven, 165-pound junior, who at the end of spring practice had been considered the fourth-best kicker on the Irish roster, looked toward the north end-zone uprights. His farthest kick in college had been a 38-yarder in a junior varsity game against Wisconsin the previous season. Thus far this season he had attempted just one field goal, a 36-yarder in Notre Dame's 31-10 season-opening win versus Purdue. He'd made that one.

But this was a 51-yarder. And, it was for all the marbles between Michigan and Notre Dame. "It crossed my mind that I can't make this," Oliver said. "But there really wasn't time to think. Everything happened so fast."

Earlier in the week Notre Dame president Father Theodore Hesburgh had addressed the Irish at practice. "You're part of the ongoing history here," Hesburgh told them.

It was difficult to impress upon eighteen- to twenty-three-year-olds just how rich the football history between Notre Dame and Michigan is. On Wednesday, November 23, 1887, a group of Michigan students took a train from Ann Arbor to South Bend to introduce the Notre Dame students to the new game. Michigan won, 8-0, after which they were treated to lunch by their hosts.

> Earlier in the week Notre Dame president Father Theodore Hesburgh had addressed the Irish at practice. "YOU'RE PART OF THE ONGOING HISTORY HERE," Hesburgh told them.

The following spring Michigan visited the Notre Dame campus for a pair of contests on April 20 and 21. While the Irish scored the first touchdown (trivia buffs: it was fullback Harry Jewett) in school history, they lost, 26-6 and 10-4.

Since that trio of games in 1887 and 1888—the first three in Notre Dame history—both programs have flourished prodigiously. Through the end of the 2003 season, Michigan was No. 1 in all-time winning percentage (.7465) while Notre Dame was No. 2 (.7461). The Wolverines also are No. 1 in all-time victories (833) ahead of the Irish at No. 2 (796).

And yet, since the students from Ann Arbor departed South Bend after that third win in 1888, the two schools had played only ten other times before Oliver trotted onto the field to attempt his 51-yarder.

The year before, the Irish won, 12-10, at Michigan Stadium. In that contest Chuck Male, a walk-on, kicked four field goals in front of 105,000 fans; and teammate Bob Crable blocked Michigan's last-second, 37-yard field-goal try to preserve the victory.

"Crable never blocked the ball," Michigan's legendary coach, Bo Schembechler, said with a mock scowl. "The ball never got more than two feet off the ground."

Thus Michigan, 1-0 and ranked fourteenth in the nation, came to Notre Dame, also 1-0 and ranked eighth, on this day. The Wolverines owned a 9-5 lead in the series and were 5-0 when playing at Notre Dame. A wind of ten to fifteen miles per hour blew as the temperature soared above eighty degrees.

The opening quarter was played to a 0-0 standstill. The 59,075 in attendance were likely still buzzing about Devine's having announced his retirement, quite unexpectedly, one month earlier. "I've talked this over at great length with Father Hesburgh, and that's that," Devine told a stunned room at the weekly Quarterback Club luncheon in mid-August. "I am leaving Notre Dame at the end of the season."

Late in the first quarter the Irish embarked on a sixteen-play, 70-yard touchdown drive that lasted 7:49. Halfback Phil Carter carried the ball ten times for 45 yards during the possession, including the final six-yard scoring run with 13:05 left in the second quarter.

Michigan quickly punted and this time the Irish offense, behind the second-string offensive line, played ball control again. Notre Dame marched 51 yards in eleven plays, using up 5:56, in putting their second touchdown on the board. Senior quarterback Mike Courey hit flanker Pete Holohan on a 10-yard completion for the score. Oliver converted his second point-after of the game (he was now six for six on the season) to put the Irish ahead, 14-0, with exactly five minutes remaining in the first half.

Schembechler, unhappy with his offense, removed option quarterback Rich Hewlett and inserted John Wangler, a better passer. The Wolverines responded immediately, as Wangler found running back Larry Ricks on an eight-yard pass for a touchdown with 1:50 until halftime. Ricks's 28-yard run had been the key play of the drive.

Devine was not content to have his offense sit on the ball in the half's waning moments. He directed Courey to throw a pass on first down, but it fell incomplete. The Irish passed again on second down, but Courey's throw intended for six-foot-five split end Tony Hunter was intercepted by Wolverine defensive back Marion Body. After a 20-yard return, Michigan had the ball on the Irish 27.

Five plays later Wangler tossed his second touchdown pass of the quarter, a nine-yarder

> "I've talked this over at great length with Father Hesburgh, and that's that," Devine told a stunned room at the weekly Quarterback Club luncheon in mid-August. "I am LEAVING NOTRE DAME at the end of the season."

to tight end Norm Betts. All-American kicker Ali Haji-Sheikh converted the extra point, and it was 14-14 at the half. "I made a lot of snap decisions out there today," Devine said. "Not all of them the right ones."

The Wolverines lost no momentum during the intermission. Two weeks earlier against Purdue, Notre Dame strong safety Steve Cichy, who doubled as the team's kick-off specialist, had been lost for the season with a neck injury. Oliver, taking Cichy's place, kicked off to All-American Wolverine wideout Anthony Carter. The six-foot, 175-pound speedster wowed the audience with a reversal-of-field, 67-yard return to the Irish 32. Michigan scored six plays later on a two-yard run by Stan Edwards to take the lead, 21-14.

The wind continued to bluster, but the Irish offense was dead calm in the third quarter. Notre Dame failed to make one first down. The wind was at their backs, though, allowing freshman punter Blair Kiel (a blue-chip recruit at quarterback as well) to

Harry Oliver had his good and his bad moments against Michigan, and he saved the best for last.

unleash punts of 69 and 59 yards, respectively. Each punt was attempted with the Irish pinned deep in their own territory (the latter from a shotgun formation on third down) and each left the Wolverines with the ball at their own 26-yard line.

"We had the momentum, and it looked as if we'd wind up with good field position," Schembechler said. "I see [those punts] as one of the turning points."

On Michigan's drive following Kiel's 59-yard punt, Wangler dropped back to pass. He underthrew his intended target, Carter. Notre Dame cornerback John Krimm stole the pass and sprinted 49 yards for the touchdown.

Oliver, kicking with the wind, missed the extra point, leaving Michigan with a 21-20 lead. "A kicker's worst nightmare," Oliver said. "You lose by one point because you miss the extra point. I was embarrassed and upset. It was my fault. I didn't point my toe."

The fourth quarter came. Carter, playing with bruised ribs and a contusion on his

Irish cornerback John Krimm intercepted an underthrown Michigan pass and returned it 49 yards for a touchdown.

knee, served mainly as a decoy for the Maize and Blue. Still, Michigan was driving for another touchdown when running back Butch Woolfolk was stripped of the ball at the Notre Dame 26. Irish safety Dave Duerson recovered.

On the ensuing play Devine called for an end-around pass. Split end Tony Hunter took the handoff from Courey and threw a perfect spiral on the run to Holohan. The play covered 31 yards, and Hunter's pass into the wind may have been the best anyone threw all afternoon. Ten plays later Carter, on his thirtieth and final carry of the game, scored from four yards out. Carter went over 100 yards on the play (103 total) and the Irish, with 3:03 remaining, took a 26-21 lead. The two-point conversion failed.

Michigan's Woolfolk, whose fumble had launched Notre Dame's go-ahead touchdown drive, returned to the field with a vengeance. With Michigan on its own 29-yard line, Wangler connected with Woolfolk for a 12-yard pass. Then he gained 20 yards on a draw play. On third and 10 from the Irish 40, Woolfolk's number was called yet again. He gained 37 yards on a draw. The ball was now on the Notre Dame four with 1:06 left to play. The crowd grew silent.

Schembechler, an avowed disciple of the run, called rushing plays on first and second down. Neither worked. Now it was third and goal.

Wangler dropped back to pass. His wobbler intended for Woolfolk was too high, but the Wolverine tailback tipped it into the air. Tight end Craig Dunaway lunged for the ball and caught it, barely, in the end zone. The Wolverines missed the two-pointer, but after Ali Haji-Sheikh, kicking with the wind, boomed the ball deep into the south end zone, it did not appear to matter. Michigan, unbeaten at Notre Dame, led, 27-26, with only 0:41 remaining.

Devine's next gambit, had it not worked, would have been second-guessed for a long time. The lame-duck coach replaced Courey with the freshman Kiel, who had yet to throw a pass in a college game. "We had worked on that [shotgun] formation all week with Blair," Devine said. "He was the only one who could make it work. I felt it was the only way we could win the game. Kiel has as much confidence as anybody I've ever seen."

Kiel almost lost the game on his first throw. The freshman from Columbus, Indiana, threw a cloud-scraper that wobbled like a wounded mallard as it descended toward Hunter at midfield. The six-foot-five receiver leaped for it as did Michigan defenders Body and Keith Bostic. No one caught it, but a referee threw a flag. Pass interference, Michigan. A 32-yard penalty. Notre Dame had a first down on the Wolverine 48 with 0:31 left. There still was time.

Kiel's next pass went right into the arms of Jeff Reeves, but he played for Michigan. Reeves dropped the sure interception. "At that point I figured if I was lucky enough for those two passes not to be intercepted," recalled Kiel, "somebody was up there helping me out."

Kiel's second-down pass was also dropped, this time by tight end Dean Masztak. Third down. A short pass to Carter gained nine yards. It was fourth and one at the

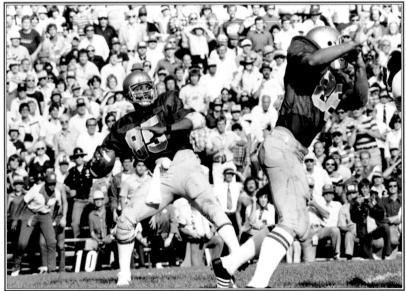

Split end Tony Hunter, on the option, heaves a pass to Pete Holohan that would cover 31 yards and set up Notre Dame's go-ahead touchdown with just over three minutes left in the game.

Michigan 39 with 0:09 left. Devine had to decide whether to go for it and risk time expiring or send in Oliver for a 56-yard attempt.

He went for it. Hunter caught a short out pattern and, though he tried to turn upfield, stepped out of bounds at the 34 with 0:04 left. Had Hunter not inadvertently stepped out, the Irish would have been doomed.

"I went out of bounds," said Hunter. "Then I tried to come back and get some more. But the ref saw I'd gone out. I was glad he did."

Now it was up to Oliver, whose missed extra point in the third quarter was now the difference in the game. The wind, and the odds, were against him. "In the pregame warmups, I was kicking with the wind," he said. "To give you an idea of how strong it was, I made a field goal from 65 yards out."

> "We had worked on that [shotgun] formation all week with Blair," Devine said. "He was the only one who could make it work. I felt it was the only way WE COULD WIN THE GAME. Kiel has as much confidence as anybody I've ever seen."

But this would be, as the popular Bob Seger song of that year proclaimed, "Against the Wind." And Seger was from Michigan.

"Well," announced Tony Roberts on Mutual Radio to the listeners nationwide, "it's miracle time for Notre Dame."

The holder, Koegel, or "Kegs" as Oliver referred to his old buddy, looked up at Oliver. "Are you ready?" Koegel asked. "Sure, why?" asked Oliver. "Because I have a better chance of running this thing in than you do of kicking it there," Koegel answered. "Just kick the hell out of it, and kick it straight."

Oliver, a soccer-style left-footed kicker, took two steps back and two steps to the side. Then long snapper Bill Siewe snapped the ball back to Koegel. The snap and hold were perfect.

"I prayed. Oh, how I prayed," Oliver said. "I kept reminding myself, 'Point your toe, point your toe.' I said my Hail Marys and made sure I pointed my toe."

Oliver, wearing number three, propelled his left foot forward with magnificent torque. His body lean was forward, his eyes focused directly down at the ball.

"I just tried to lean over the ball," Oliver said, "to put a lower trajectory on it for more distance."

Whether you attribute what those who were there say happened next to the prayer, the Notre Dame mystique, or simply blarney depends upon your point of view. "You know," Koegel said, "just as I placed the ball down, the wind died down. Almost stopped. I knew then we'd make it!"

Until he came on in relief of starting quarterback Mike Courey to lead Notre Dame's last-ditch drive, Blair Kiel had had his best moments in the game booming long punts.

Oliver's kick sailed into orbit. It cleared the crossbar with just inches to spare. "Somebody started jumping on me and shouting, 'It's good! It's good!'" Oliver remembered. "I think it was Kegs and he landed on my leg. But as I was falling down I saw it go through."

In all the years and all the games at Notre Dame Stadium, only one other Irish victory had been gained with 0:00 showing on the clock. That was in 1961, a 17-15 win against tenth-ranked Syracuse. This one, because it was Michigan, and because Oliver had kicked the second-longest field goal in Irish history (Dave Reeve made a 53-yarder versus Pittsburgh in 1976) was sweeter. The same Harry Oliver who had never kicked a field goal in a game beyond 38 yards previously.

Oliver's kick catapulted him, and the Irish, to a memorable year. Oliver would kick two more 50-yarders (he has three of the seven longest field goals in school history) while converting a then-record eighteen field goals in the 1980 season. The Irish would finish 9-2-1 in Devine's final season.

"Harry's a heckuva nice kid," Devine said in the locker room following the game. "He was a nice kid even before he kicked it."

Notre Dame 29, Michigan 27
Notre Dame Stadium, South Bend, Indiana
September 20, 1980

SCORING SUMMARY

	1	2	3	4	
Michigan	0	14	7	6	27
Notre Dame	0	14	6	9	29

Team	Qtr.	Time Left	Play	Score
ND	2	13:05	Phil Carter 6 run (Harry Oliver kick)	ND 7-0
ND	2	5:00	Pete Holohan 10 pass from Mike Courey (Oliver kick)	ND 14-0
UM	2	1:50	Larry Ricks 8 pass from John Wangler (Ali Haji-Sheikh kick)	ND 14-7
UM	2	0:31	Norm Betts 9 pass from Wangler (Ali Haji-Sheikh kick)	14-14
UM	3	11:57	Stan Edwards 2 run (Ali Haji-Sheikh kick)	UM 21-14
ND	3	1:03	John Krimm 49 interception return (Oliver kick failed)	UM 21-20
ND	4	3:03	Carter 4 run (Courey pass failed)	ND 26-21
UM	4	0:41	Craig Dunaway 1 pass from Wangler (Wangler pass failed)	UM 27-26
ND	4	0:04	Oliver 51 FG	ND 29-27

Attendance: 59,075

TEAM STATISTICS

	UM	ND
First Downs	17	14
Total Net Yards	330	234
Rushes-Yards	47-221	42-127
Passing	109	107
Punt Returns	2-17	4-30
Kickoff Returns	3-110	1-26
Interceptions-Returns	2-20	1-49
Comp-Att-Int	12-24-1	9-18-2
Punts	5-44.2	6-43.5
Fumbles-Lost	2-1	0-0
Penalties-Yards	3-47	5-39
Time of Possession	30:33	29:27

INDIVIDUAL STATISTICS

Rushing: ND: Carter 30-103, Sweeney 2-11, Buchanan 3-6, J. Stone 2-4, Courey 6-3. UM: Ricks 14-83, Woofolk 9-70, Edwards 12-40, Hewlett 9-28, Ingram 1-2, Powers 0-7 (fumble recovery), Wangler 2-(-9).

Passing: ND: Courey 6-13-2-62, Kiel 2-4-0-14, Hunter 1-1-0-31. UM: Wangler 11-19-1-98, Hewlett 1-5-0-11.

Receiving: ND: Hunter 3-32, Masztak 3-25, Holohan 2-41, Carter 1-9. UM: Carter 2-30, Edwards 2-22, Betts 2-17, Ricks 2-17, Ingram 2-10, Woolfolk, 1-12, Dunaway 1-1.

FIFTY-EIGHTH CLASSIC

USF&G
SUGAR BOWL

FLORIDA

NOTRE DAME

NOTRE DAME 39, FLORIDA 28 1992 SUGAR BOWL

JANUARY 1, 1992

AS NOTRE DAME PREPARED TO PLAY IN ITS FIFTH CONSECUTIVE New Year's Day bowl despite a relatively lackluster 9-3 record and No. 18 ranking at the end of the 1991 regular season, pundits as well as opposing players protested. "I don't know why Notre Dame is so great," said All-American linebacker Keith Goganious of Penn State. "They're a good team, but why make special rules for them?"

Goganious had ample reason to complain. In mid-November the Nittany Lions had whipped Notre Dame by twenty-two points and finished the season ranked twelve spots higher than the Fighting Irish. Yet, while the Irish were headed to New Orleans to meet No. 3 Florida in the Sugar Bowl, No. 6 Penn State was headed to Tempe, Arizona, to face No. 10 Tennessee in the Fiesta Bowl. How fair was that?

"There's some teams out there more worthy than we are," Notre Dame coach Lou Holtz admitted on November 18, the day the Irish accepted the Sugar Bowl invitation.

Holtz knew better than to go on the defensive. Especially with a defense like his 1991 version. The Irish allowed 261 points this season, including 112 points in their final three games—a 35-34 loss to Tennessee, the aforementioned 35-13 loss at Penn State, and an indifferent 48-42 victory at Hawaii. No defense during Holtz's eleven seasons in South Bend surrendered more points than this one. No Irish defense had yielded more points since 1956, when a 2-8 Notre Dame team allowed 289.

Instead, the most psychologically adroit Notre Dame coach since Knute Rockne went on the offensive. When Holtz arrived in New Orleans, after a brief holiday with his family in Orlando, Florida, he came armed with a jab sharper than any that had been directed at Notre Dame in the previous month. According to Holtz, he and his family had been dining out in Orlando when a waiter recognized him.

"What's the difference between Cheerios and Notre Dame?" the waiter is said to have asked.

"I don't know," Holtz replied.

"Cheerios belong in a bowl," the waiter said. (Then, according to Holtz, he asked the waiter what was the difference between Lou Holtz and a golf pro. "A golf pro gives tips.")

Holtz's quip disarmed his critics. If the Irish were going to be a laughingstock against a 10-1 Florida squad that had the nation's most prolific passer in Shane Matthews (3,130 yards, twenty-eight touchdowns) and the Southeastern Conference's (SEC's) most prolific rusher in Errict Rhett (1,109), then Holtz wanted everyone to know that he was in on the joke. As were his players. "We face the prospect," defensive tackle Troy Ridgley said, "of being blown off the field."

The Irish, like their lisping leprechaun of a coach, had been an enigma during the 1991 season. The woeful defense was ranked seventy-third in the nation in scoring defense (yielding 21.7 points per game), yet ten of the eleven starters would eventually either be drafted by or play in the NFL. Only Ridgley did not.

The offense . . . the offense was outstanding. The Irish set a single-season team scoring record with 426 points (35.4 per game). Junior quarterback Rick Mirer threw a school-record eighteen touchdown passes while sophomore fullback Jerome Bettis scored a school-record twenty touchdowns while leading the Irish in rushing with 972 yards. The Irish had scored at least forty-two points in half their games. So full was their cupboard that the previous season's leading rusher, senior captain Rodney Culver, was the team's third-leading rusher (550 yards) behind Bettis and fellow senior Tony Brooks (894).

In early November the Irish had been 8-1 and ranked fifth in the nation. Then, on November 9, disaster struck. Leading No. 13 Tennessee, 31-7, at home just before half-time, Notre Dame self-destructed, losing, 35-34. A last-second 27-yard field goal attempt was blocked by the rump of a Volunteer lineman, adding insult to injury. Not only was it the most gut-wrenching loss of the Holtz era to that point, it extinguished any hopes the Irish entertained to win the national championship.

"No one can describe what happened in the second half of the Tennessee game," Mirer said afterward. "That kind of stuff just doesn't happen. But it happened to us."

The Irish still looked shell-shocked when they traveled to Penn State the following Saturday. The 35-13 pasting by the Nittany Lions was the worst beating the Fighting Irish had taken since the 1988 Cotton Bowl. Holtz, unable to bolster his dispirited team after the Tennessee debacle, had seen it coming. "I don't know if Rockne and Leahy and Parseghian together could have brought our players out of that," Holtz said. "I know one thing: Lou Holtz couldn't."

Six weeks later, despite entering the contest as six-and-a-half-point underdogs to the SEC champion Gators, the Irish had gained a new resolve. On December 3 defensive coordinator Gary Darnell had resigned to take an assistant's job at the University of Texas. Holtz, who normally oversaw the offense, turned his attention to the other side of the ball.

Irish quarterback Rick Mirer would set a school record with eighteen touchdown passes, but he also had a group of talented running backs to hand off to.

"Some of the young guys have been intimidated by his shouting," said junior linebacker Demetrius DuBose, "but the key thing is that he has given us a sense of urgency."

"Lou's involvement," said secondary coach Ron Cooper, "has made us turn it up a notch."

Holtz hinted that the Irish would employ a variety of blitzes in an attempt to stymie the Gators' "Fun-and-Gun" offense, but when the Fifty-eighth Sugar Bowl began in prime time on ABC, the Irish defense resembled a prevent scheme. The Irish, clad in white jerseys with green numerals and green socks—"I feel like Gumby," said All-American offensive guard Mirko Jurkovic—rushed no more than three and sometimes only two defensive linemen. The other defenders dropped into pass coverage.

> "Some of the young guys have been intimidated by his shouting," said junior linebacker Demetrius DuBose, "but the key thing is that he has GIVEN US A SENSE OF URGENCY."

Matthews, whose coach, Steve Spurrier, had won a Heisman Trophy as the Florida quarterback in 1966, wasted no time exposing the Irish defense. The Gators took the opening kickoff and, beginning from their own 15-yard line, marched 85 yards in eleven plays for a touchdown. Matthews was 5-for-7 passing on the opening drive for 60 yards, including a 15-yard touchdown pass to wide receiver Willie Jackson.

On the ensuing kickoff Notre Dame's Clint Johnson fumbled the ball. The Gators recovered at the Irish 39 and on first down wasted no time throwing into the end zone. A touchdown would've put the Gators up, 14-0, less than five minutes into the game and it would've sent the partisan Florida crowd of 76,447 into a frenzy. Matthews targeted a wide-open Alonzo Sullivan in the end zone, but misfired.

Notre Dame cornerback Willie Clark intercepted the underthrown ball and returned it to the Irish 32. A personal foul against the Gators added 15 yards to the play, giving the Irish a first down at the Notre Dame 47. The Irish would soon have to punt, but the sequence set a tone that would repeat itself for the rest of the half. The Gators would threaten repeatedly, but the Irish would dodge the bullet.

"We had the chance to score fifty points," Spurrier said, "but we didn't do it."

Florida would stage three more extended drives in the first half, but would come away with only an Arden Czyzewski field goal each time to show for it. Late in the first quarter a 71-yard, fifteen-play drive stalled at the Irish nine, where Czyzewski kicked a 26-yard field goal. In the second quarter a 75-yard, fourteen-play drive in which Matthews tucked the ball under his arm for a 20-yard keeper, stopped at the Irish eight. Florida settled for a 24-yard Czyzewski field goal. A 36-yarder at the end of a ten-play, 51-yard drive closed out Florida's first-half scoring.

The Gators entered the Notre Dame red zone four times in the first half, but came away with only one touchdown. Matthews, despite tossing for 202 first-half yards, failed to make the Irish pay for what Holtz would later call his "bend-don't-break" defense.

"Every time [Florida] got within the twenty," Irish linebacker Justin Goheen said, "they couldn't complete the damn pass because there were so many people from Notre Dame in coverage."

That was Holtz's strategy, and it contradicted everything he had intimated in the days leading up to the game. "We didn't just fool Florida," linebacker Pete Bercich said. "We fooled the media."

The Irish offense, on the other hand, showed the ill effects of Holtz's having made the defensive unit his priority in December. Notre Dame gained just one first down in the first quarter and had only 34 rushing yards in the first half, about one-fourth their average. The Irish put together just one sustained drive, largely thanks to the arm of Mirer, a talented junior raised not far from South Bend, in Goshen, Indiana. On a third-and-14 play Mirer found Tony Smith for a 19-yard completion to midfield. Two plays later, on second and one from the Florida 40, Mirer audibled out of a running play and called a stop-and-go pattern for wideout Lake Dawson, who skirted past Gator defensive back Larry Kennedy to grab the ball before racing 40 yards down the right sideline for the touchdown.

> "We had the chance to score fifty points," Spurrier said, "BUT WE DIDN'T DO IT."

At the half, Florida led, 16-7, but it might have been much worse. The Gators had more than doubled Notre Dame's offensive output, 288 yards to 142. Inside the Notre Dame locker room, Holtz turned his attention back to his offense. "We went back to Notre Dame football," Holtz later explained. "We said we're going back to basics, power off-tackle, etc."

Holtz's halftime adjustment was simply common sense. The Irish offensive line—center Gene McGuire, tackles Justin Hall and Lindsay Knapp, and guards Aaron Taylor and Mirko Jurkovic—outweighed the Florida defensive line by an average of thirty-five pounds per man. Besides, in the five-foot-eleven, 247-pound Bettis, the Irish had a human battering ram.

"I've got to fight off a 290-pound lineman to get a chance to stop a 240-pound fullback," Gator All-American defensive tackle Brad Culpepper mused before the game. "Bettis is almost as big as I am."

The Irish made no attempt to disguise their intentions in the second half. Starting at their own 30 after receiving the opening kickoff, Holtz called eleven consecutive running plays (thirty-nine of Notre Dame's forty-seven second-half plays would be runs). The drive stalled at the Florida six, which left Holtz with a bit of a dilemma. Craig Hentrich was unable to kick.

Hentrich had reinjured his right knee during the second-quarter kickoff following Notre Dame's touchdown. The senior kicking specialist had originally hurt the knee in a bizarre play during the Tennessee game in which his field-goal attempt was blocked and returned for a touchdown by the Volunteers on the final play of the first half. Afterward, Holtz had pleaded with the Notre Dame soccer team for help. Kevin Pendergast, a junior from Simsbury, Connecticut, answered the call.

Notre Dame's Jerome Bettis was practically unstoppable, rushing for 150 yards and three touchdowns, all in a span of less than three minutes in the fourth quarter.

Now Pendergast, who had never attempted a field goal at any level, was Holtz's only option.

Pendergast trotted onto the field and calmly converted the 23-yard field goal to bring the Irish within six points, 16-10.

The Irish held, forcing the Gators to punt on their next possession. Beginning at their own 20, the Irish moved 80 yards in fourteen plays, the pivotal one being a 16-yard middle screen pass to Tony Smith on third and 17 from the Gator 24. On the ensuing fourth and one, Bettis rumbled two yards for the first down. Three plays later Mirer found tight end Irv Smith all alone in the end zone for a four-yard touchdown pass. Pendergast then converted the first point-after of his life and the Irish surprisingly led, 17-16, heading into the fourth quarter.

That, in some ways, is when the game began, as the two offenses would combine for more points in the final period than they had in the previous three. Florida drove 50 yards in ten plays and took the lead on Czyzewski's fourth field goal, his longest of the night at 37 yards. The Gators led, 19-17.

On the subsequent Notre Dame series, Gator defensive tackle Darren Mickell sacked Mirer, forcing a fumble and the Gators recovered at the Notre Dame 12. The pro-Florida crowd inside the Superdome was ecstatic, but three plays later the Gators had only advanced the ball four yards. Again, Czyzewski trotted onto the field. His fifth field goal, a Sugar Bowl record, was a 24-yarder. Florida extended its lead to 22-17, but on the Irish sideline Holtz heaved a huge sigh of relief.

> The pro-Florida crowd inside the Superdome WAS ECSTATIC, but three plays later the Gators had only advanced the ball four yards.

"I thought that when we forced the field goal, when we were down, 19-17, after the turnover, that that was the critical part of the game," Holtz said. "We still only needed one score to win."

The Irish got three. By the fourth quarter the undersized Gator defense began to look like a fighter who had ill-advisedly moved up a weight class. Adding to their woes, starting linebackers Tim Paulk and Carlton Miles, the latter the team's leading tackler, were injured and out of the game. The Irish marched 64 yards in fourteen plays, a drive that devoured 6:33, to re-take the lead, 25-22. Bettis scored the touchdown on a three-yard run. Mirer passed to Tony Brooks, after calling an audible, for the two-point conversion.

Four minutes and forty-eight seconds remained. Florida took possession and moved close to midfield, but on fourth and 10 with 3:41 left Spurrier opted not to punt. Matthews's pass glanced off Jackson's fingertips. On the next play Bettis took the handoff and exploded through the Gator defensive front untouched, rambling 49 yards for a touchdown.

"My man, Jerome Bettis," Holtz said. "That is an outstanding football player."

Bettis, who would go on to a prolific NFL career with the Pittsburgh Steelers, where he would be known to all as "The Bus," was not done. Florida scored quickly on a 36-yard Matthews pass to Harrison Houston to close the gap to 32-28. Notre Dame's Culver recovered the onside kick, though, and with 2:13 left the Irish were facing third and five at the Gator 39. Two minutes allowed plenty of time for Florida to score another touchdown.

Instead Bettis, aided by a crushing block by fullback Ryan Mihalko, rambled for a 39-yard touchdown. Bettis, who would finish with 150 yards on sixteen carries (9.4 yards per carry) and would be named the game's MVP, had just scored his third touchdown in less than three minutes (164 seconds, to be exact).

"When Jerome scored that [second] one, I thought that was pretty good," said Jurkovic. "But then when I looked up from the ground and saw Jerome rolling [toward his third] . . . that whole sequence was better than . . . well . . ."

Matthews, who would set Sugar Bowl records for pass attempts (fifty-eight) and yardage (370), eclipsing the record set by his coach, Spurrier, twenty-seven years earlier, valiantly drove the Gators to the Notre Dame five-yard line. The Gators' last hope flickered out when safety Jeff Burris intercepted a Matthews pass in the end zone with 0:24 left, clinching the 39-28 upset.

Lou Holtz probably would have been even happier after the game had he known the surprise gift that General Mills had in store for him.

"If you want someone to blame, just look at me," said Matthews, who was 3-of-13 passing from inside the Notre Dame 20. "It's going to be tough to live with this game. I still think that we're a better team than they are, but we didn't show it and they beat us."

Spurrier was less critical of his quarterback. "Their plan obviously was to wear us down in the second half," he said. "And even more obviously, they did."

For six weeks the Irish had listened to the relentless harping about their swift decline. "I get letters," Holtz said. "If they're not signed, I usually don't read 'em. If they are, I read 'em. And sometimes I'll write back and tell them some idiot's writing crazy letters and signing their name."

"When we lose," Jurkovic had said, "it's a big letdown. But I keep it in perspective. We're still the winningest senior class (43-7) that's ever been here."

"Who likes Cheerios anymore?" Bettis asked. "That's the attitude we took. We felt like nobody liked us and [we] wanted to go out and prove them wrong."

The Irish finished 10-3 and ranked thirteenth in the nation. They proved everyone, including an apocryphal writer, wrong. They proved that they belonged in a bowl.

When the Irish returned to South Bend, a gift from General Mills was waiting for Holtz in his office. Two hundred boxes of Cheerios.

Notre Dame 39, Florida 28
Sugar Bowl • Louisiana Superdome
New Orleans, Louisiana
January 1, 1992

SCORING SUMMARY

	1	2	3	4	
Notre Dame	0	7	10	22	39
Florida	10	6	0	12	28

Team	Qtr.	Time Left	Play	Score
UF	1	10:40	Willie Jackson 15 pass from Shane Matthews (Arden Czyzewski kick)	UF 7-0
UF	1	3:36	Czyzewski 26 FG	UF 10-0
UF	2	10:29	Czyzewski 24 FG	UF 13-0
ND	2	8:01	Lake Dawson 40 pass from Rick Mirer (Craig Hentrich kick)	UF 13-7
UF	2	0:20	Czyzewski 36 FG	UF 16-7
ND	3	10:03	Kevin Pendergast 23 FG	UF 16-10
ND	3	2:12	Irv Smith 4 pass from Mirer (Pendergast kick)	ND 17-16
UF	4	13:42	Czyzewski 37 FG	UF 19-17
UF	4	11:21	Czyzewski 24 FG	UF 22-17
ND	4	4:48	Jerome Bettis 3 run (Tony Brooks pass from Mirer)	ND 25-22
ND	4	3:32	Bettis 49 run (Pendergast kick)	ND 32-22
UF	4	2:28	Harrison Houston 36 pass from Matthews (Matthews pass failed)	ND 32-28
ND	4	2:04	Bettis 39 run (Pendergast kick)	ND 39-28

Attendance: 76,447

TEAM STATISTICS

	ND	UF
First Downs	23	29
Total Net Yards	433	511
Rushes-Yards	49-279	33-141
Passing	154	370
Punt Returns	0-0	0-0
Kickoff Returns	7-188	6-90
Interceptions-Returns	2-31	1-4
Comp-Att-Int	14-19-1	28-58-2
Sacked By-Yards Lost	3-18	2-25
Punts	2-34.0	2-52.5
Fumbles-Lost	4-3	0-0
Penalties-Yards	3-15	4-40
Time of Possession	29:00	31:00

INDIVIDUAL STATISTICS

Rushing: ND: Bettis 16-150, Culver 13-93, T. Brooks 13-68, Failla 1-(-2), Mirer 6-(-30).
UF: Rhett 15-63, McClendon 7-34, Matthews 7-27, McNabb 4-17.

Passing: ND: Mirer 14-19-1-154.
UF: Matthews 28-58-2-370.

Receiving: ND: T. Smith 7-75, Dawson 2-49, Brown 1-11, Culver 1-6, Bettis 1-5, I. Smith, 1-4, Pollard 1-4.
UF: W. Jackson 8-148, Sullivan 4-47, Rhett 4-38, Houston 3-52, Hill 3-41, McClendon 3-19, Everett 2-18, McNabb 1-7.

PHOTO CREDITS

Program covers and tickets stubs courtesy of University of Notre Dame Archive.

DVD TRACK LISTINGS

TRACK 1 Notre Dame 31, Miami 30—Oct. 15, 1988 (2:47)

TRACK 2 *Cotton Bowl,* Notre Dame 35, Houston 34—Jan. 1, 1979 (4:18)

TRACK 3 Notre Dame 31, Florida State 24—Nov. 13, 1993 (2:47)

TRACK 4 Notre Dame 12, Army 6—Nov. 10, 1928 (2:56)

TRACK 5 Notre Dame 49, Southern Cal 19—Oct. 22, 1977 (2:50)

TRACK 6 Notre Dame 18, Ohio State 13—Nov. 2, 1935 (3:58)

TRACK 7 Notre Dame 24, Michigan 19—Sept. 16, 1989 (2:08)

TRACK 8 Notre Dame 13, Army 7—Oct. 18, 1924 (2:42)

TRACK 9 Notre Dame 10, Michigan State 10—Nov. 19, 1966 (3:16)

TRACK 10 *Sugar Bowl,* Notre Dame 24, Alabama 23—Dec. 31, 1973 (2:44)

TRACK 11 Notre Dame 7, Oklahoma 0—Nov. 16, 1957 (2:27)

TRACK 12 Notre Dame 31, Michigan State 8—Sept. 19, 1987 (4:10)

TRACK 13 Notre Dame 17, Penn State 16—Nov. 14, 1992 (3:12)

TRACK 14 Notre Dame 35, Army 13—Nov. 1, 1913 (2:50)

TRACK 15 Notre Dame 0, Army 0—Nov. 9, 1946 (3:27)

TRACK 16 *Cotton Bowl,* Notre Dame 38, Texas 10—Jan. 2, 1978 (2:55)

TRACK 17 *Fiesta Bowl,* Notre Dame 34, West Virginia 21—Jan. 2, 1989 (2:51)

TRACK 18 *Orange Bowl,* Notre Dame 13, Alabama 11—Jan. 1, 1975 (2:25)

TRACK 19 Notre Dame 29, Michigan 27—Sept. 20, 1980 (2:45)

TRACK 20 *Sugar Bowl,* Notre Dame 39, Florida 28—Jan. 1, 1992 (2:05)

Film courtesy of University of Notre Dame Archive. Video courtesy of University of Notre Dame Football Department. Radio calls courtesy of University of Notre Dame Archive, University of Notre Dame Sports Information Department, Westwood One Radio. DVD photos courtesy of Lighthouse Imaging, University of Notre Dame Archive, University of Notre Dame Sports Information Department, Joe Raymond.

Producer: Jerry Klein; *Editor:* Brian Kosisky; *Writer:* Paul Crane; *Narrator:* Brian Welch; *Music and Graphics:* Joy Kosisky
Research: Charles Lamb, Erik Dix, Tim Collins